Meat, Murder, Malfeasance, Medicine and Martyrdom

Smithfield Stories: Wat Tyler; Sweeney Todd, 'Jack the Ripper', Heinrich Himmler, & More...

MEAT, MURDER, MALFEASANCE, MEDICINE AND MARTYRDOM

SMITHFIELD STORIES: WAT TYLER; SWEENEY TODD, 'JACK THE RIPPER', HEINRICH HIMMLER, & MORE...

GRAHAM HOLDERNESS

EER

EDWARD EVERETT ROOT PUBLISHERS 2019

EER

Edward Everett Root, Publishers, Co. Ltd.,
30 New Road, Brighton, Sussex, BN1 IBN, England.

Full details of our overseas agents are given on our website.
www.eerpublishing.com

edwardeverettroot@yahoo.co.uk

Graham Holderness, *Meat, Murder, Malfeasance, Medicine and Martyrdom: Smithfield Stories: Wat Tyle; Sweeney Todd, 'Jack the Ripper', Heinrich Himmler, & More...*

First published in Great Britain in 2019.
© Graham Holderness 2019.

This edition © Edward Everett Root 2019

ISBN Paperback 978-1-913087-08-1
ISBN Hardback 978-1-911454-27-4
ISBN eBook 978-1-911454-30-4

All photographs taken by the author in and around Smithfield in the year prior to publication.

Reproduction of detail of wounded dog from William Hogarth's *The Good Samaritan* painting by kind permission of Barts NHS Health Trust.

Cover image courtesy of Extramural Activity

Cover design and typesetting by Head & Heart Book Design.

CONTENTS

INTRODUCTION

The following stories all occupy the physical, cultural and psychological territory of London's Smithfield. In an extraordinary area, measuring little more than a square mile, bounded by Farringdon Street, Charterhouse Street, Aldersgate and Ludgate, we can find in microcosm some of the key contours of British national life. Here, to borrow the name of a famous Smithfield street, in something like its entirety, is 'Little Britain'.

Originally a 'smooth field' outside the City walls, used for grazing animals, Smithfield was, from time out of mind, the site of the famous livestock market until it was moved to Islington in 1855. It thus became a place for the slaughter of animals, and for the dead meat market that still survives.

Violence against animals was extended to violence against humans. The site of animal slaughter became one of the premier arenas of public execution, for treason or heresy. Since many were judicially killed for religious rather than criminal reasons, some of their deaths may be considered martyrdom, rather than execution. The area is rich in ancient institutions of law and punishment. Newgate Prison was built nearby in 1188, and the central criminal court, better known as the Old Bailey, erected there in the 16th century. Newgate has gone, but the Bailey remains.

Between these instruments of justice, and the stench and violence of market and abattoir, stand institutions of healing and salvation: St Bartholomew's Hospital, and the Church of St Bartholomew the Great, both founded in the 12th century. And of course close by is St Paul's Cathedral, which may have roots extending as far back as the 7th century. Clerkenwell priory, the huge London base of the Knights Hospitaller, stood alongside Smithfield, entered through the still surviving Gate of St John.

These monuments of national life are not discrete but interactive. In Smithfield medicine, faith, justice, punishment and animal slaughter all share common ground.

St Bartholomew, patron of the church, was in his legends skinned like an animal, and the church of St Bartholomew the Great is adopted by the Worshipful Company of Butchers. Butchers' Hall stood near Bart's hospital, until destroyed in the Great Fire of 1666. In the church hangs a splendid banner of the Butchers' Livery Company, showing images of bulls, sheep, boar, with the Latin inscription '*omnia subiecisti sub pedibus, oves et boves*' ('Thou hast set all things under man's feet, all sheep and oxen', Ps. 8). Today in the church you can see the astounding gilded statue by Damien Hirst, 'St Bartholomew: Exquisite Pain', informed partly, according to the sculptor, by teaching aids used in anatomy studies, and clearly related also to the artist's more familiar work with dead animals and with decomposing meat.

The great advances in medical research we associate with Bart's Hospital would have been impossible without experiments, both vivisection and dissection, performed on animals. William Harvey, who served as physician in charge at Bart's, made his momentous discovery of the circulation of the blood largely through animal vivisection and the dissection of criminals condemned at the Old Bailey, and executed at Tyburn. He cites examples from animal anatomy throughout his book on the heart, *De Motu Cordis*, and his later work focused on reproduction in animals. After the Great Fire, The Royal College of Physicians occupied a headquarters next to Newgate, in which was housed an Anatomy Theatre for the public dissection of executed criminals.

I first came across these some of these interrelations in Charles Dickens' *Great Expectations:*

> When I told the clerk that I would take a turn in the air while I waited, he advised me to go round the corner and I should come into Smithfield. So, I came into Smithfield; and the shameful place, being all asmear with filth and fat and blood and foam, seemed to stick to me. So, I rubbed it off with all possible speed by turning into a street where I saw the great black dome of Saint Paul's bulging at me from behind a grim stone building which a bystander said was Newgate Prison ... While I looked about me here, an exceedingly dirty and partially drunk minister of justice asked me if I would like to step in and hear a trial or so ... As I declined the proposal on the plea of

an appointment, he was so good as to take me into a yard and show me where the gallows was kept, and also where people were publicly whipped, and then he showed me the Debtors' Door, out of which culprits came to be hanged: heightening the interest of that dreadful portal by giving me to understand that 'four on 'em' would come out at that door the day after to-morrow at eight in the morning, to be killed in a row. This was horrible, and gave me a sickening idea of London.[1]

The newly-arrived Pip undertakes a brief tour in which he encounters the interactions of animal slaughter and execution, religious worship and judicial punishment. Smithfield, Newgate, the Old Bailey, St Paul's: Little Britain. Dickens saw Smithfield as a map of exploitation, in which people and animals were treated with equal cruelty and injustice, and from which his great liberal imagination recoiled: 'A sickening idea of London'.

More recently a modern writer, Graham Swift in *Last Orders*, has revisited the same scene, and diagnosed the same overlaps. One of the narrators, Ray, recalls how his late friend Jack, a Smithfield butcher, spoke of the area:

He used to give me all that old Smithfield guff, all that Smithfield blather. How Smithfield was the true centre, the true heart of London. Bleeding heart, of course, on account of the meat. How Smithfield wasn't just Smithfield, it was Life and Death. That's what it was: Life and Death. Because just across from the meat market was St Bart's Hospital, and just across from Bart's was your Old Bailey Central Criminal Court, on the site of old Newgate Prison, where they used to string 'em up regular. So what you had in Smithfield was your three M's: Meat, Medicine and Murder.[2]

It is not only the narrator, Ray, who dismisses Smithfield's claim to national centrality as 'guff' and 'blather'. It is also the novelist, Graham Swift, whose imagination tends to occupy 'not the place from, or the place to, but the road'. (153) Typically Ray/Swift omits from his map of Smithfield the Christian church, which should have provided at least one more 'M': Mystery, or Martyrdom, also closely entwined – if one thinks of the Crucifixion, or the flaying of Bartholomew – with Meat and Murder. And if you believe in the cure of souls, Medicine.

The following stories are rooted in the ground of Smithfield, revolve around the institutions it houses, and dwell on the overlapping activities that have characterised it for centuries. They range across historical fiction, 'Restoration comedy', Gothic romance, drama, 'alternative history', and contemporary realism. Most are closely tied to the real past by the use of historical sources and documented events: the execution of William Wallace, the killing of Wat Tyler, the burning of Anne Askew, the execution of Amelia Dyer. Others explore the imaginative possibilities of Smithfield, rather than its authenticated events and characters, reanimating fictional characters such as Sweeney Todd, or the hero of Hogarth's *Four Stages of Cruelty*; or inventing a modern *Halal* butcher who is radicalised and joins Isis. Sometimes fiction is constructed in the interstices of historical record, such as the story about William Harvey and the Earl of Rochester, or the largely invented tale of the real Jack the Ripper suspect, Jewish butcher Aaron Kosminsky. At other times the imagination is wholly off the leash, as in the story of Heinrich Himmler and the Temple of Mithras, or the fantasy autobiography of St Bartholomew.

These stories explore Smithfield diachronically, from the 12th to the 20th centuries, and trace in every example the interactions of meat, murder, malfeasance, medicine and martyrdom. They take no position on the politics of animal welfare or so-called animal rights. They are concerned only with the commonalities of violence exhibited in the slaughtering of beasts, the torture and execution of criminals, the violations of the body practised on the autopsy table and in the research laboratory, the atrocities of murder and cannibalism. These stories construct an impression of Smithfield, 'Little Britain', and throw their dark light both on British national history, and on the human condition.

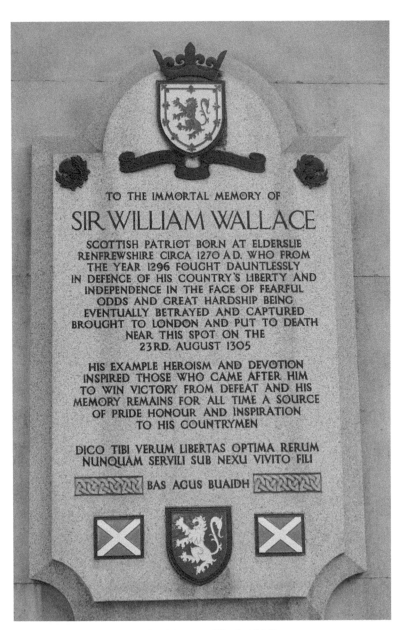

TO THE IMMORTAL MEMORY OF

SIR WILLIAM WALLACE

SCOTTISH PATRIOT BORN AT ELDERSLIE
RENFREWSHIRE CIRCA 1270 A.D. WHO FROM
THE YEAR 1296 FOUGHT DAUNTLESSLY
IN DEFENCE OF HIS COUNTRY'S LIBERTY AND
INDEPENDENCE IN THE FACE OF FEARFUL
ODDS AND GREAT HARDSHIP BEING
EVENTUALLY BETRAYED AND CAPTURED
BROUGHT TO LONDON AND PUT TO DEATH
NEAR THIS SPOT ON THE
23RD. AUGUST 1305

HIS EXAMPLE HEROISM AND DEVOTION
INSPIRED THOSE WHO CAME AFTER HIM
TO WIN VICTORY FROM DEFEAT AND HIS
MEMORY REMAINS FOR ALL TIME A SOURCE
OF PRIDE HONOUR AND INSPIRATION
TO HIS COUNTRYMEN

DICO TIBI VERUM LIBERTAS OPTIMA RERUM
NUNQUAM SERVILI SUB NEXU VIVITO FILI

BAS AGUS BUAIDH

Wallace Monument, West Smithfield

WILLIAM WALLACE

PREFACE

Scottish nationalist leader William Wallace was executed in Smithfield on 23rd of August 1305. A plaque commemorating his life and death is fixed to the wall of Bart's Hospital.

The story included in this volume is improvised around a key historical document, Wallace's sentence for treason. The story draws material parallels between the detail of Wallace's execution – he was hung, drawn and quartered – and Smithfield's primal scene of animal slaughter; and symbolic parallels between the violence applied to his body, and Wallace's own actions during the wars for Scottish independence.

Thus his being wrapped in an ox-hide (a technique used in the execution of Scottish knight Simon Fraser in 1306) for 'drawing' is compared to his flaying of Hugh de Cressingham at the Battle of Stirling Bridge; his hanging to the drowning of innocent civilians at Perth; his emasculation to the murder and mutilation of the Sheriff of Lanark, William de Heselrigg; his disembowelling to his desecration of a church in Northumberland, and his quartering to his campaign to divide the Union of England and Scotland.

The style of the tale is that of historical fiction, citing actual historical documents and imitating events accurately from the main historical sources. The scenes of execution are narrated from Wallace's point-of-view. I have systematically dissented from the heroic and sentimental view of Wallace made famous by Mel Gibson's film *Braveheart* (dir. Mel Gibson, 1995).

The Latin indictment can be found in *Documents Illustrative of Sir William Wallace, His Life and Times*, ed. Joseph Stevenson (London: Maitland Club, 1841), pp. 190-3 (*my translation*). The romantic and heroic view of Wallace now familiarised by *Braveheart* derives principally from the 15th century poem *The Actes and Deidis of the Illustre and Vallyeant Campioun Schir William Wallace* by 'Blind Harry the Minstrel': see Blind

Harry, *The Wallace* (Edinburgh: Cannongate, 2003). Other early chronicles such as those of John Fordun, Andrew of Wyntoun and Walter Bower are also strongly marked by their partiality for the Scottish cause. A more balanced view was formulated in the 16th century in John Major, *Historia Majoris Britanniae* (Paris, 1521, Edinburgh: Robert Fribarn, 1740). The modern historical accounts I have found most useful include D. J. Gray, *William Wallace, the King's Enemy* (London: Barnes and Noble, 1991); A. MacKay, *William Wallace: Brave Heart* (London: Mainstream Publishing, 1995); P. Reese, *Wallace: a Biography* (Edinburgh: Cannongate, 1996); G. Morton, *William Wallace: Man and Myth* (Stroud: Sutton Publishing, 2001); and Andrew Fisher, *William Wallace* (Edinburgh: Birlinn, 2007). There are many historical and romance fictionalisations of Wallace, but the best is still Nigel Tranter, *The Wallace* (London: Hodder and Stoughton, 1975).

WILLIAM WALLACE

Westminster Hall, 23 August 1305

> *Consideratum est quod praedictus Willelmus, pro manifesta seditione quam ipsi domino regi fecerat felonice machinando, in mortem ejus perpetrando ...* [1]

It is considered that the aforesaid William, for the manifest treason which he had made to the same lord the King by felonious contrivance, by attempting to cause his death, the annulment and enervation of the crown and of his royal authority and by raising his standard against his lord in war to the death, should be drawn on a hurdle from Westminster as far as the Tower of London, and from the Tower as far as Allegate, and thus through the middle of the city as far as [Smithfield] Elmes ...

The darkness was palpable, the smell overpowering of animal dung and urine. William Wallace was tightly wrapped inside an ox hide, his hands and feet securely bound, the skin enfolding him completely in a blackness of sensory deprivation. The pelt was lashed by rough cords at ankles and head, so he was completely enclosed, and could see nothing. Only the stench enveloped him, rank effluvia of the tanner's craft: dogshit and horsepiss, sulphurous odour of tree-bark tannin. [2]

Wallace had been rolled into the hide preparatory to the first stage of the sentence imposed upon him by the sovereign power of Edward I: to be drawn on a hurdle through the streets of London to his place of execution, where he was to suffer hanging by the neck, to be cut down while still alive and conscious, his privy members to be cut away and burned in his sight, his heart, lungs and liver to be ripped out and cast into the fire, his head to be severed from his body, and his limbs to be quartered. Since this was to be an exemplary punishment, the intention was that Wallace should be alive and fully conscious for as much of the

9

process as possible; which is why they had enfolded him in the protective sheath of ox hide. His tormentors had no intention of allowing his lolling head, as he was dragged upside down from Westminster to Smithfield, to be cracked on the hard London cobbles, or of risking the infliction of any injury that might diminish his sensitivity to pain. The protective fold of animal skin was no gesture of mercy or compassion, but a calculated method of intensifying Wallace's suffering.

Though he could see nothing, Wallace could hear clearly through the hide that swaddled his head. The contemptuous jeers of the crowd, and the shouted insults of the sheriff's officers had subsided, and a kind of lull suggested that the grim convoy was waiting for some nobleman to take his place at its head. After a few minutes of waiting, a shuffling of hooves, the swish of a horse's tail, the chink of a bridle, the procession commenced. Beneath him Wallace could feel the wooden struts of the hurdle bumping and jolting over the cobbles. Trying as best he could to take his mind off the events of the next few hours, Wallace withdrew his thoughts from the present, and retreated into the forest of memory. The leathery smell of the hide seemed comforting now, awakening in his imagination the creaking of saddles, the sharp scent of quivers and surcoats, the acrid smell of a troop of infantry fitfully sleeping in a tent on the night before a battle.

And this was not the first time William Wallace had worn a ceinct of skin.

*

Stirling, 11 September 1297

From his vantage point at the foot of the Abbey Craig, Wallace could clearly see the bridge, and in the foreground on this side the river the narrow stone and timbered causeway bulging from the low flood-plain of the Forth. The blue river looped and meandered through green bogland and waterlogged salt-marsh. Across the ford, beneath the mound of Stirling Castle, the English army was drawn up in glittering array, pennants and banners rippling in the breeze, spear-shafts of the infantry bristling against a cloudless sky. The English vanward was in the slow process of crossing the bridge onto the causeway: light cavalry, green-coated Welsh archers, a troop of infantry, and finally the heavy horse, gaily caparisoned, the knights splendid in their chainmail hauberks and heraldic surcoats, faceless behind their vizored helms. Above the cavalry flapped a red-and-white banner of St George, the English standard. Surrey must be leading them, thought Wallace. Or Cressingham.[3]

Beside Wallace on the hillside, Sir Andrew Moray carefully watched the slow and impeded advance of the English as they crowded over the narrow bridge, and spread out onto the wider causeway. Some two thousand troops had crossed the Forth, advancing to face the Scots. Macduff was hotly urging the commanders to attack, fearful of the huge army that was yet to cross. But Moray bided his time, counting and measuring and surveying the dispositions, letting the enemy come to him.

Stirling was Wallace's first experience of pitched battle in the field. For years now he had ambushed and harried, devastated and burned, murdered and looted, and by these methods chased the English from a large part of Scotland. But never before had he faced the full might of Edward's power, dispatched by the absent king under Surrey and Cressingham to teach the rebellious Scots a lesson they would not soon forget. Wisely he had ceded the command of the battle to Moray, an experienced soldier and veteran with the cool head and tactical prudence necessary in a general. Stirling was Moray's strategy, and Wallace could see it was working. But like the other Scots lords, he too was chafing and fretting sorely under the impatience of waiting, watching more and more of the English file across the Forth to join their fellows, already drawn up in battle formation along the causeway.

At last Moray turned to Wallace and nodded his approval. It was time to attack. Wallace gave the signal, and the eerie blast of a blown ram's horn rang out across the valley. Simultaneously several things happened. The bridge itself, its planks partially sawn through beforehand, collapsed at the southern end, pulled apart by men hidden in the shallow waters beneath. A clump of English knights on their massive destriers slipped and foundered into the river, splashing clumsily into the water. Alarm spread through the English advance guard, and all heads turned to the rear. They were cut off from the rest of the army, and about to be surrounded.

At the same time a detachment of Scots, bare-legged and lightly-armed, but defended with shields against the deadly shafts of the Welsh bowmen, slipped and slid their way through the marsh to flank the causeway on both sides. Taken by surprise, the enemy was too thickly crowded together to defend themselves effectively. The archers had no room to draw their bows, the infantry no space to wield their spears. Slashing and stabbing with dirks and short swords, the Scots cut down the English spearmen and seized their long shafts. These they used against the mounted troops, pushing their scrambling and floundering horses into the marsh, leaping on the dismounted men and slashing their throats. Moray's strategy was brilliant: to use the terrain as a weapon, and to turn the enemy's strength against him.

Meanwhile the heavy cavalry, the knights on their war-horses, were rendered useless, unable to advance or retreat, incapable of engaging. Cooped and cramped on the narrow causeway, they dared not move aside for fear their horses would sink into the soft bog-turf of the marsh. Still they remained immune from assault, easily splintering the Scottish spears, casually with their long broadswords cutting down any man who came near them.

With extraordinary patience, Wallace had watched and waited, recognising the brilliance of Moray's plan, understanding the need for delay. Now however, with the support troops broken, their slaughtered bodies piled on the causeway, the survivors fleeing panic-stricken into the marsh and seeking the shelter of the river, the commanders had a clear view of their primary objective, the heart of Edward's host. Above all Wallace could see their commander, a stout middle-aged man in yellow-and-black livery. So it was not the younger Surrey, but Hugh de Cressingham, Edward's treasurer: the most hated man in England. Cut-off and undefended as they were, the knightly troops were still a disciplined force, capable of repelling the attackers, of falling back towards the river and holding their position. It would not take long to repair the bridge, allow the rest of the army to cross, and turn the tide of battle. This force had to be disabled if the Scots were to win the day. Wallace carefully measured the distance between himself and the enemy flag.

Spurring his mount down the hillside, closely followed by Moray and the Scots knights, Wallace hurled himself onto the causeway and made straight for the English cavalry. The English saw them coming, and assumed a position of defence. But before reaching range of sword or spear, Wallace slid down from his saddle, and slipped into the marsh alongside the causeway. Above him he could hear the two forces meet in the shock of battle. Pushing his way through the morass, he came alongside the commander's banner, the cross of St George flapping proudly above the melee. Stealthily he pulled himself up onto the causeway, and sneaked under the bellies of the horses, weaving through their trailing linen mantlings, avoiding their rearing legs and pawing hooves, to reach the centre of the host. Guided by the heraldic colours and badges, he found his target, and slipped under the belly of Cressingham's horse. The destrier was strongly protected with chain mail around its flanks and head, but its soft under-belly was exposed and undefended. Swiftly Wallace ripped upwards with his dirk, slitting the horse's abdomen. Pink and purple entrails cascaded from the incision. Quickly he dodged the collapsing bulk of the horse as it fell, and performed the same operation on the horse of Cressingham's esquire, who bore the English standard. The treasurer lay prone, pinioned under his screaming and dying mount. Wallace slid across the pulsing, flailing body of the squire's horse, leapt on Cressingham, hauled up his visor, and struck at his face with a vicious thrust that splintered his teeth, rammed the point through to the back of his throat, and severed his spinal cord.

Wallace then retreated to the marsh, again dodging under the bellies of the horses, glancing back to observe the results of his guerrilla assault. The English banner lay trampled in the mud, the English commander lay lifeless beside it. Panic spread rapidly through the host, as they lost sight of the standard, and word passed through of the commander's fall. Cavalrymen tried to urge their horses off the causeway, and foundered in the marsh. Some even dismounted and tried to ford the river. Encumbered by their armour, none lasted long under the flashing dirks of the Scots, now closing in, confident of victory.

Moray, catching up with Wallace and hugging a wound in his side[4], had calculated that the huge army on the southern side of the river would withdraw once Surrey had observed the shambles on the northern bank, and calculated his losses. They could see commands being given, and the front ranks beginning to turn about. But before the English could leave the field, the Scots treated them to a graphic display of exemplary punishment and vindictive revenge. Wallace commanded that the corpulent body of Cressingham be stripped naked, tied at the ankles, and hauled up into the low branches of a tree, full in the sight of the English host. Two Scots butchers were then brought forward from the rear, appointed to flay the cadaver, as if it were the carcase of a slaughtered beast. They slit the skin around the ankles, then cut in straight lines down the calves and thighs. Slowly the whole covering of skin was ripped downwards, and finally pulled over Cressingham's head, like the removal of a tight-fitting garment.

Skilfully one of the butchers sliced into the hide to produce a long narrow strip of human skin, which he then handed up to Wallace, with loud cheers from the victorious Scots, and shocked silence from the English across the river. Wallace knotted the skin at its ends, and proudly slipped the grisly trophy around his shoulder like a baldric. I'll have it tanned, he thought to himself: and use it as a belt for my sword.

*

Smithfield, 23 August 1305

> ... *et pro roberiis et homicidiis et feloniis, quas in regni Angliae et terra Scotiae fecit, ibidem suspendatur ...*
>
> ... and for the robberies and murders and felonies which he carried out both in the kingdom of England and in the land of Scotland he should be hanged there ...

The naked Wallace was hauled up onto a wooden platform and jostled into position beneath the gallows. At his feet on the rough boards stood a great iron cauldron in which blazed a fire, and a low wooden block spread with the grim tools of the executioner's craft. Beyond the platform edge pressed the crowd, hoarse with their jeering and booing, now silent and hushed with roused expectation of the main event.

Wallace had been dragged on the hurdle from Westminster Hall, up King Street, along the Strand, up Ludgate, past St Paul's to the Tower of London; then through the Minories, along Aldgate and Leadenhall Street, past Cornhill, down Cheapside and through Newgate to the great open space of Smithfield Elms, cattle market and place of execution.

The hangman quickly slipped the noose over Wallace's head, placing the knot under his ear so as not to break his neck, and tautened the rope against the beam. Wallace braced himself, but the proceedings were paused again for the whole long sentence to be read through:

> *Consideratum est quod praedictus Willelmus, pro manifesta seditione quam ipsi domino regi fecerat felonice machinando, in mortem ejus perpetrando ...* [6]

As the Latin peroration reached its end, the crowd yelled and jeered and shook their fists in contempt of the traitor. Then again they fell silent. Three executioners manned the rope, and hauled Wallace's big body off the platform and into the air. The noose throttled him, stopping his windpipe, and a choking red mist blurred his vision. His legs danced and kicked helplessly beneath him. The pain of the constricting rope around his neck was intense: but it was nothing compared to the terrible vacuous helplessness of being unable to breathe, the mouth gaping wide to bite on air, the gasping lungs burning like hot coals inside his empty chest.

Again he tried to turn his mind to the past. Again he visualised the bridge at Stirling, tried to dwell on the moment of his victory, the scene of his triumph. But it was a different bridge that coalesced in his memory, choked as it was by the dreadful imminence of breathlessness.

*

Perth, 23 May 1297

Vividly he could see the old stone bridge across the Tay at Perth, on the road to Scone. After the murder in Lanark of Hazelrigg the sheriff, and the declaration of Wallace as an outlaw, he had conducted a reign of terror across the north, killing such of the English as he could catch, and intimidating the Scots into joining his cause. At Perth he had seized a group of villagers who had, according to report, received his followers with little enthusiasm, and refused them food. The helpless captives, a dozen men and a handful of women, now stood shivering on the bank of the river, their hands and feet tied with ropes, their faces ashen with terror. Wallace's soldiers were enjoying the spectacle, laughing and jeering at the captives, slapping the men with the flats of their swords, roughly manhandling the women. Wallace rode up to the bridge with his henchman John Blair, and watched from the saddle. Blair leaned over and muttered something in Wallace's ear. Blair was himself descended from peasant stock, and knew the minds of these people. They cared nothing about the nation or its politics, wanting only to be left in peace to farm their land. They felt no differently about the Scottish army than they did about the English, knowing only that from time to time big, loud-voiced men would appear in their midst, seizing their crops and their food, pressing their sons into military service, as often as not raping their women. It seemed to Blair an injustice that these simple folk should be punished over again for their poverty and ignorance. He asked Wallace to show mercy.

But Wallace was in the mood to teach the people a lesson. They must learn the simple truth: if they were not on his side, they were on Edward's. Whoso is not with us, is against us. Impoverished and hopeless they may be, but they had to learn the importance of loyalty, or the future of Scotland was lost. So these poor wretches would be made an example, for the greater good, that others might observe and act differently in the moment of decision.

Wallace nodded to the captain of the troop holding the captives. In response to the captain's orders, the troopers seized the bound bodies of the villagers, ignoring their screams of terror, heaved them up onto the parapet of the bridge, and tossed them into the water. Tied up as they were, the poor wretches could not swim, and instead thrashed and twisted to stay afloat. Wallace could see their heads, one by one, stretching up from the surface to gasp desperately for air, while the weight of their bodies dragged them inexorably under. For a moment he thought about what it must feel like to be down there, drawing cold water into suffocating lungs, seeing your last breath belch in bubbles from your mouth and burst above you on the surface of the water.

*

Smithfield, 23 August 1305

> *Praedictus Willelmum de Waleys … felonice et contra pacem … Willelmum de Hesebregg … insultavit, vulneravit et interfecit …*[7]
>
> The aforesaid William Wallace … feloniously and against the King's peace … insulted, wounded and killed William de Heselrigg, sheriff of Lanark, who represented the King in the regular meeting of the county court …

As suddenly as they had yanked him up, the hangmen let the rope go, and Wallace fell heavily back onto the platform. Quickly they slackened the noose to keep him breathing and conscious, but without removing it from his neck. Roughly they helped him upright again, and Wallace stood, unsteady on his legs, the noose still round his throat, the rope just taut enough to steady his position. Brief as it was, the pressure of the noose on his cerebellum had been enough to induce priapism, the strangled nerves forcing blood into the penis, so it protruded, turgid and erect, wreathed with auburn hair, from his naked groin. The crowd whooped and cheered at the sight: they knew what was coming next.

Two executioners seized Wallace's arms and held him fast. A third, a big butcher of a man, then held up before him a pair of blunt-edged and strong-jawed iron pincers, such as are used for the castration of bulls. Wallace could not keep the expression of horror from darting across his face as the dreadful implement was thrust towards him. Nothing daunted, the executioner slipped the tool over Wallace's cock, clamping its jaws down at the base of the shaft, ensuring the dangling balls were trapped in the pincers' grip. To howls of delirious delight from the spectators, he slowly squeezed the handles of the pincers together. Wallace yelled in agony, and the executioners were hard pressed to keep hold of his thrashing arms. The pincers bit more deeply, and blood began to flow swiftly from the wound and trickle down Wallace's legs. The implement was designed for crushing the blood vessels in an animal, rendering the organ useless, not for slicing the tissue, so there was no clean cutting, but rather a dull and brutal riving and tearing of the sensitive flesh. At last the executioner gave the pincers a vicious twist, and Wallace's genitals dropped with a soft thud onto the platform, lying there like a piece of offal, leaching blood and urine onto the dry boards.

They had made him an outlaw; now they had made him less than a man. Soon his body would be food for the kites and crows. But for a little while, his mind remained free, and flashed back to that night in 1296 when he had stealthily crept, under cover of darkness, upon the Governor's lodging in Lanark, the old Priory of St John in Friar Lane.

*

Lanark, 21 May 1296

They had made short work of the sentries, and forced the wooden door in the curtain wall. Passing through the building's many corridors and rooms, dirking to death any who came against them, they reached a central chamber, and paused before the threshold. The door swung open from within, and Heselrigg himself appeared in the doorway. big and red-faced, in a loose dressing-gown, sword in hand. Seeing Wallace before him, and the strength of the company at his back, the Sheriff dropped his sword and stepped back into the room. Wallace appointed guards through the house, and with two of his closest retainers, Hamish and Dougal, entered the room to face Heselrigg.

The sheriff showed no trace of fear. It was this resolution and hardihood, more than anything else, that goaded Wallace to cruelty. Hazelrigg could have no doubt as to the only possible outcome of this encounter, as he faced the man he had himself declared an outlaw at the previous day's assizes. He must know that Wallace would show no mercy, would kill him and everyone else in the house, and burn it to the ground. To expect anything else was foolishness. And that certainty absolved him from fear.

Wallace's hatred of the man who had thrust him beyond all protection of the law corroded like lust in his veins, and he yearned with a drymouthed desire to see Hazelrigg flinch, tremble, wince, recoil in terror. The sheriff did nothing of the kind, and his courage made Wallace's blood seethe with vindictive fury.

'Hold out your right hand', he commanded. Hazelrigg sat on the bed with that same expression of amused contempt, and made no attempt to comply. Wallace gestured to Hamish, who seized Heselrigg's right wrist and stretched out the sheriff's arm. The hand that had signed away Wallace's freedom should be the first to suffer. Slowly Wallace unsheathed his great sword, staring at Hazelrigg in the hope of seeing at least a flash of fear, a trace of humiliation. Nothing. Furious with frustration, Wallace lifted the blade and brought it down with a vicious stroke that cleft Heselrigg's hand from his forearm. Blood splashed from the wound.

Hazelrigg stared for a moment at the severed limb, then turned and looked at Wallace with that cool, supercilious expression that drove the big man mad. Wallace commanded that the other arm be extended in the same way, and with another hurtling blow sliced off the left hand. Hazelrigg crossed his two bleeding stumps and gripped them beneath his arms to control the pain and the bleeding. His red face was paler now, as the blood began to ebb rapidly from his wounds.

In spite of all his courage, eventually bodily weakness did what fear could not do, and the Sheriff slowly fell back against the cushions of the bed, his mutilated arms folded, legs stretched out at angles. Mercilessly Wallace slashed at his legs below the knee and severed both limbs, the blade biting deep into the mattress, spilling white goose feathers, their candid purity stained with blood. By now Heselrigg had passed the point of pain, so his face remained innocent of the agony visited on his body.

Wallace hacked at his shoulders and severed the arms, then lopped off the thighs. The dismembered torso lay on the bed like the carcase of a slaughtered beast. In a burst of cruelty, Wallace struck Heselrigg's head from his body. Then Dougal with his dirk sliced off Heselrigg's genitals, and stuffed them in a final indignity into the corpse's mouth. Unable to stop himself, Wallace cut and chopped, slashed and sliced, mincing the sheriff into an unrecognisable bloodstained heap, like a pile of minced meat lying on a butcher's block.

Subsequently, Wallace briefly recalled, as with a kind of detached curiosity he watched the executioner scoop up his penis and cast it into the flames, the murder of Heselrigg would become his founding legend, his myth of origin. But the gratuitous cruelty and ugly violence did not sit well with Wallace's mythology as the chivalric champion of the nation, the heroic saviour of Scotland. Some individual grievance had to be found, some more personal grudge invented, to justify that frenzy of blood-soaked rage inflicted on an unarmed captive.

And so the myth of Marion Braidfoot was born. Wallace's sweetheart, his sworn fiancée, even in some versions his wife (though his wife and mother of their daughter was yet living). There never was a Marion Braidfoot, and Wallace had slaughtered Hazelrigg for political rather than personal reasons. But the story grew of its own accord, and in fireside tales and tavern yarns, the hero would be seen running headlong through the Braidfoot house, out of the back door with the English soldiery giving chase, losing him in the winding streets and alleys of the city. Cheated of their prey, the invaders then turned on the household, slaughtering them all, men, women and children, and putting the dwelling to the torch. Wallace's love, his flower of Scotland, perished in the flames.

The story had no more substance than the floating flakes of fire that sparked out from that collapsing house of dreams. But the tale fed the insatiable appetite for atrocity: that which did happen, or might have happened, to someone else, long ago, far away – at Berwick, at Irvine, at Lanark – is felt as a personal wound, nursed as an individual grievance, and cited again and again to justify an equivalence of violence, an equity of retribution. Remember what the oppressors did to us; now let us return his cruelty with interest.

*

Smithfield, 23 August 1305

Et postea pro immense vilitate, quam Deo et sacrosanctae ecclesiae fecit comburendo ecclesias, vasa et feretra in quibus Corpus Christi et corpora sanctorum et reliquiae eorundum collocabantur ...[8]

And afterwards for the immense wickedness he did to God and to the Holy Church, by burning the churches, the vessels and the shrines in which the body of Christ and the bodies and relics of the saints were kept together, the heart, liver, lungs and all internal parts of the same William, from whom such evil thoughts proceeded, should be cast into the fire and burned.

For the next part of the execution the noose was removed from Wallace's neck, and his body forcibly spread-eagled onto the wooden block that had held the executioners' tools. Ropes were lashed tightly around his throat and hips, leaving the torso exposed. His mouth was fixed in a long grimace of pain, his eyes bleared with suffering, his face growing pale from loss of blood. He remained, as his captors had intended, sensate and vulnerable. But not for much longer.

Above him the blue cloudless sky of August promised liberation and peace. But between him and the heavens was cruelly interposed the final implement of death: the curved sharp blade of an axe, held in front of his face where he could not avoid seeing it. The polished blade glinted and flashed in the sun, and the sharp edge held out to him its certain promise of pain.

The evisceration had to be quick in order to be effective. The axe was raised, and brought down with a soft crunch, once and then again, to split Wallace's rib-cage in two, splintering the sternum. With grappling hooks two men clamped the severed edges and ripped apart his chest, exposing the heaving lungs and pulsing heart. With a long, sharp blade the butcher-executioner severed the trachea, gullet, aorta and hepatic artery, then cut and sliced quickly around the major organs to free them from their embedding tissue. Roughly the heart, lungs and liver were ripped out of the cavity, and quickly flung into the flames of the brazier. The human offal sputtered and crackled, streams of hot fat running down the sides of the vessel like lava from an erupting volcano, and thick black smoke gusted upwards, carrying a noxious smell of burning meat into the bestial Smithfield air.

They twisted Wallace's head so his eyes could see the brazier: his internal parts to be burned before his face. There was enough consciousness left in him for one brief glimpse of the obscene spectacle of his own evisceration. And for the awakening of one more memory from his past.

*

Hexham Priory, 30 October 1297

The priest, standing at the altar, took the paten with the bread and held it slightly raised above the altar with both hands, saying in a low voice:

Suscipe, Sancta Trinitas, hanc oblationem, quam ego indignus peccator offero in honore tuo, beata Mariae et omnium Sanctorum tuorum, pro peccatis et offensionibus meis: et pro salute vivorum et requie omnium fidelium defunctorum. In nomine Patris et Filii et Spiritus Sancti acceptum sit Omnipotenti Deo hoc sacrificium novum.

Receive, Holy Trinity, this offering, which I, an unworthy sinner, offer in honour of thee, of the blessed Virgin and all the saints, for my sins and offences, and for the salvation of the living, and the rest of all the faithful departed. In the name of the Father, and the Son, and the Holy Spirit. May this new sacrifice be acceptable to the omnipotent God.[9]

Wallace, kneeling at the altar-rail, crossed himself and held out his cupped hands to receive the host. The paten was a heavy vessel of silver inlaid with gold, its centre a gold circle like the boss of a shield, surrounded by chased silver images of Christ and His angels. On it lay an unassuming piece of bread: ostia, the victim. The body of Christ.

The priest, vested in splendid robes of gold and silver thread, raised the chalice, also fashioned from pure silver and elaborately fretted with gold, declared the words of Institution, and took a sip of the communion wine. This is my blood.

Wallace had ridden up to Hexham Priory with no particular expectations. After the victory at Stirling, the Scots had crossed the border into England, devastating the land as they advanced. Wallace had thought it prudent to circumvent the heavily-fortified walls of Newcastle, and restrict his attacks to weaker targets. As the chronicles record, the population of Northumbria fled before the marauding Scots, leaving their homes and farms to be pillaged and burnt, content to escape with nothing but their lives. The churches and monasteries were left empty as the priests and canons, monks and nuns fled before the relentlessly advancing host.

Wallace knew that the Priory at Hexham had been looted by Scots a year before, so he expected to find nothing and nobody there. To his surprise he came upon a band of his own men surrounding three white-robed Augustinian friars, who were shaking their heads in denial of some allegation. The soldiers were convinced that the monks would have returned for only one purpose: to recover valuables successfully hidden from the previous marauders. We have nothing left, they protested; everything has been stolen. The Scots did not believe them, and were beginning to handle them roughly. Wallace ordered them to cease, and to hand the clerics over to him. Dismounting, he asked them courteously to lead him into the church.

Relieved, the monks bustled into the building ahead of Wallace, confident in the surety of his protection. His mission was to weaken English power over Scotland, he assured them, not to assault the edifice of Holy Church. No man loved the church more than he, as his previous conduct had shown. Now he wished to stay a while, in the umbrageous gloom of the great Gothic abbey. In fact nothing would please him more than for the fathers to celebrate Mass, here among the flickering candles and the sweet smell of incense. The monks whispered amongst themselves, and came to some decision. One of them disappeared in the direction of the sanctuary, was gone for some time, and reappeared bearing the vessels of the Eucharist, paten and chalice, together with richly embroidered tunicles for the priest and deacon.

And so they robed and prepared the altar with bread and wine and water, while Wallace knelt to receive. No sooner had the priest administered the sacrament, than the Scots soldiers who had held the monks at bay rushed into the church, seized the paten and chalice, ripped the gold vestments over the heads of the clergy, and made off through a side door.

Wallace had remained kneeling, eyes closed as if in prayer. When he opened them again, it was to see the monks standing bereft of their sacred vessels and stripped of their vestments, appealing to Wallace to arrest the thieves and recover their property.

'The Lord giveth', said Wallace as he rose to leave, 'and the Lord taketh away. Blessed be the name of the Lord'.

*

Smithfield, 23 August 1305

Et etiam, quia non solum ipsi domino regi, sed toti plebi Angliae et Scotiae, praedicta seditionem, depraedationes, incendia et homicidia et felias fecerat corpus illius Wellelmi in quatuor quarteria scindatur et dividatur ... [10]

And also, because he had committed the aforesaid treason, destruction, burnings and murders, not only against the lord the King himself, but against the entire people of England and Scotland, the body of that William should be cut and divided into four quarters, and the head thus cut off should be fixed upon London Bridge ...

Wallace was little more than a lifeless lump of flesh when they struck his head from his body. The quartering followed swiftly, the limbs dismembered from the headless chest and vacant abdomen. Like so many cuts of meat, chuck and rib, brisket and shank, his limbs were hacked from the blood-boltered shambles of a body and laid on hides for packing and transportation: one quarter to Berwick, one to Newcastle, one to Stirling, one to Perth. The head in pride of place on London Bridge.

There seems little point, given that Wallace was most assuredly dead from the moment his major organs were detached and removed, in continuing that narrative convention that alternates the sensations of execution with memories of Wallace's past. Nor do we know enough about the process of death to start constructing fantasies of out-of-body experience, the spirit moving through a cornfield to the soft sound of pipes, Wallace hovering over Smithfield and looking down on the scene of his own execution, the soul like a bird on the wing, soaring over hill and glen, taking the high road back to Scotland. So I will stop pretending I know what Wallace thought and felt, suffered and remembered, and complete this story in the voice of an omniscient narrator.

Wallace was mutilated and dismembered, according to his sentence, because he had committed crimes against the bodies of the nation and the state, the people and the crown. But there was a deeper logic, in his case, to that sundering of the body that had been visited on every traitor guilty of high treason from 1238 onwards. Wallace was dismembered because he had sought to divide the realm; he was split into pieces because he had attempted to fragment the united kingdom, imposed in 1296 by Edward I, King of England and Scotland.

Of course from the perspective of Scottish independence this argument is meaningless. The two nations were yoked together by main force; you cannot divide what is already separate. Wallace would not have understood this logic, any more than he was prepared to acknowledge the charge of treason against a king to whom he had never sworn fealty.

But the congruence of crime and punishment, the division of the body that had sought to divide the realm, was not only an English, imperial point-of-view. After his defeat at Falkirk, a bitter subjugation that eclipsed the triumph of Stirling, Wallace resigned the Guardianship and became something of an embarrassment to his fellow Scots. He was sent abroad on fruitless diplomatic missions, hoping to enlist King Philip IV of France and Pope Boniface VIII into a conspiracy against England. He was insultingly ignored by Edward, until ignominiously betrayed by his own countrymen.

Wallace was, in short, no Robert the Bruce. Bruce knew when to fight, and when to compromise. He collaborated and survived, had the patience to see the great soldier Edward into his grave, and trounced his weakling son Edward II on the field of Bannockburn. Bruce lived a Machiavellian existence in a strategic space between the two kingdoms, availed himself of opportunities from both, played them off against one another, and fathered the Stuart dynasty. In 1601 a descendent of King Robert sealed a personal union of the two crowns: under James I, Scotland had in effect colonised England.

Was Wallace's execution at Smithfield the colonialist atrocity that demands resistance and reparation? Or was it rather the spelling out, in the brutal language of the time, indelibly written on the body, of an imperative of reconciliation?

'Peasants' Revolt' Monument, West Smithfield

WALTER TYLER

PREFACE

In the summer of 1381 thousands of armed commoners from Kent and Essex, Hertfordshire and further afield, inflamed by the hated poll-tax, converged on London with a programme of radical social demands, and compelled the governing elite to hide in the Tower of London: the misnamed 'Peasants Revolt', which historians prefer now to call the 'Great Rising'. Under their leaders Walter ('Wat') Tyler, Jack Straw and the visionary preacher John Ball, the rebels demanded that the king should intercede on their behalf against the landlords. The fourteen-year old Richard II went out to speak to them from his boat on the Thames at Rotherhithe, but the meeting was aborted. The rebels pillaged Southwark and penetrated the city, destroying the great Savoy Palace and the Priory of Clerkenwell. The king met them at Mile End, listened to their demands for the abolition of feudal bondage, and conceded to all of them. Some of the rebels were satisfied and left London: but Tyler and Ball demanded another meeting with the king, which took place in Smithfield. Presenting ever more radical demands, the meeting became violent when Tyler attacked either the king or the London Mayor William Walworth, who promptly slew the rebel leader.

Recent historical analysis of the Rising has proposed that Richard fully intended to implement his agreements, and to carry through the programme of radical social reform demanded by the commons, but was prevented from doing so by his nobility. The following story assigns most of the blame to the rebel leaders themselves, who persisted in provocative challenges that could never conceivably have been granted, and in doing so lost the opportunity of far-reaching social reform that would have benefited their hapless followers. I have made use of the following historical studies: J.G. Bellamy, *The Law of Treason in England in the Later Middle Ages* (Cambridge: Cambridge University Press, 1970);

Martha Carlin, *Mediaeval Southwark* (London: Hambledon Press, 1996); S.B. Chrimes and A.L. Brown, *Select Documents of Mediaeval History* (London: Adam and Charles Black, 1961); Alistair Dunn, *The Peasants' Revolt: England's Failed Revolution of 1381* (Stroud: Tempus Publishing, 2002); Gerald Harris, *Shaping the Nation: England 1360-1461* (Oxford: Clarendon Press, 2005); Rodney Hilton, *Bond Men Made Free: Medieval Peasant Movements and the English Rising of 1381* (London: Routledge, 2003); Charles Oman, *The Great Revolt of 1381* (Oxford, 1906, London: Forgotten Books, 2003); but based my interpretation of the Rising largely on Juliet Barker's brilliant *England, Arise: the People, the King and the Great Revolt of 1381* (London: Little, Brown, 2014). The main primary sources – Thomas Walsingham's *Chronica Maiora*, Froissart's *Chronicles, the Anonimalle Chronicle* – are conveniently collected in. R.B. Dobson, *The Peasants' Revolt of 1381* (London: Macmillan, 1970). Among fictional narratives of the Revolt Melvyn Bragg's *Now is the Time* (London: Hodder and Stoughton, 2015) is probably the most distinguished.

The story that follows is firmly based in history, but uses the techniques of historical fiction, employing some 'mediaevalism' of language and vision. The portrait of Richard II owes something to Shakespeare's history play. The charter included in the story is a historical document. The dialogue has been constructed so that the speech of the 'peasants' resembles English alliterative verse such as that of *Piers the Ploughman*, while that of the aristocrats sounds more like the iambic pentameter of Marlowe or Shakespeare.

WALTER TYLER

1

Blackheath, 12 June 1381

Wat Tyler hoisted himself in his stirrups and looked down from the heights of Blackheath onto the circumambient panorama of London.[1] From his vantage point, the ground sloped steeply away and cascaded in bright green fields towards the fertile marshlands around Deptford, lush wetlands dotted with placidly grazing beasts. The Thames ran blue in the June sunshine, and insouciantly arced its great southern loop around the Isle of Dogs. At the foot of the hill, a patchwork of fields and woods broke up the meadows, and fronting the river he could see the palaces, grounds and parklands of siegneural and ecclesiastical manors. Directly below, the rich royal manor of Greenwich perched proudly on its point. Due westwards, from the crowded dwellings of Southwark, old London Bridge forded the river, leading directly into the solid, stubborn mass of the Tower. Beyond, the tall spire of St Paul's lanced into the blue sky, and over the river's meandering loops he could see the twin towers of Westminster Abbey. The Thames was crowded with vessels, carrying goods from across the seas: gold cloth from Florence, lace from Ypres, tapestries from Bruges, wine from Guienne, all being busily unloaded at one of the river's many wharves.

Riches and beauty conspired to render the landscape as captivating as an illumination in a missal or psalter. Tyler had seen such images in books of hours, glowing in preternatural colours of gold and silver leaf, red lead and white lead, azurite and orpiment and ultramarine, verdigris and vermilion, pigments that turned the workaday world into a series of scenes from heaven. The city radiated an unearthly splendour, bright as glass, as if it were the New Jerusalem, the Holy City, prepared as a bride for her husband.[2]

Behind Tyler, on the heath, John Ball was addressing the Kentish rebels, nigh on a thousand strong, drawn up in a semblance of military array.

'My brothers and sisters, not a thing in this realm can ever come right, till in common our goods are, in England all equal, no nobles nor villeins, all one and the same. When Adam and Eve, our grandparents past, as Piers the Ploughman the furrow followed, Paradise ploughed, and God's good garden together tended, all things were in common, no rich and no poor. The earth in its infancy, the age in its innocence was equal for all. When Adam delved, and Eve span, who was then the gentleman?'³

Wat Tyler looked again on London, and saw a network of property and possession, ownership and deprivation, enclosure and exclusion. The land was no longer the earthly paradise originally granted to Adam and Eve for their mutual enjoyment, but a commodity divided and parcelled up between powerful churchmen and nobles. Fields were partitioned and enclosed, manors separated from one another by hedges. He saw the king's manor of Greenwich, rich in rents and revenues. He saw, down in Southwark, the palace of the Bishop of Winchester, with its elegant courtyards, surrounded by an extensive park, fertile gardens and fishponds, and a private landing-stage and wharf on the river-front. He saw the commodities of trade, disgorged from the Thames, bound for the great houses of the landowners, such as John of Gaunt's Savoy, the most splendid palace in Europe. He saw the Tower, the royal stronghold, where the owners of all this land, the king and his nobles and churchmen, were probably at this very moment sheltering from the human tide that encroached from Middlesex and Hertfordshire and Essex, threatening to engulf them. And everywhere, crawling on this landscape of private property, he saw the teeming tiny figures of the dispossessed, of those who owned nothing, not even their own bodies or the fruits of their labour: the serfs, villeins, bondsmen and bondswomen, going about their everyday work, labouring from sunrise to sunset, and reaching the end of the day as poor as they were in its beginning.

A bank of high clouds began to obscure the sun, and a shadow fell over the land. Again he turned to hear the words of John Ball.

'How are the lords larger than we, more mighty the masters, notwithstanding their meed? In bondage they bind us, in fetters enfold. Adam and Eve were parents of all, father and mother of all mankind. How can they prove their position above us, unless they compel us to produce what they spend, and grab what we grow, all the wealth of the world? Their coats are of camlet, their vestments of velvet, with squirrel and ermine all richly lined, while we wear coarse cloth. They drink the wine and we drink the water; they eat the spices, we gnaw on rye bread. My brothers and sisters, is not the world made for the many, not fashioned for the few?'[4]

And now for a third time Wat Tyler looked down upon London, and saw a great cruel mechanism of exploitation, the rich using their property and possessions to grind the faces of the poor. The land was nothing more than an instrument of power, held in private so as to compel the labourers to work not for themselves, or the common good, but only for the profit and pleasure of their masters. The royal estates, the lordly manors, the immense holdings of the church, all existed to maintain the many in servitude, for the good of the few. Slaves in everything but name and legal status, the poor owed to the rich their dwellings, their use of the land, even the liberty of their own bodies. Each man and woman compelled by law to work the land of the lord, forced by custom to buy and sell where the landowner decreed, tied to a little spot of earth that would never be their own. And obliged to deliver outrageously exacting dues and taxes to the landowners, the government, the king, whenever and wherever their need for money arose, for foreign wars, for palatial buildings, for all the pleasures and privileges of the rich.

This was the true meaning of the landscape that lay so placid and beautiful under his penetrating eyes: England was a vast system of legitimised robbery, where the wretched of the earth groaned beneath the yoke of tyranny, held down by brutal force and the threat of punishment. Among the estate buildings and crowded dwelling-houses, the gorgeous palaces and lofty steeples, he picked out the dark outlines of the prisons. So many, visible even from here: the Clink, set in the Bishop of Winchester's palace grounds; in Southwark the royal prisons, the King's Bench and the Marshalsea; across the river the Fleet and Newgate. Houses of correction, where men and women bold or desperate enough to resist despotism were deprived of what little liberty they possessed, cast into darkness, whipped, mutilated, even put to death.

Tyler felt the first chill of evening as the sun touched the horizon, and darkness began to cover the face of the earth. We must put an end to this, he said to himself; this condition of England can no longer be borne. We must transform society, raise a new world from the ashes of the old. For the many, not the few.

The time is out of joint. And there is only one man who can set it right. John Ball was reaching the peroration of his sermon.

'Let us go, then, comrades, let us go to the King. Let us show our oppression, reveal our wrongs, and tell him the world must be changed for the better, or we will make changes to better ourselves. When the King hears us, he'll heed our lamenting, and offer us remedies to right our ills, or else we'll compel him to come to our aid. The time is come, my comrades-in-arms, now the time is come.'[5]

2

Rotherhithe, 13 June 1381

Richard Plantagenet sat in the prow of the royal barge and surveyed the army massed before him on the southern bank. Between a thousand and two thousand men. Some were mounted, and armed in helmet and mail, with bucklers at their backs and swords at their sides. This disciplined militia formed the heart of the rebel host, but flanking them were hundreds and hundreds more, villeins on foot, equipped with agricultural tools serving as weapons: long-handled bills, pitchforks, sickles and scythes, short axes. Among the coarse-clothed mass of earth-coloured peasantry he could discern the richer clothing of London craftsmen, artisans and apprentices who had already joined the insurrection.

The long oars swept the craft along the river, bringing them closer and closer to the shore. Now Richard could make out the rebel leaders, horsed and positioned in the van, waiting for him on the bank. He identified John Ball by his black clerical garb: a gentle-looking man, grizzled and avuncular, with close-trimmed grey beard and soulful expression, his compassionate eyes drooping solicitously at the corners. The other he guessed must be Tyler: older than he had imagined, with a head of flat white hair incongruously matched by thick black eyebrows, sinister black eyes set in a weathered red face, and a strange fixed grin, malicious and amused.

As they came within bow-shot distance, Richard felt the barge slowing down at some whispered command from the stern. He rose to his feet in order to see better, and to show himself to his people. The effect on the waiting host was astonishing. As one man they vented a tumultuous roar of greeting, aimed at the slim young figure, richly clad in ermine and gold, rising like the sun from a wrack of clouds, a bright figurehead in the bows of the boat. The King! They cried, the King! John Ball bowed in his saddle, but made no move to dismount and kneel. Tyler casually doffed his hat, as if welcoming a comrade, greeting an equal.

Ball and Tyler felt this to be their moment of destiny. At last they would be able to speak directly, man to man, with their young sovereign, help him to understand the severity of their wrongs, present to him in full their just demands, and rescue him from the toxic influence of his treacherous councillors. They would teach him their slogan: For the King and the True Commons!

But something was wrong. The boat had slowed its approach, and was riding gently on the tide. Suddenly they saw Richard flanked and dwarfed on either side by two big bearded men in full armour, who began hotly to remonstrate with him. There also was the Archbishop of Canterbury and the Lord Chancellor, the hated Simon of Sudbury, whispering urgently in the young king's ear. Meanwhile the barge was backing away with the tide, then the port oars began pulling it around, prow away from the shore, pointing back across the river towards the Tower.[6]

As the rebels realised that the king was retreating, refusing to meet with them, hurrying back to shelter behind the walls of the Tower, they voiced as one man a great cry of rage and disappointment. They had trusted him, believed in him, accepted him as their true king. He was to hear their grievances, right their wrongs, give them the justice they deserved. He had promised. Tyler had assured them. Now the reward for all their pains was to watch the wake of the king's barge creaming behind as he turned tail and bolted to safety. Had the king betrayed them? Or was he still in the thrall of his wicked councillors, the lords Salisbury and Warwick and Oxford, Chancellor Simon of Sudbury, Prior of the Hospitallers Robert Hales, and above all the king's despised uncle, John of Gaunt, now in the north campaigning against the Scots, and out of their reach, but still grasping the young Richard tightly in his mailed fist?

Ball bowed his head, muttering silent prayers. Tyler's face was a still mask of white anger, patches of red rage showing on his cheeks. Betrayed. Humiliated in front of his followers. Made to look a fool.

He would have those royal advisors. He would have their heads. And maybe the King's too, if he proved recalcitrant. For now, it was still the King and the True Commons. Tomorrow, perhaps, the Commons without the King.

3

The Tower of London, 13 June 1381

Richard stood on the high wall of the White Tower and watched his city burn.

Frustrated by their failure to meet the king at Rotherhithe, the rebels had smashed their way through Southwark, burning the houses of crown officials, breaking open the prisons and freeing the captives, and sacking the Archbishop's palace at Lambeth. Here they destroyed everything they could, burning every scrap of paper from the offices, every charter and bond and muniment, every roll and record and remembrance. Since the chains of their bondage were inscribed on parchment, they would put every written record in England to the torch, reduce every document to ashes, and so liberate themselves from the servitude of paper.

A few minor officials were dragged out to summary execution, but the major leaders of the realm had already fled to the shelter of the Tower. The realisation that the birds had flown turned Tyler's mind to the city across the river. The Tower was said to be impregnable. But who could have predicted that such a host of the common people could ever have advanced so far without resistance? There were armed men, loyalist retainers, palace guards everywhere in London. Where were they? Why were they not resisting? What force was holding them back?

Let us find out, thought Tyler to himself. And with a series of peremptory commands he had drawn his forces off from their orgy of destruction, and led them to London Bridge. Across the river the bulk of the Tower rose against the blue June sky. A column of full two thousand men, swollen with new recruits cheered by their success, filed across the river and approached Bridge Ward. Tyler paused. Again, no resistance. There must be archers inside; but not a single shaft flew through the air to threaten them. Not a banner was raised, not a drum-beat sounded. Their rulers seemed to be responding to their progress with silence and inactivity.

By contrast, crowds of the common people lined the bridge as they rode past, applauding and cheering, welcoming them as liberators. And as he picked his way carefully through the throng, ducking his head to avoid the low-hanging shop-signs, Tyler saw with his own eyes what his mind told him could not be true.

The drawbridge was down. The gate was open. Who it was who had ruptured the defences, and whether it had been done out of solidarity or fear, he would never know. The moment he realised that London was open to them, he had spurred his horse onwards and ridden at the head of his host through the outer gateway of the Tower, and into the city.

Once inside the Kentishmen soon encountered their comrades from the other counties, who had also easily penetrated London's open defences. Tyler's force linked up with the men from Essex, who had entered the city through the Aldgate. Together they had descended on John of Gaunt's great Savoy Palace on the Strand, looting and pillaging and destroying everything they could find, and burning the building to the ground. Again every scrap of parchment was torched, and the hapless clerks who kept Gaunt's accounts were dragged out into the street and mercilessly slaughtered.

From there the rebel armies, now turned into little more than a terrorising mob, turned their attention to the great priory of the Knights of St John at Clerkenwell, and went in search of its preceptor, the Treasurer Robert Hales, the official linked most closely in their minds with the hated poll-tax. Unable to find Hales himself, they destroyed the priory and butchered its few occupants. Who are you with? They would demand of anyone who did not immediately join them. The correct answer was 'With King Richard and the True Commons'. Anything other than this reply resulted in a summary and brutal beheading.[7]

From the walls of the Tower Richard watched his city on fire. To the west the sky was bright with flame and darkened with smoke from the ruins of the Savoy Palace, the Temple, the Priory of St John. London was burning. They could hear the howls of the mob as they cut down another victim, the crashing sound of buildings collapsing in the flames, even a violent percussion from the direction of the Savoy Palace, where barrels of gunpowder had been tossed unwittingly into the fire.

Behind him Salisbury was reading from the petition the rebels had delivered to the king. It was a statement of their demands. The abolition of villeinage and villain tenure. Land held in return for service to be commuted to rental, at no more than four pence an acre. The people to be given freedom of employment, and freedom of trade. Free pardons to all for any crimes committed during the prosecution of the uprising.

The rest was a lengthy death list of 'traitors' whose lives were to be surrendered to the peoples' justice. 'We demand the heads of John of

Gaunt; Chancellor Sudbury; Treasurer Hales; keeper of the Privy Seal John Fordham; chief justice Robert Bealknapp; baron of the exchequer John Plesyngton ...' And so it went on, enumerating the names of fifteen nobles, churchmen and officers of the crown, all of whom, except for John of Gaunt, were there, gathered around the King, huddled in the relative safety of the Tower. Enemies of the people, in the eyes of the rebels, who should be held to account for their crimes: for the exaction of unjust taxes, for the imposition of unwarranted servitude, for the crushing burdens of bondage.[8]

Salisbury screwed the paper into a ball and tossed it aside, before spitting contemptuously over the wall. 'Peasants' was all he had to say. 'A peasants' revolt. We must end it now. Let us strike hard at them, tonight in their sleep, take them when weary and bleary from drink. Here I can marshal a troop of men who will think nothing of slitting their throats, while they are snoring, under cover of dark'.

Richard had listened to the reading of the petition and to Salisbury's commentary with only half his mind. With the other half he was thinking through his experiences of the last few days. Out there were his people, his loyal subjects, who protested that they loved him, and were acting only in his interests. He knew them to be normally gentle, peace-loving, hard-working family men. Surely the extremity of their actions spoke of their desperation, not of any depravity of nature or malicious intent. They had begged him for justice, and he was being prevented from delivering justice to them. He was their King. To whom else could they appeal?

Prevented by whom? Richard's admiration for the rebels had grown in proportion to his mistrust of his barons and officials. He looked around the circle of suspicious and inquisitive faces, carefully watching him. Big men, well dressed, well fed, well educated. Why were they all so wealthy? Was it not obvious that they had enriched themselves at the expense of the people and the state, robbing the commons, and embezzling from the crown?

They were confident, arrogant, secure of their power, certain of their right to hold sway. He felt very young and small beside them, a slim fourteen-year old boy. He was the son of the Black Prince, with an absolute right to rule. But he knew that would mean nothing if his powerful subjects turned against him. He had read his history. They could choose another king in a heartbeat, deposing him before he was possessed. There were other candidates, even here. He saw the sharp eyes of his cousin Henry observing him critically. The young Earl of Derby, son of the great John of Gaunt.[9] A grandson of Edward III, like himself. Like his father, hungry for power; another boy who would be king: as were our England in reversion his, and he our subjects' next degree in hope. And who would care a jot for primogeniture, if the interests of the rich and powerful were really threatened? Richard would be nothing, a snowman king, melting away to vapour in the searing heat of rebellion.

Richard looked down over the walls to the east, into the precincts of St Katherine by the Tower, where the sisters and brethren of the hospital cared for the sick and indigent. There a large number of rebels had set up camp, circling the walls like a besieging army. But he could see no sign of violence or intimidation. The buildings of the hospital were left unscathed. The insurgents seemed to view the religious as equals rather than oppressors, and offered them no harm. Richard could see monks and nuns bringing food to the rebels, clearly on friendly terms. Meanwhile one of the rebels was helping a sister to care for a sick child: he watched the countryman go off to the well, and carry back a bucket of water. This was what England should be: a community of reciprocity and mutual compassion. Instead it was a divided society, in which the labourers toiled in fear of the rich and powerful. Did the rebels have a cause? Could the face of England be changed?

At that moment Richard Plantagenet came to a decision. 'On the morrow I will meet them. At Mile End.' He cut off any further remonstrance – 'Enough! We were not born to sue, but to command!'[10] – and raising his hand to block any resistance, strode regally towards his chambers.

4

Mile End, 14 June 1381

The royal cavalcade swept under the arch of Aldgate and out onto the Colchester Road. Preceding Richard rode Aubrey de Vere, bearing the sword of state. Accompanying him were all the great lords, Salisbury, Warwick and Oxford, knights such as Sir Thomas Percy and Sir Robert Knolles, city officials like the mayor William Walworth, and many knights and esquires beside. Even the men of war were lightly armed, prepared for parley, not ready for battle. Strangely, given the dangerous circumstances, Richard's mother rode with them in a carriage. A substantial detachment of guards from the Tower afforded military protection. And bringing up the rear were a troop of some thirty men, clad in clerical black, who seemed unused to riding, and had difficulty keeping up.

Only a small retinue remained, by Richard's explicit command, in the Tower: Archbishop Sudbury, who had resigned as Chancellor and handed Richard back the Great Seal; Thomas Hales, Prior of St John; and against his own wishes, young Henry Bolingbroke, who stood petulantly on the walls to watch them ride away, and wondered at the strange silence and eye-avoiding glances of the guards who remained to protect the few left behind.

Richard rode out onto the green meadow of Mile End to meet the rebel army, amassed at their full strength of some ten thousand, with only a small detachment left behind in St Katherine's to secure the Tower.[11] Waiting for him were their commanders. John Ball was there, and Jack Straw, leader of the Essex revolt, and Wat Tyler. Richard reined in his horse opposite Tyler, the lords, knights and esquires forming a rank around him.

And then, to the amazement of the rebels, and the shock of his own retainers, Richard quickly dismounted and stood beside his horse, bridle in hand. After a few seconds Tyler did the same. The man and the boy stared across the meadow between them; and then slowly walked towards one another, leading their horses, until they stood not more than six feet apart.

'Welcome, your Majesty', said Tyler courteously. 'You are our prince, and we are your people. No other king will we have, but only you'.[12]

'Thanks, Master Tyler', said Richard. 'You see I am here, ready to listen to all your requests'.

'Demands', retorted Tyler more abruptly. 'Not negotiable'.

Richard glanced back at the frowning faces of his lords, then forwards to behold the hopeful and expectant expressions of the people. No other king but you.

'Proceed, let me hear them'.

And Tyler listed the same demands Richard had already heard, and could recite himself if need be. There should be no more serfs. Men and women should be free to work by contract for whoever they chose. No land should be held in return for bondage or customary service, only for rent. There should be no new taxes beyond the established tithes, and no tolls, monopolies, privileges or fines exacted over the means of production. A free people should exchange labour freely for wages, and trade freely throughout all the cities, boroughs and market-towns of England. Lastly, the King should permit the Commons to deal with traitors who had broken the law and shamed the king's majesty; and guarantee free pardons to all involved.

'Freely I grant to you all that you ask', said the king.

Tyler did not seem to hear him. There was something about the youth that fascinated and disarmed him. He continued to stare him up and down, studying the costliness of his clothes, the pale beauty of his face. 'Know now', he said, as if collecting himself, 'that we will not withdraw from this field, until … what did you say?'

'All this I grant', Richard replied. 'It is just, and fair, and what England should be. No more serfdom. Land for rent. No new taxes. Freedom to sell the work of your bodies, freedom to trade your labour's fruits. Free pardons to all. I will have letters swiftly drawn up, by clerks I have brought here to that same end. The Great Seal is here, held in my hand, to seal and secure them. Banners will I give you, one for each county, bearing the emblem of your King. Take now these letters, and under my banners ride you back home. A new world begins. Is there anything else?'

Tyler was still struggling to comprehend what had happened, like a man stumbling forward after kicking an open door. The voice of John Ball sounded over Tyler's head. 'One omission there is, my potent prince. The heads of the traitors we must have, or justice will not be seen to be done'.

Richard nodded slightly, and took one step closer to Tyler. 'I am no fool, young as I am. Here we have left the safety of the Tower; tonight at Blackfriars we take our rest. The Tower is yours. Should you find traitors within its walls, bring them to trial, and do what you will. Now I bid you good day. It is time to be home'.

Richard sprung onto his horse, waved to the cheering rebel army, pulled sharply round on his bridle, and disappeared into the midst of his retinue. At his command thirty clerks began busily writing.

5

Mile End, 14 June 1381, Night

Richard by the grace of God, king of England and France, and lord of Ireland, to all his bailiffs and faithful men to whom these present letters come, greetings. Know that by our special grace we have manumitted all our liegemen, subjects and others of the county of Kent; and we have freed and quitted each of them from bondage by these present letters. Henceforward no man shall be a serf nor make homage nor any kind of service to any lord, but shall give four pence for an acre of land. And no man shall serve any man except at his own will and by means of regular covenant. Henceforward all my subjects shall be free to buy or sell throughout the realm of England. We also pardon our said liege men and subjects for all felonies, acts of treason, transgressions and extortions performed by them or any one of them in whatsoever way. We also withdraw sentences of outlawry declared against them or any of them because of these offences. And we hereby grant our complete peace to them and each of them. In testimony of which we order these letters of ours to be made patent. Witnessed by myself at London on 14 June in the fourth year of my reign.[13]

Sitting under the canvas of a tent, by the light of a fire, Tyler had read the letter a dozen times, studied every clause, pored intensively over the stamp of the Great Seal. Usually, he knew, the king would use his own privy seal. But by Sudbury's resignation Richard held the Great Seal in his own hands, conferring on these letters the unique and potent joint authority of state and crown, Chancellor and King.

As soon as the royal party had left Mile End, Tyler had taken a troop of Kentishmen and raced towards the Tower. There he found little or no defence, and they were able easily to penetrate the fortress and search for the traitors. They soon discovered Sudbury and Hale, dragged them unceremoniously onto Tower Hill and subjected them to summary execution. The king's sergeant-at-arms, a physician and a lawyer met the same fate. Tyler had hoped to find John of Gaunt's son Henry, and to take him hostage; but somehow he had been spirited out of the Tower and away. They chose not to return to the fortress, having no intention of being trapped inside the Tower as the king and court had been. And so Tyler rode to re-join the Essex rebels in their camp at Mile End.

The camp was a carnival of feasting and rejoicing. Word of the king's concessions had spread through the host, and most of the rebels considered their objectives achieved. They were free; England was free; the young King was a true king. Who are you with? With King Richard and the true Commons!

But Tyler was gnawing at his lower lip. It had been too easy. He would like to have suspected treachery, but the letters patent lay undeniably in his hand, signed by the King, carrying the wax impression of the Great Seal.[14] Absolute, ultimate, irrevocable. Why then was he dissatisfied? Had they not realised their vision, the dream of John Ball, a free people in a free realm?

No, he thought to himself. It cannot be so. The nobles still possess their lands, the rich their wealth, the powerful their armies. The people may be free to work and trade, buy, and sell, but still there was no equality. Sooner or later those in power would find new ways of oppressing the poor.

We have to cut deeper. We must have more than freedom; we must have power. Where does power lie? In land, in the law, in armies. The people had shown they could raise an army, and take London by force. They had shown they could wrest the law to their own ends, by executing the enemies of the people. But they had no land.

There had been a balancing, but not a reversal. The commons must expropriate the land, or they would never be truly free. All land to the commons. Agriculture, commerce, government, the military, all must be taken into public ownership. All power to the people. We will have a king bound by constitution to rule on behalf of the people. Or better still, no king at all, but a republic, ruled by a senate. *Senatus atque Populus Anglicus.* The Senate and the people of England.

'How goes it, Wat?' asked John Ball. 'You are pensive and pale. What ails you, my man?'

'The battle is won', Tyler said, 'but not the war. We must force the king to forfeit the land, to take it away from the lords and the church. All land to the commons. If he countermands, then we shall depose him, and throw down his throne. A council of the Commons shall rule in his stead'.

'But he is our king!' protested Jack Straw.

'And what does it mean, to be our king? What do *you* mean by it, you, Jack Straw? The king who binds us in fealty's fetters? The king to whom homage we're forced to pay? The king to whom basely we bend the knee?

If truly *our* king, he belongs to us: he is our creature; our puppet; our servant. We need a king to do our bidding, against the nobles, against the church. A king who'll oppose all those who oppress us'.

'A King of kindness, liberty, love', came the dreamy voice of John Ball. 'Who will bring us back to the golden age. Back to the garden; back to God. As the prophets sang: 'a little child shall lead them there'.

'Too far you go, man', cried Straw to Tyler. 'Miles too far. This follow a fantasy. Damn you, the only end to this, is death to all'.

Tyler leaned over and seized Straw by the cloak, his white face incandescent in the firelight, his wild black eyes staring like those of a madman. 'All power to the people', he gabbled feverishly. 'All land to the commons. If you are not with us, you are against us. If thine eye offend thee, pluck it out. Now the time is come. Now the time is come. Now the time is ...'.

'Back to Essex I mean to take my men', interrupted Jack Straw. 'Now. Tonight. This is folly, and follow we will not. It is not for this that we have fought'.

Tyler leapt to his feet, pushed Straw aside and stood in the doorway of the tent. 'Send word to the king. On the morrow we'll meet him. There is more to be said'. He thought for a moment. 'Close to the city. Smithfield. Quickly, send'.

6

Smithfield, 15 June 1381

Early in the warm, fresh June morning King Richard with his train and a troop of armed men trotted swiftly along the Strand. His high-stepping roan horse, chestnut brown flecked with white, seemed to disdain the ground. The charred remains of his uncle's Savoy Palace were still smoking. There were few people in the streets; the crowds seemed to have dispersed.

At Westminster Abbey Richard knelt and prayed at the shrine of Edward the Confessor.

'Deus qui miro ordine angelorum ministeria hominumque dispensas ...' [15]

'God, who in miraculous order arranged the ministry of angels and men, mercifully grant that by those ministering eternally to you in heaven, our life here on earth may be attended and defended. Through Christ Our Lord, Amen'.

Remounting outside the Abbey, with great jingling of spurs and clinking of bridles the royal procession rode on to Smithfield. Stopping by the gate of the Priory, they could see the rebels drawn up in formation under the wall of St Bartholomew's Hospital. Not so many of them now as there had been, their ranks depleted since the moderate Straw, satisfied with the king's promises, had led his men back to Essex. Tyler and Ball had divided the movement with their excessive and importunate demands, confusing the people, breaking their ranks. The balance of power had shifted, and the King's forces seemed no longer so manifestly outnumbered.

Tyler and Ball kept in their saddles and made no move the cross the ground between themselves and the king. But neither was Richard in a moving frame of mind. 'Walworth', he said to the Mayor. 'Go bring these rebels to confront us here'.

Mayor of London William Walworth kneed his mount forward, and crossed the grassy space between the armies.

'Tyler', he shouted, with no pretence of courtesy, 'you are to come and meet the king'.

Tyler glanced sideways at Ball, and both together slowly advanced across Smithfield towards Richard, following Walworth's horse.

Richard looked them over, his pale face expressionless. Ball looked even more unkempt than before, his wrinkled face stamped with new lines. But his previously gentle eyes had hardened, and his face had a haunted look. Tyler returned the King's gaze with a defiant stare of open hostility.

'Why are we here', asked Richard, 'when all should be at home? What do you lack I've not already given?'

'We cannot be content', Tyler began, omitting any formal address, 'till we have all we ask. The fruits of the field were made for all mankind: the fish and the fowl, the flesh and the fruit. Therefore all parks and preserves, all warrens and brakes, all waters and woods, must be common to all. Throughout the realm, both the rich and the poor must be free to take game, to fish in the ponds, hunt hares in the fields, and feed their families. Only such freedom of the lakes and the land will induce us to hie back to our homes'.[16]

By the time Tyler ceased speaking, Richard could scarcely hear his voice over the noise of remonstrance and recrimination from his own side. All the land in common? Ownership abolished? But Tyler had not finished.

'There is more, your majesty, for you to hear. The law of this land is all for the rich, none pleads for the poor. We therefore demand a commons' commission, to arraign and to execute all attorneys and escheators. We will kill all the lawyers, all those trained in law. From that day forth there shall be no more law, only the power of the peoples' courts. All decrees shall derive from popular power. My mandate shall rule, I will be Justice, and all who oppose us, we will have their heads'.[17]

The groundswell of opposition was growing all around Richard, who felt trapped in a vice between the intractable commons and the implacable lords. Slowly, quietly, mounted men were moving alongside, by-passing the King, and targeting Tyler.

'Fellow', Richard said, 'these are but wild and whirling words. No realm on earth has such a rule of law. The innocent would be sacrificed together with the guilty. Can you be serious in your demands?'

Thoughtfully Tyler drew a bottle from his saddle-bag, and raising it high took a long and noisy draught. And then he spat the dregs onto the ground in front of the King. There was an audible gasp of astonishment from the royal train.

Emboldened by Tyler's extremism, John Ball pushed his horse forward and began to speak.

'As well as the law, we must reform the Church. All priests must lose their place, and their possessions pass to the people. All goods of the clergy shall be confiscate, all their pelf given to the parish. All property of the Church to be expropriated, for the Commons. There shall be but one prelate to rule over all; his master is God, and his name is John Ball'.

The young King did not know what to do. Only the day before he had given the rebels everything they asked. Against the wishes of his own lords, he had offered to transform England from a feudal kingdom based on serfdom, to an open society with free movement of goods and labour. And now these men had come to him again, with new demands impossible for him to deliver: to abolish private property, to replace the law with anarchy, to grant spiritual supremacy to a hedge-priest. How could they possibly expect him to help them?

Tyler and Ball remained immovable in their defiance. Out of the corner of his eye Richard could see horses moving forward from the flanks of his host, circling around behind the rebel leaders.

Richard was beginning to panic. 'We will consider all that you have said. Only retire from this field, return to Kent, go back to your homes, and we will answer you'.

A look of cunning came over Tyler's face, and he edged his horse forward until its nose was almost touching Richard's. 'You see, your Majesty, that will not do. You have served us well, and we would keep you as our king. But the Commons must have their courts, the laity their church. Tyler will share your throne, and Ball will be your Bishop. You will be the peoples' prince. You will have our mandate; we shall be your masters'.

During this speech the rebel leader had been surreptitiously reaching inside his jacket, and now suddenly drew out a long dagger, which he hefted in his hand as he grabbed the bridle of Richard's horse. But Walworth was too quick for him: his grip was on Tyler's bridle, and violently he was pulling the rebel's horse away from the King. 'All power to the people', shouted Tyler, as he turned on his attacker, leaned across and slashed at Walworth's chest. But the Mayor wore mail beneath his cloak, and the sharp blade glanced aside. The King's Esquire, Ralph Standish, had also ridden between Tyler and the King, and now flanked the rebel leader on the other side. The three horses bumped ungainly together, the mounts whinnied and snickered and jerked at the reins. The Mayor reached across and thumped his own dagger deep into Tyler's head, while Ralph Standish, trained in arms, drew his sword, and ran the rebel through. Helplessly Tyler lolled out of his saddle, blood coursing from two mortal wounds. Royal retainers swiftly dismounted, pulled Tyler from his horse, and dragged him across the grass. Reaching the place where beasts were slaughtered, where the grass was black with the blood of lambs and pigs, cattle and goats, they pushed Tyler to his knees, and with a single axe blow, hacked off his head.[18]

Everything changed, in the twinkling of an eye. The front rank of the King's army drew their swords, dropped their shields into place, and riding past the King began to canter towards the rebel horde. John Ball had disappeared. A few brave bowmen of the Commons drew their shafts and launched ineffectual darts. But the death of their leader robbed most of them of their courage. Many broke ranks and began to run. Others dropped to their knees in surrender, casting their weapons aside. Those bold enough to keep the field in arms were mercilessly cut down.

Richard's horse, panicked by the melee, was thrashing round in circles, held on a tight rein. In a moment everything was lost: all his royal promises, all the aspirations of the Commons, all the hopes of a new society based on freedom and justice. He felt his power leaching away. A mockery king of snow in the hot June sun, his authority soaked up by the thirsty Smithfield earth along with Tyler's blood. Helplessly he turned his horse and spurred it towards Clerkenwell. His bodyguards followed him, while the rest of his army chased the peasants from the field.

7

Smithfield, 15 June 1381. Evening

Later that day Richard returned to Smithfield to re-join and reward his followers. Walworth and Standish were knighted, right there on the field, to acknowledge their courage in defending the King's life and destroying his enemies. The pale young monarch moved and spoke like an automaton, merely performing the tasks assigned to him by the victorious lords. He felt that his first attempt at personal rule might well have been his last. He had hoped to deliver justice to the people; but the peoples' leaders had preferred revolution to reform, threatened to depose him, compromised his safety and left him helpless in the face of his followers.

And now he was an impotent spectator as the nobility restored equilibrium, reinforced its power and began to strike back against the Commons with a terrible revenge: show trials, imprisonment, torture, executions. Tyler's head on its spike blackened on London Bridge, and the dream of John Ball was borne away like so much flotsam on the swift Thames tide. The aspirations of the people for liberty in employment and trade, access to land and business, were set back centuries.

He knew the nobles would never trust him again, and that he would live out his reign in continual fear of plots and conspiracies. At night he dreamed that he was in prison, fighting with an unseen assailant; or standing in Westminster Abbey, reluctantly handing over his crown. He trusted no-one, and knew that no-one trusted him. Sometimes he would feel upon him the watchful eyes of his cousin Henry Bolingbroke.

Uneasy lies the head that wears the crown.[19] But there was never any shortage of ambitious men eager to endure exactly such unease. Ah, Richard, with the eyes of heavy mind, I see thy glory, like a shooting star, fall to the base earth from the firmament. The sun sits weeping in the lowly west, witnessing storms to come, woe and unrest.[20]

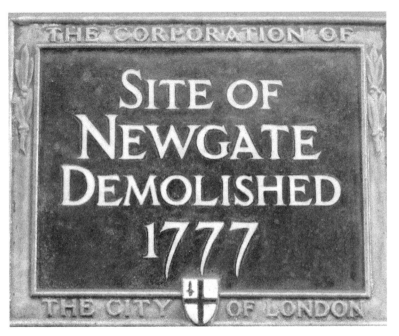

Site of Old Newgate, Newgate Street

ANNE ASKEW

PREFACE

Anne Askew was a remarkable woman, one of the 'Protestant martyrs', executed along with others for heresy on 16th July 1546, during the reign of Henry VIII. She was one of only two women to have been both tortured in the Tower of London, and burnt at the stake. She was the first Englishwoman to demand a divorce, and one of the earliest female poets. She was held in Newgate, interrogated in the Saddler's Hall in Cheapside, the Guildhall and St Paul's, and burnt to death in Smithfield.

Anne was interrogated in the Tower by Richard Rich (better known for his role in the conviction of St Thomas More), and the Lord Chancellor Thomas Wriothsley (grandfather of Shakespeare's patron the Earl of Southampton). They were seeking to implicate certain ladies of the court, even possibly Queen Katherine Parr herself, in Protestant heresy. They put Anne on the rack, but she would not talk. When the Lieutenant of the Tower refused to continue, Rich and Wriothsley took off their coats and racked her themselves. Anne told them nothing.

Anne told her own story in a work entitled *The Examinations*, published in 1546. This story imitates her writing, using some sentences from the original and extending and adapting it with additional historical evidence. Anne knew the Bible by heart, and could quote chapter and verse when debating with the leading theologians of the land. In her autobiographical narrative she often quotes passages from the Psalms. I have used Psalm 22, with its powerful expressions of physical agony and spiritual suffering, as a kind of refrain to the confessional narrative.

Protestant polemicist John Bale published Anne Askew's narrative after her death, together with a voluminous commentary, as *The First Examynacion* (Wesel, 1546) and *The lattre examinacyon* (Wesel, 1547). John Foxe published the *Examinations* in Latin in *Rerum, in Ecclesia Gestarum Commentari* (1559), and in English – as 'The two examinations of the worthy servant of God, Maistris An Askew' – in his *Acts and Monuments of these latter and perillous dayes, touching matters of the Church* (London: John Day, 1563) (better known as Foxe's *Book of Martyrs*). Both texts are reprinted in Elaine V. Beilin, *The Examinations of Anne Askew* (Oxford: Oxford University Press, 1996).

ANNE ASKEW

I

Truth is laid in prison. The law is turned to wormwood. And there can no right judgment go forth.[1]

Anne Askew

Newgate Prison, 2 July 1554

My God, my God, look upon me; why hast thou forsaken me: and art so far from my health, and from the words of my complaint? (Ps. 22)

The words of the Psalmist are a great comfort to me, as I lie here broken in body, knowing that my own dear Saviour himself spoke them from the Cross. No sorrow was like unto his sorrow, no pain so great as the pain he endured. What then that I, a poor weak woman, should suffer a little hurt in the few days before my death? For I hope by His grace very soon, at Smithfield, to pass through my torments, and end the long course of my agony, being compassed in with flames of fire, as a blessed sacrifice unto God.[2]

This writing, the work of my hands, always such a pleasure to me, I can scarcely perform, injured as I am from the tortures of the rack. I can scarcely move my fingers, and the pain at my wrists troubles me sore.

I am poured out like water, and all my bones are out of joint. (Ps. 22)

On Tuesday last I was sent from Newgate to the Tower, where Master Richard Rich, with Lord Chancellor Wriothsley, charged me upon my obedience to reveal the names of any of my sect at court. My answer was, that I knew none. He asked me of many ladies, such as my Lady of Suffolk, my Lady of Sussex, my Lady of Hertford, my Lady Denny, and my Lady Fitzwilliam. I told him that even if I were to pronounce anything against any of them, he would be able to prove nothing.[3]

Though my words were bold, I was sorely afraid.

My heart also in the midst of my body is even like melting wax. (Ps. 22)

For I knew that they had already condemned me as a heretic, from my opinion on the Eucharist alone, and that only God's mercy, or the King's, could save me from the flames. I had told them, that after the priest has spoken the words of consecration, the bread remains but bread, though the same is a most necessary remembrance of his glorious sufferings and death. They say, and teach as a necessary article of faith, that after those words be once spoken, there remains no bread, but even the self-same body that hung upon the cross on Good Friday, both flesh, blood, and bone. To this belief of theirs say I, nay. Christ sits at the hand of the Father Almighty; he is not baked into a common loaf. Lo, this is the heresy that I hold, and for it must suffer the death.[4]

As I was already condemned, they needed no further confession from me, and no need to put me to the pain. So it was clear that their intent in torturing me was for the purpose of gaining information, not for the purpose of proving guilt. I knew they would stint nothing in applying their punishments, since they were merely breaking a body soon to be burned; and I knew that since I should tell them nothing, the suffering they would visit on me would be most severe.

They told me that the king knew of a great number of my sect in his own court. I replied that in this he was deceived, as in many other matters. Meaning by this, the dissemblance and untruth that such creatures as they practised on his majesty. They demanded to know how I had been supported while in the Counter prison, if certain gentlewomen had sent me money. I said there was no creature that therein did strengthen me, that I was left abandoned and alone.[5]

All they that see me laugh me to scorn: they shoot out their lips, and shake their heads, saying, He trusted in God, that he would deliver him: let him deliver him, if he will have him. (Ps. 22)

And so because I confessed no ladies or gentlewomen to be of my opinion, then they did put me on the rack.

2

I was taken to a dungeon by the jailor. There waiting for me were Sir Richard Rich, and the Lord Chancellor, and the Lieutenant of the Tower, Sir Anthony. First they showed me the instrument, trusting that fear alone would induce me to tell them what they wished to know. It is a terrible thing to see, a great iron bed with planks across, and two wooden rollers with ratchets and ropes. At top and bottom were rings to hold the chains on my ankles and wrists, and a long lever on the top roller to pull and stretch the prisoner. I stared at the rack, and could scarcely hear their questions. The jailer shook me, and slapped me, and bade me answer. This is your chance, he whispered fiercely in my ear. Tell them what they want to know.

But I would say nothing. For all their exhibition of terror they misjudged me, for my fear is of the Lord alone. To Him I prayed:

Be not thou far from me, O Lord: thou art my succour, haste thee to help me. (Ps. 22)

Once it became clear that I would tell them nothing out of mere timidity, they determined to subject me to the pain. First the Lieutenant had me stripped of my clothes, down to my shift. What their purpose was to uncover my nakedness, I knew not. Or rather I knew only too well. I know myself to be a handsome woman, for in the days of my preaching they called me 'The Fair Gospeller'. Many men have desired me, even my beast of a husband, at first. I knew those men in the Tower looked on me with lust in their hearts, watching with greedy eyes as the jailer pulled off my gown, and slit my stays. I stood before them with my face downcast, fair hair falling about my face, my shift so thin they could see through it to the contours of my breasts and legs. What manner of men, beasts rather I may call them, would look on a woman with bodily desire, and at the same time visit her with such cruelty and violence? I could see them relish the vision of my vulnerability. But I held fast to a remembrance of my Lord at his Passion:

They part my garments among them: and cast lots upon my vesture. (Ps. 22)

Then Sir Anthony commanded the jailor to pinch me with the rack. This is the word they use to mean an application of pain without the extremity of injury. First they made me climb up onto the rack, which with some difficulty I managed, encumbered as I was with irons and chains about my wrists and ankles, and then to lie down on my back and lift my hands above my head. In doing so I could not avoid, for all my efforts at modesty, exposing my privacy to their prying gaze. Then the jailer made fast the chains to the rings on the rollers. Though pressing so close upon me, his chest against my breasts, he took care not to touch me indecently, and his eyes avoided my eyes, as if he took little pleasure in the work he was compelled to do. Gently and discreetly he pulled my shift down over my legs, as if to guard what little modesty was left to me. Sir Anthony gave the order, the jailor seized the long lever and pulled it over, and my ordeal began.

As the roller revolved, the chains at my wrists and ankles tightened, and began to pull my limbs contrariwise. The pain at first was bearable, a stretching only of the joints, and so I lay quiet and replied nothing to their questions. Who were my acquaintances at court? Who sent me money when I was in the Counter? What gentlewomen were of my sect? with whom was I in secret communication? All this time I lay quiet with my eyes closed, and teeth clenched against the pinching of the rack.

Again, the Lieutenant commanded the jailor to pull on the lever. This time the chains lifted me bodily off the bed, so I was suspended six inches in the air, the mechanism of the rack locked against any relenting, and the torment at my shoulders and hips felt like flames of fire. Still I did not cry out, though my body rocked and trembled in the agonising air, and still I refused to give answer to their questions. How many other heretics could I name? who else was of my opinion?

At last I heard the Lieutenant order the jailer to cease the torture and loose me from the rack, since I was clearly not going to talk.[6] We have done enough, he said: let her be taken down. But then I heard Wriothesley, the chancellor, saying hotly that he was not content I should be loosed so soon, confessing nothing, and commanding the lieutenant to strain me on the rack again. I will not do it, said the Lieutenant, boldly remonstrating against the chancellor. No woman has ever been treated so in England, and if I had my way, no woman should ever be treated so again. The chancellor was angry, and threatened Sir Anthony that his disobedience should be signified to the king. Do what you will, said Sir Anthony: I will have nothing further to do with it. And so, he left the dungeon, taking the jailer with him, and slamming the great iron-studded door behind.

Well master Rich, said Wriothsley to his companion, we have her to ourselves. Let us get to work. And both threw off their gowns, as if they meant to play the tormentors themselves.[7] By now all my fear had been chased out by anger. These men of power knew full well they were proceeding far beyond anything the law allowed. The good Sir Anthony, a man of honour, had done his duty as commanded, and resolved to do no more when his conscience told him they were in the wrong. But Rich and Wriothsley were ready to do anything to further their ambitions, and foment their plots. I hated so their bare-faced iniquity, their cruelty and violence towards a woman, that I cared nothing for their terror. Let them do with me what they will, and let us all answer to God.

Thou art he that took me out of my mother's womb: thou wast my hope, when I hanged yet upon my mother's breasts. (Ps. 22)

First, they asked me if I was with child. Much you care for that, I said, for if you will do this to the tender body of a woman, you would do it to a child to serve your purpose. Rich laughed, and said that it seemed she was not with child, meaning that no man would desire me. Ye shall not need to spare for that, I said, but do your wills upon me. And so they did, pulling the lever over to tighten the chains again, over and over, and with each pull repeating their questions. I cried aloud, I could not help it, not to them for mercy, but only to the Lord.

O go not from me, for trouble is hard at hand, and there is none to help me. (Ps. 22)

Now the pain was grievous, and I knew my body could not much longer withstand the stress. I heard strange noises, cracking and popping, not knowing whence they came, and realising they were the sounds of my own joints, the cartilages and ligaments snapping under the strain. I could see Rich and Wriothsley, red in the face, taking turns to pull the lever. Their eyes were incensed with cruelty, like the eyes of wild beasts, excited by the scent of blood.

They gape upon me with their mouths: as it were a ramping and a roaring lion. (Ps. 22)

And then my joints themselves began to give way, torn asunder by the rack, the bones dislocated and dragged from their sockets. I felt the bones of my arms coming away from the shoulder, my leg bones parting company with my hips. My elbows and knees were pulled apart, my wrists snapped.

They pierced my hands and feet: I may tell all my bones. (Ps. 22)

Quietly and patiently I prayed to the Lord that he would deliver me. I knew that very soon the rack would pluck my body asunder, and I would bleed to death, that cruel wooden couch my deathbed. My tormentors knew this also, and just at the point where I felt I could truly bear no more, and would have said anything at all to stop the pain, they desisted and loosed the chains. I could not move, and I heard them call for assistance in taking me from the rack. I could not stand, so they set me in a chair and carried me back to my cell. I abode their tyranny, and I told them nothing.

3

Newgate Prison, 2 July 1545

You will think it strange, gentle reader of the future, that such cruelty should be used by men of authority on the tender body of a woman, for no reason other than her holding fast to a true and honest opinion. It is my hope that sufferings such as mine may move the consciences of some of those in power, and that the spirit of God my Saviour will prompt them to bring the people of England back to true religion. I have seen that spirit at work, even in some of those who have been set on to torment me: such as the jailor who tried to guard my modesty, even on the rack; or the brave Lieutenant of the Tower, who put himself in danger by refusing to torture me further. For nothing I have ever preached, or said, or confessed to my accusers, is in any way contrary to the truths of scripture. Nor have I ever broken any laws, knowing better than my accusers the laws of God as laid down in that same holy gospel.

I cherish the hope, that after my death, these my beliefs will become in the future as familiar and uncontested, as today they are held heretical and unlawful. Let me here rehearse some of the interrogations to which I was subjected before my ordeal in the Tower, so that you may see the common sense of my opinions, and the absurdities of those set upon to question me.

My first examination took place at Saddler's Hall in Cheapside.[8] I was asked by the Lord Mayor whether the sacrament of the altar was indeed the very body of Christ? In return I asked my interrogator why St Stephen was put to death, and he said he knew not.[9] He asked me if I believed that God did not dwell in temples made of hands?[10] I cited to him chapters 7 and 17 of the Acts of the Apostles. He said it was reported of me that I had said, I had rather read five lines of the Bible than hear five masses in the church.[11] I confessed that I said no less, and offered to defend this opinion from the text of holy scripture. If my lord knew the scripture as well as the Mass, I told him, he would better be able to debate theology with me.

Then he asked me a question designed to trap me: whether a mouse, eating the host, received God or no? I made him no answer, but smiled. For if I said no, they would take that as proof that I disbelieved in the sacrament of the Eucharist. If I said yes, I would be speaking folly, that a mouse can receive Christ.[12]

Then the bishop's chancellor rebuked me, and said that I was much to blame for preaching on the Scriptures. For St. Paul, he said, forbade women to speak or to talk of the word of God. I answered him that I knew Paul's meaning as well as he, which is, in 1 Corinthians xiv., that a woman ought not to speak in the congregation by the way of teaching: and then I asked him how many women he had seen go into the pulpit and preach? He said he never saw any. Then I said, he ought to find no fault in poor women, unless they had offended the law, which for my own part I never had.[13]

All they were able to allege against me, is that I often read the Bible in the minster at Lincoln. Some had told me beforehand that the priests would harass and assault me if they found me reading, so when I heard that, I went swiftly there, not being afraid, because I knew my matter to be good. Moreover I remained there nine days, to see what would be said unto me. And as I was in the minster, reading upon the Bible, they approached me, two by two, and stared at me, but said nothing, and went their ways again without words speaking. Not one of those priests had the knowledge to challenge my understanding, or the courage to forbid me to read the word of the Lord.[14]

In several examinations, at Saddler's Hall, the Guildhall, in St Paul's Church, great lords of the realm, bishops, priests and doctors again and again questioned me, and sought to compel me to acknowledge the bread of the sacrament to be the body of Christ, flesh, blood and bone. This doctrine was both the king's will, they said, written in his own work called the *King's Book,* and the law, as enacted by Parliament in the Six Articles some five years past. If I did not believe in this transubstantiation, then I was a heretic, damned by the church, and condemned by the law to death at the stake.[15]

Now it was my earnest desire that they should fully understand my opinion on this doctrine, and so I took trouble to explain it to them. Christ said unto his apostles, I reminded them, 'Take, eat, this is my body which is given for you'. He gave them bread as a visible sign or token to receive his body, which would be crucified for them, and to understand his death to be the only health and salvation of their souls. The bread and the wine were left us for a sacramental communion, or a mutual participation of the inestimable benefits of his most precious death and blood-shedding, and that we should, in the end thereof, be thankful together for that most necessary grace of our redemption. And I referred them to the scriptures where St. Paul says, 'The letter slayeth, the Spirit giveth life'; and to the sixth chapter of John, where all is applied unto faith; and to the fourth chapter of St. Paul's Second Epistle to the Corinthians, which says that things which are seen are temporal, but they that are not seen are everlasting.[16]

Is the consecrated bread the body of Christ? They repeated their question. 'My belief is', I said, 'that the sacramental bread was left us to be received with thanksgiving, in remembrance of Christ's death, the only remedy of our soul's recovery; and that thereby we also receive the whole benefits and fruits of his most glorious passion'. But still they urged, is the bread in the box, God, or no? I said, 'God is a Spirit, and will be worshipped in spirit and truth.' Then they demanded, 'Will you plainly deny Christ to be in the sacrament?' I answered, that I believe faithfully the eternal Son of God not to dwell there; in witness whereof I recited again the history of Bel, Daniel xix., Acts vii. and xvii., and Matt. xxiv.[17]

Still they persisted, becoming more and more angry, ignoring my arguments, and demanded to know, if I would deny the sacrament to be Christ's body and blood? I said, 'Yes, I deny it. For the Son of God, that was born of the Virgin Mary, is now glorious in heaven, and will come again from thence at the latter day, to judge both the quick and the dead. And as for that ye call your God, it is a piece of bread. Let it but lie in the box three months, and it will be mouldy, and so turn to nothing that is good. Whereupon I am persuaded that it cannot be God'.[18]

At last they were satisfied. They had their answer. And so I was condemned.

Will you have a priest, they asked, thinking that facing death I would wish to confess. I smiled. Why do you smile, they said?[19] Is it not good to confess? I said, I would confess my faults unto God, for I was sure that He would hear me with favour. They shook their heads, and laughed me to scorn.

'I neither wish death' I said in conclusion, 'nor yet fear his might. God have the praise thereof'.

4

Newgate Prison, 10 July 1545

After my condemnation I was sent again to Newgate for present execution at Smithfield. But first they had me to the Tower to be laid on the rack, in the hope that I would betray my fellow Protestants by informing on them. Since I was now a condemned heretic, any connection or correspondence they could discover between myself and others could be used to condemn them to the same fate. In the event they showed no interest in the common people I knew to be engaged in the Lord's work of Reformation, and I was scarcely acquainted with any great ladies at court. Rumours had reached me that my lady Queen Catherine herself was secretly of our number, that she had the tutelage of the young prince Edward, and that once he succeeded his father he would complete the great work of Reform. But I knew no more of this than every man or woman with eyes to see, and ears to hear. God is at work in the world, and he is preparing the way for his faithful children. I am only sorry that like Moses, I will not live to see the Promised Land. So in refusing to provide them with the damning evidence they sought, and testifying to the truth of the Gospel, I was only speaking the truth, though the truth has condemned me to the fire.

After my racking I was returned to the prison, and laid in a bed, with as weary and painful bones as ever had patient Job.[20]

> *My strength is dried up like a potsherd, and my tongue cleaveth to my gums: and thou shalt bring me into the dust of death.* (Ps. 22)

And here in great pain and anguish I have written this confession, and this prayer.[21]

O Lord! I have more enemies now, than there be hairs on my head. With all the spite they can imagine, they fall upon me, who am thy poor creature. Yet, sweet Lord, I heartily desire of thee that thou wilt of thy most merciful goodness forgive them that violence which they do, and have done, unto me. Open also thou their blind hearts, that they may hereafter do that thing in thy sight, which is only acceptable before thee, and to set forth thy verity aright, without all vain fantasies of sinful men. So be it, O Lord, so be it!

– By me, ANNE ASKEW.

5

Newgate Prison, 16 July 1545

This day is the day appointed for my execution, so presently this narrative will, perhaps abruptly, cease. Be of good comfort,[22] gentle reader: for know that once my presence has departed this page, I will be looking upon the face of God. My Lord said, on the Cross, to the penitent thief, this day you will be with me in Paradise (Luke 23.43). I too, like him, have been so tormented, that I cannot live long in such great distress. And so I yearn for death, and the release from suffering it brings. For He shall wipe away every tear from my eyes. (Rev. 21.4).

I have looked upon the scene of my death, and found strange comfort in the sight. Since I cannot stand or walk, I begged my friend the jailor to lift me up to the window so I could behold the place of execution. He urged me not to do so, saying it was better not to dwell on bodily things, but to think only of heaven. I assured him that it would be of comfort for me to see the shape of the future, and I should fear it less. And so he lifted me in my chair, so I could gaze down at Smithfield.

There in the centre of the market-place stood the stake, surrounded by a great pile of faggots and straw. Heaps of fuel lay nearby, ready to cast onto the flames should they be needed. Men were busy at work constructing a dais under the wall of the hospital, which provided a covered platform for the nobles, churchmen and court officials to sit and watch the spectacle of my burning. I knew that Wriothsley the Lord Chancellor would be there, and the Dukes of Norfolk and Bedford, the Lord Mayor of London, sundry bishops and priests and lawyers. All eager to see the immolation of this woman whose mouth they could not shut, this 'fair Gospeller' who would speak out of turn, and shame men by showing she knew more than they; whose beauty thy both desired and hated, and whose voice they could neither ignore, nor harness to their own will. Well, they have marred my fairness, and soon my voice will be stilled for ever.

Facing the stake in the marketplace was a pulpit, from which a priest will deliver a sermon before I am put to the fire. I believe it will be Dr Nicholas Shaxton, that great Judas who professed our reformed faith, and then recanted to save his skin.[23] I told him it were better he had never been born. If I am able, I will answer his discourse, and correct his learning, a still small voice speaking out of the whirlwind of flame.

I must needs be carried to the stake in a chair, since I cannot go on my feet, by means of my great torments. They will tie me to the stake with a chain about my middle, to hold up my body.[24] Other Protestants who have seen their friends go to the stake tell me that the common practice is to lay gunpowder about the body of the condemned, to shorten the suffering. In my case, I can tell, there will be no such relief. Those bold and honourable men, my accusers, would not sit so close to the site of an explosion. Because of my intransigence, because I would not submit to their will, say what they want me to say, tell them what they wanted to hear, they have resolved to prolong my torment, and deliver me here to a slow and agonising death.

Perhaps they will offer me a reprieve, the king's pardon, if I will recant. But even in the face of such terror, I must say to them that I have not come here to deny my Lord and Master. The priest will finish his sermon, and commend my soul to the mercy of God. The lord mayor will command that fire be put to me, and cry with a loud voice, *fiat justitia*.

And so I, Anne Askew, having passed through so many torments, will there end the long course of my agonies, being compassed in with flames of fire, as a blessed sacrifice unto God.[25] And so at last I will sleep in the Lord.

6

It is time. They are come. I must go.

Pray for me, gentle reader. Pray for my soul.

Henry VIII Gate, St Bartholomew's Hospital, Smithfield

JOHN WILMOT

PREFACE

William Harvey is acknowledged as one of the greatest medical researchers in history. He put an end to millennia of misunderstanding by demonstrating the function of the heart, and the continuous circulation of the blood. Harvey was physician in charge at St Bartholomew's Hospital from 1609, and an important Fellow of the Royal College of Physicians, based at that time in Knight Ryder Street alongside St Paul's. Harvey was personal physician to both James I and Charles I, and a mentor to Charles II. He lived in Ludgate, but also occupied a house belonging to the hospital in Smithfield.

Harvey himself has proved resistant to fictionalising, as demonstrated by the clumsy 'Imaginary Journal' *The Diary of William Harvey* by Jean Hamburger (1983, trans. Barbara Wright, NJ: Rutgers University Press, 1992). In his *England and Other Stories* (London: Simon and Schuster, 2014), Graham Swift includes an attempt – 'Haematology' – to conscript the lifelong Royalist Harvey for the Commonwealth.

Harvey provides only the background to the following story, a comic fantasia about the Restoration poet and libertine John Wilmot, Earl of Rochester. Some obscure and unexplained facts link Rochester with Harvey. When Charles II sent Rochester abroad in 1661, it was in the company of Scots physician Andrew Balfour, a pupil of Harvey's. Rochester ended up enrolling in the medical school at the University of Padua, where Harvey had taken his degree in 1602. During one of his many periods of exile from court for bad behaviour, Rochester set himself up as a physician, 'Dr Bendo', in a makeshift surgery on Tower Hill.

I have linked Harvey's theories on circulation, essential to understanding the physiology of the male erection, with the Restoration obsession with male sexual performance and impotence that is so prominent in Rochester's poems and plays. Both Aristotle and Galen, who still provided the theoretical basis for medical understanding in the 17th century, taught that the erection was caused by air and heat. The role of the nerves began to be understood in the 18th century, and the pathology of smooth muscle relaxation in the 19th. Astonishingly the physiology of the erection was not fully understood and accepted until 1984. Viagra was patented in 1996.[1]

In this story Charles II believes that Harvey had discovered the secret of the male erection, and sends Rochester to Europe to find it.[2] Comic, erotic, satirical and scientific, the story concludes with a performance of Rochester's obscene farce *Sodom, or the Quintessence of Debauchery* (1684) where he puts Harvey's medical discoveries to good use. This farce features largely in Stephen Jeffrey's play *The Libertine* (1994, London: Nick Hern Books, 2014) and the film of the same title (dir. Laurence Dunmore, 2004).

I have cited Rochester's poems as well as the play, and drawn some of Charles II's speech from historical record. The European journey is chronicled in Balfour's posthumous *Letters written to a Friend, by the Learned and Judicious Sir Andrew Balfour, M. D., containing excellent Directions and Advices for Travelling thro' France and Italy … Published from the Author's Original M.S.* (Edinburgh, 1700). Harvey's invented case notes use the style of his manuscript Lumleian Lecture notes.

Harvey's great work is *The Anatomical Exercises: De Motu Cordis and De Circulatione Sanguinis in English Translation*, edited by Geoffrey Keynes (London: Nonesuch Press, 1956), and his Lumleian Lectures are published in *Lectures on the Whole of Anatomy*, by C.D. O'Malley, F.N.L. Poynter, and K.F. Russell (Berkeley and Los Angeles: University of California Press, 1961). His life and career are examined in the biography of Geoffrey Keynes, *The Life of William Harvey* (Oxford: Clarendon Press, 1978), and by Thomas Wright in *William Harvey: a Life in Circulation* (Oxford: Oxford University Press, 2013).

The biography of Rochester by Vivian de Sola Pinto remains definitive: *Enthusiast in Wit: a portrait of John Wilmot, Earl of Rochester, 1647-1680* (London: Routledge and Kegan Paul, 1962), while Graham Greene's *Lord Rochester's Monkey* (London: Bodley Head, 1974) is brilliant and compelling. I have also used the more recent biography by James William Johnson, *A Profane Wit: The Life of John Wilmot, Earl of Rochester* (NY: University of Rochester Press, 2004). I have quoted Rochester's poems from John Wilmot, Earl of Rochester, *Selected Works*, ed. Frank H. Ellis (London,

Penguin, 1994, new edition 2004). For the brief appearance of Charles II, I have drawn on Antonia Fraser, *King Charles II* (1979, London: Phoenix, 2002), and Don Jordan and Michael Walsh, *The King's Bed: Sex, Power and the Court of Charles II* (2015, London: Abacus, 2016).

JOHN WILMOT

1

Around midnight on the 5th November 1662, King Charles II found himself, not for the first time, unable to get it up.

Or rather unable to keep it up, since his customary prodigious tumescence had collapsed into an unseasonably premature, though copiously abundant, ejaculation.

Leaving the Queen to her unintelligible Portuguese prayers, he slid out of bed, grasped a candle-stick and made his way moodily to his study. Such repeated disappointments in the royal bed were proving particularly humiliating to Charles. To start with, he was the king. His primary purpose in life was to produce erections with which to inseminate his queen and to generate heirs. As the poet Rochester put it, Charles ruled by a unique combination of sexual and political potency: 'his sceptre and his prick were of a length'.[3] Any diminution in the dimensions of the one might conceivably cause attenuation in the other.

Secondly, Charles was a world-famous lover, a man prodigiously endowed with a superhuman capacity for pleasing women. Should it become common knowledge that he was experiencing even a localised failure in that department, his reputation as both king and rakehell, the eponymous 'merry monarch',[4] would lie in tatters. He would be a king of shreds and patches, his high desires far exceeding his strength. He would be seen as a fool, the 'great natural' described by Mercutio in one of his favourite Shakespeare plays, 'that runs lolling up and down to hide his bauble in a hole'.[5]

His grandfather King James had drooled and dribbled at the mouth, and coveted arse much more than cunt, but managed to father three children, including his own martyred father of blessed memory, Charles I. Now James's flamboyantly heterosexual grandson found himself dribbling from another organ, and like Onan spilling his seed in the ground, instead of depositing it securely where it belonged, inside the tight and chaste uterus of his wedded spouse, Her Royal Majesty Queen Catherine.

Still in his night-shirt, a damp patch of sticky semen drying in his lap, Charles sat at his desk and irritably rifled through a sheaf of papers. One particular manuscript caught his eye, and he pulled it from the pile towards him. A poem in a familiar hand: 'The Imperfect Enjoyment'.

Naked she lay, clasped in my longing arms,
I filled with love, and she all over charms;
… But whilst her busy hand would guide that part
Which should convey my soul up to her heart,
In liquid raptures I dissolve all o'er,
Melt into sperm, and spend at every pore.[6]

He read it, and read it again. Then he called a messenger and sent for the Earl of Rochester.

2

The equerry accepted the task with mixed emotions. Not that it was ever difficult to locate John Wilmot, 2nd Earl of Rochester: such was his celebrity; his whereabouts in London were always common knowledge. Nor were the premises in which Rochester would invariably be found in any way unpleasant or forbidding to enter. Quite the reverse: a royal servant dispatched on such a mission could count on being treated with copious rounds of drink, extravagant pinches of snuff, and his free choice for a basic servicing package from among a gallery of the most attractive whores. The problem was not to find Rochester, but to extricate him from his pleasures, and get him safely back to Whitehall. The king's command, usually so decisive a motivator, seemed to fall with Rochester on ears of studied but impenetrable deafness. Just one more, he would say with that graceful, irresistible charm: just one more drink, one more blow-job, one more fingering of fundament and fanny. Rochester seemed to care more if anything for his reputation as a spark among the drunks and sluts of Covent Garden, than for his standing as a peer of the realm with his king and patron.

On this occasion however, much to the equerry's relief, the young Earl was disposed to come quietly. Having started the day's dissipation unusually early, in honour of the late King James' deliverance from the unnatural conspiracy of the Gunpowder Treason, and of the same king's sterling services to buggery and pederasty, Rochester had peaked early, slept through most of the evening, and was now at his most lucid and cynical. His beautiful face, like the face of a newly-fallen angel, had not yet lost all its original brightness, and displayed as yet few of the harsh lineaments and dark shadows of debauchery. A devil in him, as Etherege put it, but an angel undefaced.[7] His mind was clear, diamond-sharp, splenetive and bitter, as he declaimed, extempore, uncompleted verses of an uncomposed satire:

> I'd be a dog, a monkey, or a bear,
> Or anything but that vain animal,
> Who is so proud of being – rational![8]

Putting the poem aside, and fully conscious of the irony, the poet came along meekly enough at his great master's summons.

3

'Rochester, my good fellow. Come in, come in. I hope my knave didn't drag you away from anything important?'

'Always at your majesty's service', said Rochester, as he slid gracefully into a chair. Framed by the mane of long black hair, the king's saturnine features seemed harsh, Italianate, even gloomier than usual. Rochester felt overdressed, and wondered if he should remove his wig and red silk coat. Such gestures might however be misinterpreted, and the king didn't look in the mood for folly.

'Good. Good. Now' – after the briefest of hesitations Charles plunged straight in – 'You're the expert on impotence'.

'Expert?' Rochester replied, trying to sound modest rather than defensive. 'Expert in description, I would hope, rather than experience'.

'Never mind that', said Charles. 'This isn't about you'. He paused again, pushing the manuscript of the poem around on the desk. 'I'm going to confide in you now, John. I have a problem I think you might be able to help me with. But I don't want it written up in one of your damned poems and passed around the whole court. It's too serious for that. We're talking international crisis, diplomatic breakdown, war. Understand?'

Rochester assumed sincerity, and disarmingly shook his head.

'As you know, I married her Majesty a month ago. But as yet – strictly between us now – the marriage remains – unconsummated'.[9]

Sincerity gave way to disbelief on Rochester's plausible features.

'Yes, I know, I know. I boast the proudest, peremptoriest prick alive. Oh yes, I read that scurrilous poem I took out of your pocket. "T'would break through all to make its way to cunt".[10] But not, unfortunately, to the queen's. I've never had this problem before. Every whore in London, from the orange-girl in Drury-Lane to the Countess of Castlemaine, can make it spring up like a jack-in-the box with minimal stimulation. And it stays up all night, however many women hitch a ride. Only when I approach her Majesty's bed does it fail to rise to the occasion. Or rather it flips up like a howitzer, and then blows its wad before I can even take aim. It's here in your poem. Look.'

What oyster-cinder-beggar-common whore
Didst thou e'er fail in all thy life before?
When vice, disease, and scandal lead the way,
With what officious haste doest thou obey![11]

'It's all there, don't you see? The one place you're really supposed to be able to use your prick – marriage being ordained for procreation, and all that – is in the conjugal bed. But that's the one place where the bloody thing doesn't work'.

'Tell me, your Majesty', put in Rochester, placing his palms together with an air of judicious pondering. 'What are your feelings towards her Majesty?'

'Oh, I like her well enough. People are determined to think I don't. They'll tell you she's ugly. Most of my mistresses have been really beautiful, and she's not in their league. Her face is not exact enough to be called a beauty, but her eyes are excellent good.[12] Can't see her in the dark anyway. And they don't like her because she's Catholic. I could do without the incessant praying, in all honesty. And the invocations of saints. And the rosary beads. And the relics. But I can hardly say I'm not used to all that with dear Mamma. Not to mention my damned incorrigibly papistical brother'.

'What of her Majesty's more intimate person?'

'Well she sports hairy armpits. It's a Latin thing, apparently. Not my first choice. And she doesn't shave her cunt, so her bush is like the hedges at Hampton Court when I can't afford to pay the gardeners. I'm used to a smooth passage. But it's quite fun to have to find your way sometimes.

"Through brake, through briar, etc.", as Shakespeare has it'.

'What of her Majesty's scent: does she smell sweetly?'

'Down there, you mean? No worse than any other woman. Better than most in fact. Most of the cunts I frequent are usually liberally lined with some other fellow's spunk. At least hers is clean. No, it's something else. Something like this' – and again he cited the poem. 'Here you're talking to your prick, you see …'

'Not me in person', Rochester remonstrated; 'it's just a dramatic monologue …'

'Not about you. Listen -

Like a rude, roaring hector in the streets
Who scuffles, cuffs, and justles all he meets,
But if his king or country claim his aid,
The rakehell villain shrinks and hides his head;
Ev'n so thy brutal valor is displayed,
Breaks every stew, does each small whore invade,
But when great Love the onset does command,
Base recreant to thy prince, thou dar'st not stand.[13]

That's the trouble, I think. My prick responds to the siren song of pleasure, not the stern trumpet-call of duty. It'll stay up all night long in Vauxhall Gardens, but on Horse-Guards Parade it just won't stand to attention long enough to storm the breach'.

'Your Majesty has tried aphrodisiacs, of course?'

'Christ have I not? I've tried everything. Oysters, chocolate, pumpkin seeds. Ambergris, mandrake, Spanish fly. A rhino's horn, a narwhal's tusk, a dead dog's bollocks. Half of them make you sick; the other half can kill you. All useless. This is the Age of Reason, for God's sake. The time of Rationality, Enlightenment, Science. All these potions and preparations are out of the Dark Ages: the stuff of alchemy, wizardry, demonology. There must be a scientific remedy, based on evidence, research, clinical trials. There must be doctors who understand these things'.

'But your Majesty is not consulting a doctor, but confiding in a sentimental poet and cynic philosopher. You know I have no specialist knowledge in this area'.

'There's only one doctor I know of who might have been able to help: but he died a few years ago, just before I got back. He was my father's personal physician. You might have heard of him: Dr. William Harvey?'

'*De Motu Cordis et Sanguinis in Animalibus?*' said Rochester, naming Dr Harvey's great work on the motion of the heart and the circulation of the blood, which he had read at Oxford. 'Yes of course. My father spoke very highly of him. But I can't recall anything in his book about the anatomy of the erection'.

'No there isn't. He wrote it up in another book, *Love, Lust and Act of Generation of Animals*.[14] But it was never published. When he was in Oxford during the Rebellion the Commonwealth troops smashed their way into his London lodgings and took all his papers. Destroyed them, most likely. At any rate they were never seen again. I was very fond of Harvey: he used to take care of my brother and me. He was looking after us at the Battle of Edgehill.[15] It was so funny: James and I watching the battle, old Harvey sitting under a hedge trying to read a book. This cannonball comes whizzing and smoking towards us, and lands right at his feet. He looked at it as if he didn't know what it was. We thought it was going to explode, and were out of there double quick, I can tell you, with Harvey scrambling after us through the hedge. Anyway, when we were besieged in Oxford,[16] I was about 14 or 15, and I used to suffer from 'priapism'. Know what that is?'

'No, but I'm sure I've got it. It sounds like the sort of thing I would have'.

'I doubt it. Uncontrollable night-time erections. And nowhere to put them at the time, of course. Can't imagine that troubles you. I consulted Harvey about them. He examined me, and gave me some foul brew to drink that had no effect whatsoever. Some disgusting African tree-bark. Ugh. He said that the male erection was one of the greatest mysteries of human physiology, but that he was very close to reaching an understanding of its mechanisms, and devising a method of controlling them. Do you know how erections work?'

'Only what we've always understood from Galen', Rochester replied. 'Spirit is pumped into the prick along with the semen. It blows up like a balloon filled with air. When the seed is expelled, the air evaporates, and down it comes'.

'Yes, we're still guided by a 2nd century Roman physician whose patients were gladiators. "My arm's been cut off, Dr Galen. Can you sew it back on for me?" But old Harvey told me that the erection is caused by blood, not air. That's why all the old aphrodisiacs don't work: they're targeted at the emotions, or the nervous system, or the spirit. Or they're designed to increase the wind in the body, so some of it goes to the penis. Barbaric. They don't have any physiological impact on the flow of blood. I got the impression that Harvey had some idea of how to control the mechanism. So we'd be able to get it up, keep it up and let it down on command. He told me that in Paradise Adam was able to get an erection at will; and that it became involuntary with the Fall. Science, he said, would regain Paradise for man. But I was too young to understand. And later, once I'd learned what to do with an erection, I never felt the need. My concern was only never to waste one. Afterwards things got pretty busy, you know, what with recovering the crown and all. When this – problem – started I thought of old Harvey. But found that his heart had finally stopped beating and his blood circulated no more'.

'So how can I help?' asked Rochester.

'I'm sending you on a mission. To track down Harvey's work on the physiology of the erection. To recover his theory, and to find out if he had any solution to the problem. This should help'.

Charles took a key from a desk drawer, turned to open a beautiful lacquered Chinese cabinet that stood behind him, opened one of the nested drawers, and drew out a single sheet of paper.

'Harvey wrote up my case, and started to set down his theory. He never finished it. He was called out to see a patient. That was the night I had to leave Oxford in a hurry with my troop of horse, taking the road to the West. Anxious to avoid meeting my Lord Essex and Sir William Waller. It was a dark night, pouring. I remember looking back at Oxford, melancholy in the rain. I never saw old Harvey again. Nor, for that matter, my father'.[17]

The king paused in his speech, his eyes downcast. Then as quickly shook away the rare current of emotion.

'Harvey left my case notes on his desk. Here they are. I'm entrusting them to you'.

Rochester took the paper and glanced over it. A spidery secretary hand. Unfamiliar technical terms. Latin and English. Macrotic. Cryptic.

'Not now', said Charles peremptorily. 'Take it with you'.

The interview was at an end. 'Where do I start?' Rochester asked.

'Padua'.

'Padua – in Italy? " Fair nursery of arts"?'

'The same. Harvey studied there, around 1600. The paper mentions it. Start there. I'm sending you on a Grand Tour, France and Italy. Make sure you end up in Padua'.[18]

'Your Majesty', said Rochester, rising to leave.

'Oh', added Charles. 'And I've appointed a guardian to accompany you, seeing as you're under age. A nice fellow, you'll like him. Dr Andrew Balfour. Scots. Taught by Harvey. Studied in Padua'.

'And does Dr Balfour know the reason ...'

'Christ no. Not a word. Just string him along. His expertise should come in useful'.

Charles was reading something else by the time Rochester reached the door, but the king glanced up to call after him.

'Don't forget, John. Paradise Regained. Don't let me down'.

4

Dr William Harvey his Case Notes, 1644.

Patient

His Royal Highness Charles, Prince of Wales.

Condition

Priapism.

Symptoms

Uncontrollable nocturnal hardening, without emission. Disturbs the prince's sleep, renders him uneasy.

Examination

Anatomy normal, though penis of unusual length and thickness. Ballocks large and unusually blue. *Genitalia viri:* two stones and a yard.[19] In this case barely an exaggeration.

Authorities.

Causes of erection, per Aristotle.[20] Material cause, stimuli; formal cause, excitation; efficient cause, *vaginam entrare;*[21] final cause, generation.

Hippocrates saith that vital spirits flow to the penis, which fills with *pneuma*[22] like a blown bladder. Galen saith the corpora cavernosa are the 'hollow nerves'. *Pneuma* attracted to the penis which expands, heat distends the yard from the body. Priapism caused by excess of *pneuma* in the nerves: too much of a good thing. Errors all.

A young man's problem. For every boy who wants his member down, there's a man who wants his up. Impotence, premature ejaculation, flaccidity: the problems of the age. Hence aphrodisiacs, per Galen: rich food generates wind, and thus air to the penis.

The penis hath a will of its own. In Paradise Adam controlled it. Now a man gets it when he wills it not, and cannot will it when he would.

Evidence.

But there is no air. *Demonstrare propria illius cadaveris, nova vel noviter inventa.*[23] The ancients wrong, as in so many things. Leonardo da Vinci and the hanged man: the erect prick filled with blood, not air.[24] Blood circulates into the corpora cavernosa and out again, via the femoral artery and dorsal vein. But circulation is rapid. Why the retention? What blocks the venous return? Variolo writes of *musculi erectores penis.*[25] But what are these muscles that we cannot control? Why do they relax and constrict at the same time? Biblioteca di Palazzo Bo. At the sign of the Ox.

Treatment.

To understand the physiology of erection: the motion of blood to the penis, the means of blocking its return. What acts upon these motions? And what remedy?

What herb can reduce blood flow to the penis, and assist its passage thither? And what plant of our herbarium can both enhance the flow of blood, and work on the muscles to secure its retention in the penis?

Viriditas capri cornum.[26] A bull's pizzle in Smithfield …

5

The sign of the Ox. That part of the puzzle at least had been fairly easy to decipher, if disappointing in the denouement. For the sign of the Ox did not denote some low-ceilinged tavern, full of fragrant smoke and beautiful Italian wenches: but the elegant headquarters of the University of Padua, where William Harvey had taken his medical degree. The Palazzo Bo, palace of the Ox, was built over the site of a famous mediaeval inn, the Ox's Head. The imagery of animals seemed to be pervasive as Rochester strolled through the arched gateway of the old palace: staring down at him from above the gateway was the winged lion of St Mark, emblem of the Venetian republic, of which Padua was a vassal city-state. Beyond the gate the courtyard featured a double loggia held up by Doric and Ionic columns, and was refreshingly cool and shady after the dusty streets, hot and bright even in October. In the porter's lodge Rochester was met by a university official who greeted Balfour as a returning alumnus, and witnessed the Earl's signature in the *Registro del viaggiatori inglese in Italia.*[27] That was it: he was a medical student at the University of Padua, just as William Harvey had been sixty years earlier.

'Well done, laddie', said Balfour, earnestly shaking Rochester's hand. 'Ye've done the right thing, and ah'm reel prood of ye'.

If only he knew, thought Rochester to himself. If only he knew.

6

Rochester had expected Balfour's guardianship to be tedious, but he had grown to enjoy the company of this studious polymath, with his antiquarian curiosity and scientific enthusiasms. Since his father, the loyal Cavalier John Wilmot, had died when the boy was only ten, Rochester had already had his fair share of guardians. There was Francis Giffard, his boyhood tutor, who lay with him for six years and introduced him to sodomy; and his Oxford mentor, the red-faced Robert Whitehall, who both extended his sexual experience, and introduced him to the delights of drinking.[28] Balfour was like neither of these depraved pederasts, having as little interest in wine as he had in his charge's slim buttocks and prodigious cock. His interests were intellectual and cultural: he loved bookshops and classical ruins, gardens and palaces, as well as the fascinating lore of his own profession of medicine. Botanist and bibliophile, physician and philologist, he lectured his companion continually on subjects from Petrarch to plant biology, Ariosto to architecture, chemistry to Cicero. Balfour almost rekindled the young man's love of learning and study, which had been so signally broken off at Oxford.[29] Rochester found this period of respite from incessant debauchery curiously refreshing: his health improved, his interests broadened and his knowledge increased. And whenever the temptations of wine and women overcame him, it was easy enough to wait until Balfour had fallen asleep over his book to steal out into the warm and perfumed Italian night, and spend some of the annual pension of £500 granted to him by the king on wine, women and song.

Their Grand Tour had taken them through France and Italy, by way of Rouen, Paris, Cannes, Genoa, Naples, Rome, to Venice and finally Padua. Everywhere they observed the obligatory sights, made polite visits to the local nobility, delivered and received correspondence. In Turin they witnessed the miraculous Shroud; in Naples they admired the crucifix of St Thomas Aquinas; and in Loreto they wondered at the birthplace of the Holy Virgin Mary. They rode through boiling lava on Vesuvius, laboured up the steeple of San Marco in Venice, and dodged the tumbling rockfalls of Mont Cenis.[30] And arrived at last in Padua, where Rochester hoped to solve the mystery entrusted to him by His Majesty, to discover the secret that all men desire, the control of the erection.

Charles had proved characteristically judicious in his choice of guardian for the young Earl. Although no libertine, Balfour was also no prude, and had a healthy if abstract interest in the literature of sex, consisting more of scientific curiosity than of personal prurience. Confiding to the Earl that it was possible in Venice to acquire books quite unobtainable elsewhere, and prohibited even in Italy, he guided Rochester to a bookshop that unabashedly displayed a treasure-trove of erotica and pornography. Rochester managed to acquire quite cheaply a copy of *I Modi*, the set of sixteen copper engravings by Marcantonio Raimondi after Giulio Romano of the postures of sexual congress.[31] Side-by-Side, Man on Top, Woman on Top, Standing Missionary, Leapfrog, Fingering with Left-hand Index Finger ... Leafing through them Rochester reflected ruefully that none of the gods and heroes depicted so brazenly *in flagrante* seemed to share King Charles' problem, endowed as they were with huge, priapic, prodigiously tumescent members, sufficiently sturdy to ensure confident management of all the various physically challenging positions. Admittedly they were gods, equipped therefore with prelapsarian capabilities, or at least legendary lovers like Mark Antony and Paris, as famous for their prowess in the bedroom as their courage on the battle-field.

So it was not difficult to engage Balfour in discussions about sexual physiology, without revealing the true cause of his interest. By general reading in books of anatomy, and circumspect conversation with the knowledgeable Scot, Rochester had puzzled out much of Harvey's cryptic document, arriving at a fairly firm understanding of antique errors and modern discoveries. Perusing the ancient text-books of Aristotle and Galen, he soon grasped the now discredited notion that the arteries filled with air, or spirit, mingled with the blood. Harvey's theory of the circulation had demonstrated the fallacy of that belief: the arteries and veins are filled with blood that moves around the body in a continuous circulation.

What this meant for the physiology of erection was that blood was the key; that the erection is produced by blood circulating in and out of the penis; and that the erection is held in place by some mysterious mechanism of retention. Poring over diagrams in his text-books Rochester learned about the structure of the penis, about the corpus cavernosa and the corpus spongiosum. Both these channels fill with blood in the aroused member by dilatation of the arteries. Long before Harvey revealed the truth about the circulation, the great Italian artist Leonardo da Vinci had studied the erections of criminals who had been hanged, and found them to be full of blood. Simple unprejudiced observation by the Florentine master had been enough to dispense with centuries of Greek and Roman superstition.

But in this case modern scientific knowledge remained of purely theoretical value. Knowing that the erection is caused by blood, and lacking Harvey's crucial observations on 'lust and love', brought men no closer to an understanding of how to control it. Balfour clearly had no answer, though he was interested in the problem. Rochester talked to the doctor about the topic as if it applied to himself, without disclosing the true objective of the quest. Balfour took him to an apothecary in a dark *sottoporteggio* in Venice, whose dingy shop housed numerous 'marital aids', dildos, aphrodisiacs strange-looking plugs, the purpose of which one could only imagine. As connoisseurs of sex, the Italians had invented mechanical devices to assist the erection: here Rochester obtained a small tool known locally as an *'anello di gallo'*, a kind of ligature of leather that fitted over the base of the penis, designed to prevent the blood from withdrawing. He tried it out on a complaisant and voluptuous whore: but the results were disappointing. External compression simply caused loss of sensation, and did nothing to prevent premature ejaculation.

When asked if he wanted to accompany his ward on such nocturnal adventures, Balfour politely declined. 'It's no that I don't like a good screw as much as the next mon', he said. 'But I've seen too many cases of syphilis. Ye ought to be more careful. Have ye tried wearing a sheath?'

Rochester admitted he had tried wrapping a linen rag around his member, but was unable to do anything at all with the uncomfortably swathed and swaddled organ.

'Aye, they're pretty rudimentary, but they do work. There was an old chap here at the university, Fallopio by name, who tested them on over a thousand men. A sort of clinical trial, I suppose you'd call it. None of them contracted syphilis'.[32]

'But did any of them enjoy what they were doing?' asked Rochester sceptically.

'I don't think he was testing for that variable. Now there's a doctor I know at home whose been experimenting with tissue from a pig's bladder. A foreigner, French I think. An odd name, he had, can't recall it. Something like 'Condom'. Very promising. A second skin, so to speak. Most of the sensation, none of the risk. Dr Condom. He'll make a packet one day.'

But none of this was getting Rochester any closer to his goal. And so it was that, at something of a loss, he complied with Balfour's proposal that he should enrol as a student at the medical school of Padua. In that capacity, the Scotsman recommended, he would have access to lectures by brilliant professors, a library that was an unrivalled treasury of medical knowledge, public dissections performed for the students on the corpses of executed criminals, and visits to the sick and dying in the San Francesco Hospital. In a matter of a few months in this one place the student could acquire medical theory, practical knowledge and clinical expertise.

7

A rank smell of putrefaction wafted upwards, and Rochester held a perfumed handkerchief to his nose. Below him in the Anatomical Theatre the Cutter had slit, with a huge butcher's knife, the abdomen of the executed criminal who lay supine on the wooden dissection table. The cadaver was that of a burly man, hirsuite and muscular, his glistening yellow face swarthy with a stubble of beard, his entrails now on display. Above and around Rochester, thronging the galleries of the theatre, students of all nations, German, French, Italian, hanging over the railings to get the best view they could, choked and gagged on the fetid stench.

At 8 o'clock on that bitter cold January morning Rochester had filed alongside the other students into the Anatomical Theatre, the first of its kind in Europe, a beautifully designed wooden auditorium encircled by stacked galleries, and centred on the dissection table at floor level. His rank enabled him to score a place in the first gallery, as close as possible to the scene of the anatomy. When the theatre was full, the porters had called for silence and announced the entrance of the Rector, splendid in his gold and purple robes, followed by a small group of university professors and government officials, who all took their seats in the cramped space around the dissection table. The porters again called for silence, and issued stern warnings to the students to preserve decorum.

At last the lecture had begun, with the ceremonial entry of the Professor and his two assistants, the Cutter and the Demonstrator. The Professor called for the cadaver, which was handed up from a pit through a trap-door and laid on the dissection table. Then he began to read from an anatomical text-book, while the Cutter continued his grisly work, and the Demonstrator pointed out the body parts being discussed and analysed.

At last the lecture reached that part of the body in which Rochester was interested: the genitals. The man had obviously been well endowed, since his member demonstrated a convenient thickness and turgidity. The Cutter sliced it vertically in half with a razor, peeling the two sides apart like the skin of a banana. Rochester could clearly see the corpus spongiosum, with the urethra running through it, and the two corpora cavernosa, still retaining some traces of blood. Monotonously the Professor read from his text-book, naming the parts of the organ, but displaying little interest in its functions. Reading in Latin and ad-libbing in Venetian Italian, his discourse was hard to follow.

But it was at precisely at that point that Rochester learnt something. The Professor began to describe the muscles at the base of the penis, naming them: ischiocavernosus, bulbospongiosus, tubica albigensis. But what's their function. Rochester asked himself, finding no clarification in the drone of the Professor's voice; what do they do? Then the Professor mentioned a name, a name that had featured in Harvey's notes, and Rochester's ears instantly pricked up: Variolo. Variolo, he said, had described the function of these muscles, and the student should seek there for further wisdom.

Rochester lost no time in repairing to the library, where with some difficulty he found Constantine Variolo's work.[33] There it was, a complete description of the penile muscles. But the account only confused Rochester more. For Variolo seemed ignorant of the contribution to the erection of circulating blood, and believed that the muscles alone generated an erection. If anything he seemed to adhere to the old Galenic idea that the penis filled with air.

Nonetheless the thoughts of the old physician from Bologna stayed with him and grew into the germ of an idea. It was impossible to believe that the muscles alone caused the erection, since they had no influence on the flow of blood. But could they not have a role in maintaining it? If these muscles were to tighten at the base of the shaft after the blood had flowed into it, might they not operate as a ligature, just like the *anello di gallo*, keeping the blood-filled penis engorged and firm?

8

At first sight it looked as if the boy had no penis at all, only a kind of hollow cavity above his balls, surrounded by a loose flap of ragged skin like the end of an elephant's trunk. A patient in Padua's San Francesco Hospital, he had been bitten by a dog.[34] Rochester couldn't help wondering what had happened to the severed organ: had the dog eaten it? Or carried it off in his mouth to bury somewhere? Could it have been sewn back on if retrieved in time? The thought of going through life without a penis caused Rochester an involuntary shudder. But then women managed it somehow …

Hospital visits were part of the medical curriculum at Padua, and Rochester was dutifully accompanying the professor on his rounds. The case of the boy naturally interested him, but initially seemed unpromising. The root of the penis had retracted completely into the body, like that of a eunuch. He is like a monkey, the old doctor said coarsely, referring to the fact that some animals can withdraw the whole penis into the body: two stones and no yard. The students laughed at the professor's insensitive joke, and the whole entourage moved on to the next patient.

Rochester hung back, unnoticed, until the group had left the ward. The boy had clearly not enjoyed the experience of being not only examined, but laughed at, by a crowd of strangers. A few kind words got a smile out of him, which broadened when the Earl produced a few coins from his purse. Then he called over one of the Sisters, a young girl whose lovely olive face showed to advantage in her black and white habit. At Rochester's bidding she drew the curtains around the boy's bed, and listened carefully to his whispered instructions.

The patient, a handsome boy in his early teens, was by now growing increasingly nervous. What were they going to do to him, this strange foreigner in his rich silk garments, and the nurse who was clearly putting herself under his direction? A shadow of fear crossed his face: more pain, more humiliation? He was pleasantly surprised, however, when the nurse, at Rochester's bidding, took his balls into her cool fingers and began to squeeze and palpate them. Bending over him, her breasts brushed against his mouth. Softly she inserted her thumb into the hole where his prick should have been. Meanwhile Rochester was observing the aperture, and was rewarded by the sight of a bitten stump emerging from the hole, exactly as the head of a tortoise peeps out from beneath its shell. The nurse closed her hand around the truncated shaft, encircling it with her fingers, and masturbating it at first slowly, then with increasing speed and vigour. At Rochester's request she slowed the stimulation down, and the penis swelled red and angry between her fingers. It was some time before her efforts were rewarded when, with a stifled groan, the boy fetched liberally into her hand. Quickly the stiff little stump subsided, and disappeared again into its cavernous retreat.

Satisfied by the results of his experiment, Rochester generously rewarded them both, giving the pretty nurse the bonus of a kiss. The Sister went off to wash her hands, and left the boy grinning broadly. Perhaps life as a mutant was not going to be so bad after all.

Back in his rooms in the Palazzo Bo, Rochester contemplated the results of his experiment. The anatomy of the boy's penis was so abnormal that he appeared to have none. In fact his member had simply retracted into his body, as is normal in animals; but still retained the capacity for engorgement and protrusion when stimulated. Although the blood vessels had clearly been severed by the dog's bite, they appeared to have healed and re-united, and normal blood circulation could occur even in so unusual a penis. The erection had lasted for some time, so the muscles at the base of the penis were still intact, and able to operate normally. The shape and size of the organ seemed irrelevant to sexual function, which depended anatomically on only two factors: blood flow and muscle activity. So in their different ways, both Harvey and Variolo were right. Erection was all about the flow of blood into the corpora, and about the capacity of the muscles to delay its return.

9

At last it was time to return. Their money was running out, and there were reports of plague in Venice. Rochester was sure he had discovered all he could in Padua. They resolved to travel back overland, crossing the Alps into France and thence across the channel to England.

Back in London, Rochester felt he had little choice but to surrender his quest, and throw himself on the king's mercy. He had tried, God knows, as hard as any man could try, but he had failed. The secret had eluded him.

On a warm July evening in 1664 he wandered disconsolately through Harvey's London: his house in Ludgate in the shadow of the old Roman wall, the College of Physicians in Knyght Ryder Street by St Paul's, and at last the precincts of St. Bartholomew's Hospital. He passed under the baroque stone gate with its stained glass windows and curious round clock, where he met by appointment with an elderly hospital porter who had known Harvey. Wearing a white overall lightly speckled with blood, the old retainer led Rochester through a maze of courtyards and cloisters and gardens to a little house that stood at the hospital's perimeter, and on the edge of Smithfield. Harvey, he was told, had used these premises as consulting rooms. Nobody lived here anymore. The ground floor being given over to farm animals, Rochester ascended to the first floor, but here too the rooms were deserted, empty of furniture, dusty and cobwebbed. He opened a cupboard, but it contained nothing but spiders. All Harvey's papers, books and instruments had been handed over to the Royal College, and were neatly organised in the Harveian Library, where Rochester had already spent many hours of fruitless research. He closed the cupboard door. No secrets hidden here. Peering through the grimy panes of the window he looked down into a small garden, now profusely overgrown, bordered by a low wall that separated it from Smithfield. The evening sun gilded the meadow and struck shadows into the clustering vegetation of the garden.

Descending the stairs, Rochester found his way into the walled enclosure, and sat down on an old wooden bench among the profusion of plants to admire the prospect and gather his thoughts. This part of

Smithfield remained a 'smooth field', deep with clover and studded with yellow buttercups. A herd of cattle browsed placidly in the meadow, their tails rhythmically swishing away the swarming summer flies.

The cattle were of the old English breed White Park, as Rochester had learned from the knowledgeable Balfour, distinguished by their speckled white hides and long curved horns. Among the docile, preoccupied cows, contentedly feeding in the pasture, he observed a big bull, startlingly white in colour, with thick muscled withers and immense sloping horns. The very image of virility. Clearly aroused by the females, he seemed indecisive as to which lady to choose as the object of his desire. At last he selected one, a beautiful milk-white creature who might have posed for Coreggio when painting Io, seduced by Zeus and transformed by the jealous Hera into a beautiful white heifer, and began to snuffle and slobber enthusiastically about her pink swollen arse. She feigned indifference, but seemed in no way averse to his advances, and presently crouched her back legs in a posture of submission. The bull mounted, placing his broad hooves on her shoulders, and gathered his great haunches for penetration. But nothing happened. His thick stubby penis, with its tuft of black bristles, remained retracted, twitching helplessly, but failing to make an entrance.

The lessons of comparative anatomy, thought Rochester. It can happen to anyone. Kings and cattle, monkeys and monarchs, we all suffer from the same plague of impotence. The cow, irritated by this failure of masculinity, shook him irritably off her back. Moodily the bull stood and peered around, as if looking for someone to blame.

Then seeming to make up his mind, the bull trotted over towards the wall of Harvey's garden, and proceeded to strip with his rubbery lips the leaves of a plant whose clustering branches overhung the wall. Rochester gazed idly at the shrub, wondering what it tasted like. Leaves of bright green, with a brown speckling on the underside, and delicate yellow flowers dangling like the bells of a fuchsia. Methodically the bull munched his way through all the leaves he could reach, and turned back towards the herd.

After an interval, Rochester was astonished to see the same cow, the object of his earlier attentions, trotting towards him across the field. The bull, apparently energised with a new confidence, turned his great head superbly away. But she came close to him as if in courtship, rubbing her head alongside his flanks, their mouths even touching as in a bovine kiss. Then in an even more extraordinary turn, the cow planted herself in front of the bull, and crooked her legs in an unmistakable gesture of self-offering.

This time there was no hesitation: the bull promptly mounted, and his great red penis shot out from its retraction, and slid unerringly into the moist pink vulva of his receptive mate. Her flanks quivered and her back arched as the bull's massive hindquarters thrust and pumped into her until, with a great wrenching bellow, he came, withdrew, and pulled unceremoniously away.

Good Christ, said Rochester to himself: what's he been eating? An excitement of discovery began to grow in him. This had been Harvey's garden. Perhaps it was a herbarium. Who knew what properties pertained to these simples? Well the cattle seemed to. He examined the plant. It had no particular scent, and its leaves were nothing extraordinary. Pushing aside the thick shrubby growth with his stick, Rochester sought around the base of the plant for any kind of label or sign. Sure enough, there it was, a faded card tied to the stem by a piece of string. He could make out the word 'Epimedium' in an unfamiliar hand. None the wiser, Rochester cut the card away with his pen-knife, and examined it in the rays of the setting sun. On the reverse, there in Harvey's own spidery writing, were the words he had hoped to see: '*Viriditas capri cornum*'.[35] Weed of the Horned Goat; Horny Goat Weed.

A bull's pizzle in Smithfield. Harvey had watched this identical drama of bovine sexuality played out by his own garden wall. Rochester was able to follow his train of thought, and at last realise the solution. The herb clearly acted upon the flow of blood to the penis, and simultaneously relaxed the muscles at the base of the shaft. Blood flow engorged the member, and the muscles compressed the veins, impeding outflow. Constricting the base of the penis was exactly the wrong thing to do, since the more the blood flowed in, and the more the muscles relaxed, the more the veins were restricted, and the blood stayed where it was. This was the answer all men sought: Horny Goat Weed. Erection at will. Paradise Regained.

Quickly Rochester began to strip leaves from the bush, and with his pen-knife began to slice slivers for cuttings. I must give it a name, he thought. Something vital, vigorous, virile. This problem actually taxed his knowledge and imagination for several days afterwards, as he sifted his way through countless words in innumerable languages. In the end he chose a word from Sanskrit, with the exact connotations of strength, fierceness, power; the name of the most sexually potent beast in the whole animal kingdom, the tiger.

'I shall call it' he said triumphantly, 'I shall call it: Vyaghra'.

10

The rest is history. King Charles II recovered his virility, and remained capable of simultaneously servicing multiple women, whether for duty or pleasure. Regrettably his queen proved unable to bear him a living child, and the king's loyalty to her sealed the fate of his dynasty.

The Earl of Rochester made equal use of his discovery, proving himself a champion in the lists of love, until syphilis brought a predictable but unseasonable end to his amorous career. He never managed to locate M. Condom.

At one point during one of his frequent periods of exile from court, he set up on Tower Hill as a physician, specialising particularly in female complaints, but covertly offering to men advice on virility, accompanied by prescriptions of his patent (and potent) powder, Vyaghra. Dr Bendo he called himself, the soubriquet slyly hinting at the origins of his medical training in the problems of erectile dysfunction. Dr Bendo will straighten you out.

11

Then dance six naked men and women, the men doing obedience to the women's cunts, kissing and touching them often, the women in like manner to the men's Pricks, kissing and dandling their Codds, and then fall to fucking, after which the women sigh and the men look simple and so sneak off. [37]

Rochester was rehearsing his obscene play *The Farce of Sodom, or the Quintessence of Debauchery*. Bolloxinian, King of Sodom, has developed an aversion to sex with his Queen, Cuntigratia, and decrees that all his male subjects should stick to buggery with one another. The men welcome this change, since they save money on prostitutes; but the women become helplessly dependent on 'dildos and dogs'. At last the court physician

Dr. Flux prescribes a reversal of the king's policy: 'Fuck women, and let buggery be no more'.

One of the actors cast to dance among the six naked men approached Rochester, script in hand, and a puzzled expression on his face. 'My Lord' he said tentatively: 'I have a question about this scene'.

'What is it?' asked Rochester innocently.

'Is it your intention that there should be more than one performance in any one day?'

'Why yes. On Wednesday we will do a dress rehearsal, a matinee and an evening show'.

'And you did say that the stage directions are to be executed in full, exactly as written?'

'Indeed'.

'*"They fall to fucking, after which the women sigh and the men look simple"*. And this is to be done – three times in one day?'

'Don't underestimate your powers, my friend', said Rochester reassuringly. From his pocket he drew a small jar of some blue-green powder, and held it up to the light. The actor could see a strange, unfamiliar name, neatly-written in red ink on the label: 'Vyaghra'.

'An hour before each performance', Rochester advised, in the practised voice of Dr Bendo, 'take one spoonful of this. You'll be back up – on stage, I mean – in no time at all'.

Wounded dog from William Hogarth, The Good Samaritan,
St Bartholomew's Hospital, Smithfield

TOM NERO

PREFACE

William Hogarth was born in Bartholomew Close in 1697, and lived in Smithfield until he was apprenticed at the age of fourteen. His father ran a coffee shop for gentleman in St John's gate. Hogarth's paintings and engravings often feature Smithfield, as in his famous painting of the Newgate scene in *The Beggar's Opera*. Later in life he painted two great murals, still there to see, in the entrance-hall of St Bartholomew's Hospital. From 1749 to his death in 1764 Hogarth lived partly in his country house in Chiswick, West London, now known as "Hogarth's House", and only a mile from where I live. He is buried in St Nicholas Churchyard in Chiswick.

Shortly after the publication of his famous *Gin Lane* print, Hogarth published in four plates, under the title *The Four Stages of Cruelty*, a pictorial narrative of Tom Nero, a charity boy who in his youth and manhood torments and tortures animals, and eventually murders his lover. The final plate shows his executed body being publicly dissected in the Anatomy Theatre of the Royal College of Physicians, at that time occupying an elegant building, designed by Robert Hooke, that stood in Warwick Lane next to Newgate.

Gustave Flaubert's *Legend of St Julien L'Hopitallier*, published as one of his *Trois Contes* [*Three Tales*] (1877), based on a pictorial narrative in a stained-glass window in the cathedral of Rouen, tells a remarkably similar story. From a very early age Julien wantonly kills animals, becoming an insatiable huntsman. He tries to evade a prophecy that he will murder his parents, but eventually by accident kills them in a jealous rage.

There the similarity ends. Julien becomes a hermit dedicated to helping others, and is eventually visited by Christ Himself in the form of a leper, who receives him as a saint into heaven. For Tom Nero there is no redemption, and his death on the autopsy table is consistent with his life, the just reward (Hogarth's words) of cruelty.

The following story weaves together Hogarth's graphic tale and Flaubert's mediaevalist fable. Like Hogarth's engravings, and unlike Flaubert's hagiography, it depicts a fallen world of total depravity, with no hint of redemption. My story is drawn directly from Hogarth's plates, mainly *The Four Stages of Cruelty*, but also *Gin Lane, Beer Street*, and *Before and After*, all of which can be found reproduced in large format in *Engravings by Hogarth*, ed. Sean Shesgreen (Dover Publications, 1973). Hogarth's pictorial narrative is embellished with historical data on eighteenth-century London, especially the specific places Hogarth depicted: Seven Dials, Newgate, the Church of St Nicholas in Chiswick (close to Hogarth's House).I have used Jenny Uglow's biography *Hogarth: a Life and a World* (London: Faber, 1997), and an older source in H.B. Wheatley *Hogarth's London* (London: Constable and Co, 1909). I have drawn some descriptive details from Michael Dean's fictional *I, Hogarth* (London: Duckworth, 2012).

My narrative is also supplemented with an imitation of Flaubert's story, which ends 'And this is the story of St Julien the Hospitaller, as it is given on the stained-glass window of a church in my birthplace'. I have adapted this sign-off to 'And this is the story of Tom Nero, as it is given in the engravings of the great artist William Hogarth, of Smithfield and Chiswick, my home town'.

TOM NERO

Julian's father and mother dwelt in a castle built on the slope of a hill, in the heart of the woods.

    - Gustave Flaubert, *The Legend of St Julien the Hospitaller*[1]

1

St Giles-in-the-Fields, July 1736

Tom Nero's father and mother did not live in a castle on the slope of a hill, in the heart of the woods. They didn't live anywhere, as they had died when Tom was very small.

Tom himself, a charity school boy, lived in the Rookery of St Giles, where the Great Plague had started in 1667. He had one very vivid memory of his parents. It was a memory of falling.[2]

He was perhaps eighteen months old, and suckling at his mother's breast. There was nothing particularly intimate about this operation, as it was conducted in the open street, and the great pendulous breasts were fully exposed, literally pouring out of his mother's ragged smock. He remembered the taste of the milk, thin and bitter, but strangely warming and intoxicating. His mother sprawled helplessly on the steps of the Gin Royal, ripped bonnet awry, blotchy syphilitic sores on her extended legs, while he lay draped across her chest, one huge breast partially blocking his view. Her head nodded gently from side to side, her face disfigured by a stupefied, meaningless smile.

At the foot of the steps he could see his father, little more than a cloaked and hooded skeleton, gin-bottle clutched in one bony hand, the other limply holding a tilted glass. He was dying: shallow breaths scarcely moved the exposed ribs of his bare, emaciated chest. You could see the skull beneath the skin. A dog sat patiently by his side, staring at the empty glass, hoping the man would leave him at least some scattered drops of liquor.

Tom could see, over his mother's breast, the loud and thronging life of Seven Dials, 'the Rookery', better known from the Hogarth print as

'Gin Lane'. A man and a dog fought over a bone. Artisans were pawning the tools of their trade, exchanging their livelihoods for gin. Two men were dumping a woman's naked body into a coffin, while her baby cried alongside, unheard. Another woman sloshed gin down an infant's throat. A man was beating a blind, lame beggar with his own crutch. In an upstairs room a barber had hanged himself, his body swaying gently from side to side. A few bricks tumbled down from the leaning wall of a collapsing house.

And seeing all this, captured in a single glimpse, sharp as a steel engraving, Tom fell, as his mother, lapsing into her final stupor, let him go. Head over heels he tumbled from the steps and over a railing, his naked heels kicking at heaven, his little head destined to be dashed on the hard brick pavement below.

But two small charity girls, the badges of St Giles on their shoulders, happened to be passing, and between them caught the baby as he fell. Tom Nero was rescued. They soon established that his parents had expired, and he was already an orphan. They took him home with them.

And so Tom came to live in the charity school of St Giles. There he was housed and fed, and taught to read and write. He learned from the Bible and the Book of Common Prayer, and once a month the children were tested on their knowledge by the curate of the parish church. Tom was taught to be thankful to God, and to his benefactors; to submit himself to all governors, teachers, spiritual pastors and masters; and to order himself reverently and lowly to his betters.

In truth Tom felt no such gratitude, despised the discipline of the school, and spent most of his young life in the streets of Seven Dials. There he passed his time in the derelict warrens of the squalid slums, the shared houses and overcrowded tenancies, the open sewers and cesspits, the muck and the filth. A rudimentary education enabled him to read the signs: 'Drunk for a penny. Dead drunk for two pence. Clean straw for nothing'.[3] His companions were drunks and prostitutes, pedlars and fish-wives, news-criers and ballad-sellers. He begged from soft-hearted whores, cozened new-comers and naïve customers, stole from passed-out drunks, and acquired enough money to keep his inherited gin-habit abundantly supplied.

By the time he was fourteen he had run away from the charity school, and was living entirely on the streets. He slept under the wall of a house with rotten foundations that leaned out so far it provided shelter to many huddled forms crouching underneath. Every day they talked about their fear of the wall falling on them; and every night, dead drunk, they turned again to sleep in its shadow. Eventually the earthquake of March 1750 toppled the house, and left it in ruins. Some people may have died under the rubble, but nobody missed them, or even afterwards noticed the smell.

All day long Tom idled around the streets, which ran with filth and excrement. When it rained, the gutterless roofs cascaded water into the roadway, washing the cobbles temporarily clean.

The Rookery was normally a no-go area for the police, magistrates and parish officers. Runaway charity children could hide there with impunity. Occasionally a violent and destructive brawl would precipitate a visit from the beadles, who would break a few heads, arrest a few drunks and as quickly withdraw. The drains were full of vomit, and crows picked over the corpses of dead cats and dogs.

There were no locks on any of the doors, for the poor had nothing worth stealing. In the winter they shivered with cold, and in the summer sweltered in the heat. In December they froze to death, in July they died of infections. They lived on mouldy bread and cheap rot-gut gin. Their pockets were always empty.

When a fight broke out, over a woman or a loaf of bread, they fought with fists and feet and heads, a loose cobble from the roadway, or a length of wood splintered from a fence. The more desperate characters would have a knife hidden away somewhere in the rubble. Occasionally a real criminal, a footpad or highwayman armed with pistols, would grace the neighbourhood for a time. But they soon moved on, either to more salubrious precincts, or to the gallows at Tyburn.

The centre of neighbourhood life was the Gin Royal, where prostitutes entertained their clients under the watchful eyes of pimps. A few coins scattered across a drink-soaked table would be the catalyst for the production of food: a chicken, a rabbit, a savoury pie. The smell of burning fat crept through the bar and permeated into the street, attracting the shambling, spectral figures of the poor and hungry. Tom was often among them, taking up a prime position by the back door of the gin palace. Usually the whores would inveigle their clients upstairs before they had chance to eat, so the food would quickly be distributed around the destitute of Seven Dials. Very small portions of food seemed like a royal feast to them, and would be taken back to the ruins of the tumbled building they inhabited to be greedily devoured, once darkness had fallen, by the flaring light of torches.

At the end of one such impromptu banquet, at which Tom had managed to secure a juicy slice of roast pork, thick with crackling fat, he was weaving his way drunkenly through the rubble to find a sleeping place, when he beheld, in the light of a moonbeam, something that looked like a moving shadow. It was an old man, roughly clad, a beggar's sack on his shoulder. Without opening his lips said: 'Tom Nero, you shall be lifted up on high, and admired by many'. Then gliding along the moonbeam, he rose through the air and disappeared. Tom searched the rubble, but there was no sign of the old man, only the sound of the wind whispering through broken rafters. From that day forwards he felt that his life was charmed, and that his future held promise.[4]

2

Seven Dials, September 1750

One morning, as he woke to see the early morning light beginning to soften the plaster on the ragged remnants of a tumbled wall, he saw a mouse poke its pink nose out from a hole in what was left of the wainscot. Emboldened, the creature slipped out from its hiding place, and ran quickly across the floor, disappearing under a pile of bricks. The presence of the animal irritated Tom, and he could not stop thinking about it. Gradually as he lay there, waiting for sunrise, a kind of hatred for the mouse grew within him, and he resolved to do away with it.

The next morning he rose while it was still dark, and placed himself by the hole, armed with a stick from which protruded a rusty nail. After a long while the questing pink snout appeared again, and the mouse began to slide out of the hole. Tom struck it lightly and deftly with his stick, and stood stunned at the sight of the little, lifeless body. A drop of blood stained the floor. Casually he tossed away the stick and kicked the dead mouse out of sight. But he felt a kind of fulfilment, like the satisfying of hunger or thirst.[5]

He began to notice the swarming of animal life around him, and the desire to kill soon returned. He made himself a crude bow from a stolen bamboo cane, and fashioned sharpened arrows from splintered stair-rods. He watched the crows pecking among the rubble, searching for scraps of food and bits of decomposing body. It was easy to launch an arrow and pierce their plump breasts. He could not refrain from laughing, and being delighted with his own cleverness. He plucked glossy black feathers and used them to plume his shafts.

One morning he saw a fat pigeon sunning itself on the top of a wall. Silently drawing his bow, he let fly a sharp shaft that pierced the bird through its wings and body. It lay on the floor, its broken wings helplessly fluttering. The persistence of its life irritated the boy. He began to strangle it, and its convulsions made his heart beat quicker, and filled him with a wild, tumultuous voluptuousness, the last throb of its heart making him feel like fainting.[6]

So Tom became something of a hunter. Armed with his bow and a purloined knife, he lay in wait for cats, transfixing them with an arrow, and slitting their throats. He obtained some glue from a knacker's yard, and spread it on flat paving-stones to trap rats. He liked to watch their frenzied struggles to escape, delighting especially in one big, bold rat who preferred to gnaw off his own leg rather than accept the inevitability of death. He stamped on its head with his boot before it could break free. Once he found a badger lurching clumsily over a broken wall, fell upon it and stabbed it to the heart; and once he almost caught a fox in a carefully-placed snare, but the wily beast took the bait and eluded him in the dark. The thought of the animal escaping, getting away scot-free, yapping that high-pitched, snickering, scornful laugh, choked Tom's throat with a thick black bile of irritation.

3

Seven Dials, February 1751

One bitterly cold Sunday morning in winter, Tom left his tumbledown lodgings and walked eastwards towards the city. He still wore his charity school uniform, the tunic now flapping in rags around his knees, breeches split and stockings hanging over the tops of his boots. The round hat with its ribbon and bow was grotesquely set off by the craggy lines of his profile, the brutal protruding jaw and upturned, snub nose. His arm still bore the initials SG, for the parish of St Giles. In his hand he carried his bow, and a sheaf of arrows tucked into his belt.

As he walked along Holborn, the church bells pealed forth and called the faithful to prayer; but very few were listening. It was too cold. A stiff east wind blew hard, and icicles hung down from the branches of trees. As he crossed the Fleet River, its waters sheathed in a casing of ice, he saw a duck gripped fast, its feet pinioned to the frosty surface. Drawing his bow, he pierced its breast and left its blood pooling over the frozen stream.[7]

Nearing Newgate, he saw two cats shivering on a garden wall, trying to catch some glimpse of the sun. Softly he crept upon them, and grabbed them by the fur on their necks. Drawing a length of string from his pocket, he lashed both animals by the hind legs, and threw the cord over an iron stanchion. Desperate to free themselves, unable to reach anything but themselves, the two cats began to tear at one another, hissing and biting, clawing and scratching. Tom looked at the frenzied, spitting, screaming balls of fur, now ripping one another to shreds, and laughed out loud.[8]

Tom saw another cat, perched high on the roof of a house. Nimbly he shinned up the wall and crept over the tiled roof. The sky seemed almost black, presaging snow. Stealing upon the cat from behind, he seized it by the neck. Then with a vicious upswing of his arm he tossed the animal as high, and as far from the edge of the roof, as he could. Twisting and turning, trying its best to mount the air, it dropped onto the street, hit the cobbles with a thud and lay still. From the high roof Tom stared down at the broken corpse, and felt as if he were staring into an abyss.

At last he reached the open space of Smithfield, quiet as always on a Sunday. The pens of the beast market stood empty. A few people were about, all of them up to no good. A man was busy tying a bone to a dog's tale, so the cur would drive itself mad chasing the object he could never reach. Two men were busy provoking plumed and spurred cockerels to fight one another. The neighbourhood animals seemed indistinguishable in point of cruelty from the men: a mastiff with a huge jaw was ripping the stomach of a cat, tearing out its entrails with blunt yellow teeth.

Tom paused to watch two boys torturing a dove. One held the bird under his arm, holding in his other hand a brightly burning torch. The second was heating a length of wire in the flame, waiting until it glowed hot, orange and bright blue. Seizing the bird's neck in his left hand, the second boy pushed the red-hot wire into its eyes, first one and then the other. There was a strange hissing sound, a smell of burning flesh, and from the dove an unearthly scream of pain. Tom watched the feral faces of the boys as they laid their heads together to watch the bird's struggles. Seeing him observing them, the first boy offered an explanation.

''E won't fly away no more'.

But Tom cared nothing for any rationale. The pleasure he derived from witnessing the scene of torture was too intense, too sweet to demand any sense or reason. He walked away in a kind of delirium.

He came across a girl sitting on a flight of steps with a big dog held on a leash. Tom wanted to do something to the dog, but he did not know what it was. He sat for a moment and talked to the girl, a simple, pretty thing in the dress of a servant. The dog was not hers; she didn't know where it came from. She cared nothing for it. Two younger boys loitered up and joined them.

Slowly a realisation dawned on Tom: he knew what he must do. Taking an arrow from his belt, he bade the two younger boys grab the dog and hold it upside down. The girl kept tight hold of the leash. The dog snarled and struggled, but between them they held him fast. Tom positioned the sharp, barbed point of the arrow against the dog's stretched anus. It struggles increased. He pushed the arrow downwards, the point travelling into the dog's lower intestine. Its snarls of rage changed to howls of pain.[9]

Further and further in Tom pressed the shaft, feeling the point ripping and tearing through the dog's bowels. Blood began to gush from its arse, and dribble from its mouth. The two younger boys who held the dog had had enough of the creature's thrashing and ineffectual biting. The girl still held fast to the rope, her face a mask of indifference. The sky had turned red like a sheet of blood.

Suddenly the dog, which Tom thought was near enough dead, swivelled its head around and looked up at him. The bell of a nearby church began to toll, and the dog spoke, its voice as human as yours or mine. 'Curse you. Curse you', it said. 'By the aspersion of my blood, and the piercing of my bowels, I curse you. As you have done to the least of these my brethren, so shall it be done to you'.[10]

Tom gave a last disgusted twist to the arrow, and the dog's head fell back lifeless. He left it dumped at the foot of the steps, and started to make his way back home.

4

Thavies Inn, 20 March 1757

Tom was now twenty-one years old, and a hackney carriage driver. In spite of his youthful hardships, he had grown up physically strong. His face had set into a cruel mask, a brutal visor. Predominant among the street-bullies of Newgate and Little Britain, he managed a thriving business. Potential competitors gave him a wide berth, and turned a blind eye when he barged his coach to the front of the queue and stole their customers. If anyone objected, he would show them his whip, the long handle of which was a heavily weighted cudgel with a ballast of lead. By such methods he had become a successful London cabbie, his charity school rags and boots long since discarded, and replaced by a decent broadcloth coat, and buckled shoes.[11]

He did particularly good trade round the Inns of Court, ferrying barristers backwards and forwards from their chambers to the Old Bailey. On this particular day Tom drew up in his coach outside the portico of Thavies Inn in Holborn. Four fat, red-faced barristers, with flowing gowns and heavy wigs, emerged from the door, arguing amongst themselves. Although the carriage was designed for two passengers, all four of them squeezed inside to save money on the fare.

Tom prodded his old horse with the end of his whip. The nag did not move. Irritated, he cut it across the flanks with a vicious swipe. Still no movement. The barristers were growing impatient: they would be late for court. Get a move on, man.

Tom cursed them, and whipped his horse, again and again. At last the elderly beast, exhausted from years of overwork and ill-treatment, began to shamble forwards, trying to drag the heavy weight of the overburdened carriage behind him. The effort was too much, and he collapsed into the road in a tangle of traces, breaking one of his legs as he fell. The weight of the fallen horse dragged the carriage itself over with a noisy smash onto its side, throwing Tom off his box. The barristers flung open the door vertically, and struggled to pull themselves out.

Smarting from a hard bang on the cobbles, Tom leapt to his feet, retrieved his whip, reversed it, and began to lay into the body of the old horse with the heavy leaded cudgel. Broken leg twisted underneath him, the blinkered old nag could only try to turn its head away as the blows rained down. Harder and harder Tom beat at the beast, smashing the cudgel down onto its head. The face of the horse began to split like a ripe fruit. The rough end of the cudgel dislodged one of its eyes, which slipped down onto its tear-stained cheek.

Panting from the exertion, Tom paused to look around him. The fat barristers were still trying to get out of the coach. As he looked down the long stretch of Holborn, his own cruelty seemed to have formed the epicentre of an earthquake of violence. A drover with the face of a demon, shepherding a flock of sheep to Smithfield, had lost his temper with a laggard, and was beating it to death with a heavy club. The animal's bowels were gushing out of its mouth. Further down the road another man was goading an overburdened ass with a pointed stake. And as Tom looked around at this vista of violence, he saw on the other side of the road a dray, laden with hogsheads of beer, the fat drayman drunk and sound asleep at the reins, running over a child who had been playing in the street with his hoop. The big iron-shod wheel crunched over the little body, the boy's mouth opened in a soundless scream, and he lay still.

At the end of the road Tom could see a group of men baiting a bull. The animal stood its ground, horns lowered, as a mastiff growled and snapped at his face. The dog was afraid, keeping his distance. Impatiently a man grabbed the dog by its collar, and threw him at the bull. The dog sheared off the bull's hot flank and dodged away. But the man had come too close, and with a deft flip of his great horns the bull tossed him into the air like a bag of rags.

And then the bull turned his head, and looked down the length of the street. The horse lay dead at Tom's feet. Slowly the bull turned to face him. All the sights and sounds of the street seemed to fall away, and there was nothing but the man and the bull trotting towards him, tossing its threatening horns, pawing at the pavement with its hooves. Nothing daunted, Tom confronted the bull, and struck it between the horns with his club. But the weapon snapped as if the beast were made of bronze. The bull stared at him, and with eyes aflame and the solemn air of a patriarch and a judge, repeated thrice, while a bell tolled in the distance: 'Accursed! Accursed! Accursed! Tom Nero, you will one day kill the only thing that loves you'.[12]

5

St Nicholas Churchyard, Chiswick, July 1762[13]

An owl hooted. The moon waned gibbous. Tom crouched in the porch of the old church, lying in wait. Risking a glimpse over the boundary fence, he could see, raised on a slight incline, the lights of the big detached house where his mistress, Ann Gill, worked as a servant. Briefly the moon broke free from its integument of cloud, and frosted with silver the broken tombs and the sloping lawns beyond. Softly a bat left the church tower and began to flit among the gravestones.[14]

After the death of his horse Tom had given up his profession of cabman. But he must needs seek employment, as his wants were considerable, and his means slender. He was big, and tough, and utterly indifferent to the suffering of others. And so he became a thief.

He began in a small way by picking pockets around the markets of Cloth Fair, Leather Lane and Smithfield. From there he graduated to burglary, breaking and entering houses through a smashed window or an unhinged door. Soon he was flush enough to procure weapons, and armed himself with a brace of pistols, and a long keen knife. He aspired to join the aristocracy of crime and become a highwayman. But for that he would need a horse, and his resources did not stretch so far.

For some time he had been working on a plan to augment his capital. A year or so before he had taken up with a young serving-girl who had ridden in his coach. A naïve country girl, she was easily infatuated by Tom's flashy metropolitan assurance. He concealed his true nature from her, and seduced her with promises he never intended to keep. She trusted him, believing he would give her protection and freedom. She had no knowledge of sex, other than the impressions derived from observing the coupling of animals, so was not surprised when Tom rammed her face into the seat-cushion of his hackney coach, dragged her skirts up behind and thrust himself roughly inside her. It was what she expected: nasty, brutish and short. She did not even notice the change in his expression from optimistic alacrity to weary irritiation. *Post coito omne animal triste est.*[15] She adored him with a dog-like devotion, and wanted him to marry her. Then she fell pregnant, and became something of a nuisance. He had no intention of being saddled with a wife, and had thought of a scheme for simultaneously enriching himself, and getting rid of her. He had persuaded her to rob the house of her employer that night, and join him in the churchyard, whence they would elope and marry. He was waiting for her now, crouched in the darkness of the churchyard, two pistols hidden in his coat and the sharp dagger held in his hand. In his pocket was the letter she had sent him the day before:

Dear Tommy

My mistress has been the best of women to me, and my conscience flies in my face as often as I think of wronging her, and yet I am resolved to venture Body & Soul to do as you would have me so don't fail to meet me as you said you would. For I shall bring along with me all the things I can lay my hands on. So no more at presant but I remain yours until Death. Ann Gill.[16]

Yours until death, he thought to himself. But it may not come to that.

A big white owl swooped like a ghost over his head. He heard a faint sound, like the closing of a door. Looking over the fence, he could see Ann, carrying bags in both hands, running across the lawn. He opened the lych-gate for her and she collapsed, out of breath, into his arms. She wore her best white dress, and her blond hair, now silvered by moonlight, strayed from under her mob cap. In one hand she held a small chest bearing her initials, AG; in the other a sack that clinked as she set it down. Tom bent down over the dropped sack, and examined its contents. A fair haul: a pair of gold candle-sticks, a big silver teapot, a couple of gold watches. Enough to buy that horse. But not enough to share with a partner.

As Ann looked down at the round dome of his head, bald from hereditary syphilis, she seeemed to read the treacherous thoughts within, and grabbed the sack back from him. This was her dowry, the price of her freedom. She would not part with it so easily.

Tom stood up and looked at her, his face inscrutable in the shadows. What's your game, he thought, suspecting betrayal. A spasm of irritation shook his whole body like a tremor in the earth. Give it to me. She clasped the sack to her, along with her little monogrammed chest of trinkets, and stared at him in defiance. Give it to me, you …

Then a lifelong habit of cruelty compelled his hand, and viciously he slashed at her left wrist with his blade. Half-severed, her maimed hand dropped the bag, and she screamed in pain and fear. He had to silence her, or she would wake the dead. Casually he sliced the knife across her throat, severing the trachea and silencing her screams. She fell back among the grave stones, and began to bleed out on the green turf. Tom bent to recover the loot, and then to his surprise was seized roughly from behind by strong hands, his arms pinioned behind his back. A man with a lantern suddenly appeared before him, and held the light aloft to illuminate the scene.

The night watch, who chanced to be patrolling nearby, alarmed by Ann's cries, had rushed to the churchyard to apprehend the killer. Tom was held struggling but fast, by a group of men armed with pitchforks and muskets. His own weapons were snatched from him, the pistols from his pockets and the bloodstained knife from his hand.

The corpse of poor Ann lay at his feet, pale and bloodless, the wounds gaping at throat and wrist. The little life inside her swollen belly was fluttering its last heartbeat as her own heart slowed and stopped. The contents of her box were spilled across the grass, ribbons and trinkets and a Book of Common Prayer.

This was the perfection of Tom Nero's history of cruelty, when in fulfilment of the curse, he killed the only thing that loved him. Now he was to receive his reward.

6

Smithfield, September 1762

And so Tom Nero was hanged at Tyburn for the double murder of Ann Gill and her unborn child. His corpse was granted to the Royal College of Physicians, and in the round Anatomy Theatre in Warwick Lane, by Newgate, subjected to a public dissection.[17]

Though there is no reason to doubt the finality of Tom's death, it is tempting to imagine him sensate, responsive, feeling the dreadful violence being visited upon him: for that is what he deserved. Indeed his face, as we look at it, almost seems to register agony, his mouth stretched open as if in a silent scream, as a surgeon digs around with a sharp knife in the socket that had held his soft, gouged-out eyeball.

The end of the noose still looped raggedly around his neck, they bored two holes in his skull, and through them threaded a rope to hang him again, this time from a pulley suspended from Robert Hooke's elegant roof. There for a while he dangled and spun, lifted up on high, admired by many. Then they dropped him prone onto the oval dissecting-table, and commenced their butchers' work.

A bespectacled surgeon ripped open his abdomen with an upwards incision, and began to drag out the serpentine coils of his intestines. Below the table an assistant pulled the entrails free, coiling them into a bucket.

The presiding physician sat above in an ornate carved chair decorated with the symbol of the college, a physician's hand taking a patient's pulse. From this eminence he delivered his commentary, pointing out the organs with the tip of his long demonstration rod.

Another surgeon began work on the muscles of Tom's foot, separating them with the sharp blade of a scalpel. Members of the college crowded round the table in their wigs and mortar-boards, some disputing the anatomist's findings, others reading or talking amongst themselves. Members of the public stood further off and observed the macabre display, some with aroused curiosity, others with hardened indifference.

As the skeletal parts were removed from the cadaver they were thrown into a cauldron of boiling water and there reduced to be later re-assembled. The skeleton of a notorious murderer would grace the walls of the theatre, taking its place alongside famous specimens like that of the highwayman James McLean.[18] So for the third time the prophecy came to pass: Tom Nero was lifted up, and admired by many.

Discarded on the floor, like an inedible piece of offal, lay Tom Nero's wicked heart. A stray dog wandered unnoticed into the hall, and began voraciously to devour it.

And so Tom Nero's punishment did not end with the throttling out of his worthless life on the gibbet at Tyburn. In death he found no peaceful burial place, his breathless corpse was mourned by no sorrowing friend.[19] There in the chill Anatomy Theatre in Warwick Lane his evil heart was ripped from his body, and thrown to the dogs. He rose from the dissecting table a specimen of cruelty and violence, a monument of shame.

And this is the story of Tom Nero, as it is given in the engravings of the great artist William Hogarth, native of Smithfield, and resident of Chiswick, my home town.[20]

Meat pie, The Butcher's Hook and Cleaver, West Smithfield

SWEENEY TODD

PREFACE

Most people are familiar with the legendary Sweeney Todd from Tim Burton's 2007 film, scripted by John Logan from Stephen Sondheim's 1979 musical theatre adaptation of Christopher Bond's 1973 stage play. In all these versions Todd is a victim of injustice perpetrated by Judge Turpin, who abducts and rapes his wife and has him transported to Australia. Todd is a revenge hero who wreaks a terrible vengeance on the society that unjustly condemned him, and destroyed his wife's innocence.

The story in this volume recaptures the original Sweeney Todd, a figure of unredeemed cruelty and malice, who appeared first in a serial prose narrative entitled *The String of Pearls: a Romance* (1847). This Sweeney Todd has no sympathetic back-story to explain his vindictiveness and cruelty; he is simply an avaricious thief and murderer. 'There can be no doubt but that the love of money was the predominant feeling in Sweeney Todd's intellectual organisation … with such a man, then, no question of morality or ordinary feeling could arise, and there can be no doubt but that he would have sacrificed the whole human race, if, by doing so, he could have achieved any of the objects of his ambition'.[1] In *The String of Pearls* the barber's violent business straddles the real London, the everyday world of Fleet Street, and the subterranean domain of church vaults, prison cells, torture chambers, burial grounds, sewers, madhouses that make up London's gothic underworld. On the surface, a respectable barber's shop, a successful bakery, a parish church. Beneath them, murder, violence, crime, cannibalism, false imprisonment, slavery, exploitation.

The story in this volume follows the 1847 novel, not the modern appropriations of Sweeney Todd. Todd's domain is of course Fleet Street, linked to Smithfield by the underground River Fleet which once flowed as an open sewer past the Georgian meat market. I have shifted Mrs Lovett's pie-shop from Fleet Street to Smithfield, and adjusted the narrative's time setting from Georgian London to the date of the novel's publication, 1847.

In this story Sweeney and Mrs Lovett are pursued by two policemen, Inspector Keen and Sergeant Blunt (the names may seem too obvious, but 'Blunt' at least is the name of a magistrate in *The String of Pearls*). Here Keen is a progressive founder of the new Metropolitan detective service, Blunt an old-school professional bobby. Which of them turns out to have the better understanding of a criminal like Sweeney Todd?

The original 1847 gothic romance *The String of Pearls* is published in a modern edition in *Sweeney Todd: the Demon Barber of Fleet Street*, ed. Robert L. Mack (Oxford: Oxford University Press, 2007). In my endnotes citations of *The String of Pearls* refer to this edition. Robert L. Mack's book *The Wonderful and Surprising History of Sweeney Todd: the life and times of an urban legend* (London: Continuum, 2007) provides a comprehensive survey of Todd adaptations. The modern Sweeney Todd is manifested in Christopher Bond's play *Sweeney Todd, the Demon Barber of Fleet Street: a Melodrama* (London: Samuel French, 1974); Stephen Sondheim and Hugh Wheeler, *Sweeney Todd, the Demon Barber of Fleet Street: a Musical Thriller* (NY: Dodd, Mead and Co, 1979); and the film version *Sweeney Todd, the Demon Barber of Fleet Street*, dir. Tim Burton (2007). For the history of the Metropolitan Police I have used J.M. Beattie, *The First English Detectives: The Bow Street Runners and the Policing of London, 1750-1840* (Oxford: Oxford University Press, 2012) and Haia Shpayer-Makov, *The Ascent of the Detective: Police Sleuths in Victorian and Edwardian England* (Oxford: Oxford University Press, 2011). The historical parts of the narrative are anachronistic as to chronological sequence.

SWEENEY TODD

1

1 August 1847

'Is that him?', asked Inspector Keen, Detective Branch of the Metropolitan Police, of the Desk Sergeant on duty at Great Scotland Yard, as he peered through a dirty glass panel in the door.

Keen's companion, Detective Sergeant Blunt, craned to look over his superior's shoulder. 'What is 'e? Some kind o' Fuzzy-wuzzy?'

The man they referred to sat with his back to them in Interrogation Room no. 1. In fact, the 'room' was nothing more than a holding cell in the basement of the police station. Keen had insisted that it be labelled in this way, and furnished with a table and chairs. There was no Interrogation Room no. 2. Sergeant Blunt's graphic description was of the man's hair, a thickset rook's nest profusely and untidily overhanging.

'No', said the Desk Sergeant, as he continued writing into a big ledger on the counter before him. 'He's the barber'.

'The *barber*?' laughed DS Blunt. 'Not much of an advert for his trade, is he?'

'He's old school, he is', said the Desk Sergeant. 'No dummies in his window sporting lovely wigs. Doesn't hold with advertisements. Or beargrease. Or scented hair oil. Just a pair of scissors and a pudding basin, that's all he uses'.[2]

'Very well', said Keen. 'Let's see what he has to say. And Blunt, for God's sake don't call him a Fuzzy-wuzzy. He's a citizen, assisting us with our inquiries. He's a respectable tradesman. And he has rights'.

The two detectives sat down opposite the man, whose appearance was even more striking from the front than from the back. His body seemed badly assembled, his hands disproportionately large. Framed by the mane of black hair, his face resembled that of a wooden puppet in a Punch and Judy Show. A thin line for a mouth, eyebrows like black caterpillars, and a most peculiar cast of the left eye that made his eyes stare in different directions.[3]

'Name?' Keen asked shortly.

'I give it' was the man's reply, uttered with a sharp opening and snapping shut of the rat-trap mouth.

'Then give it again!' shouted Blunt, banging his fist on the table. Blunt tended to switch to 'hard cop' prematurely. 'And who do you think you're looking at?'

The man gave a short, sharp bark which seemed to be the way he laughed. 'I'm looking at your Guv'nor'.

Keen sighed. 'Calm down, Blunt. Can't you see he has an unusual optical obliquity?'

'A what?' asked Blunt.

'A cast in his eye'

The man again barked his peculiar, unmirthful laugh. 'It's true', said Todd, 'I am what in a horse would be called walleyed. Some say my eyes are set on either side of my head, like those of a pike. And my name's Todd. Sweeney Todd. If you're still interested'.

'And you run a hairdresser's shop in Fleet Street, yes?' Keen continued. 'Next to St Dunstan's Church?'[4]

'Barber's. Plain and simple. None of your fancy French pomade. You can see the red-and-white pole outside. A trim, a cut, a short sharp shave. That's my business'.

'Very well. Now we're investigating the disappearance of one …' – Keen looked down at the paper in front of him – 'Mr. Thornhill. About sixty years of age, country dressed, red face. Seen entering your shop at 10 am yesterday. Never came out again. According to witnesses'.[5]

Blunt banged the table again. 'Where were you at 10 am yesterday?'

'In my shop, as always', replied Todd, swivelling his right eye for the first time towards Blunt. 'Gentleman o' that description come in for a shave, it's true. I had a customer. He didn't want to wait. Left again, the same way he came in'.

'And apparently', said Keen quietly, still looking down at his papers, 'left his dog behind'.

'That yapping cur? Was it his? With its infernal barking?' Todd's big hands closed for a moment, then as quickly relaxed. 'There was a dog, making a nuisance of itself, outside my shop. I don't know if it was the gentleman's dog. Looked like a stray to me. What does that prove?'.

'You say this Mr Thornhill left your shop. Did he speak to you first?'.

'He did, as a matter of fact. Asked me if I knew of a certain lodging house in Red Lion Court. Looking for a friend of his, name of Oakley. Said they had some business to transact. Something about' – and here Todd swivelled his eye back to Keen again – 'a string of pearls'.[6]

'Pearls, eh?', interjected Blunt, trying to sound knowing. 'Pearls!'.

'Did you see these pearls', asked Keen. 'Did he have them on him?'

'I know nothing more than what I've told you', said Sweeney, with the air of a man shutting up shop. 'I mention the pearls only because he talked of them. And then disappeared. Did his vanishing have anything to do with the merchandise? I don't know. A suspicious man might think so. But I've given you the name of his partner. And where he expected to find him. If I were you, I'd start my search there. And stop detaining an honest citizen who should be about his lawful business. My shop don't run itself, you know. I should be at work'.

'Yes, yes', said Keen absent-mindedly. 'We're sorry to have kept you, Mr Todd. You're free to leave. If you hear anything more of Mr Thornhill – well, you know where to find us'.

And Todd left the Interrogation Room, eyeballing Blunt for one last time with his one straight eye.

''E done it, Guv', said Blunt. 'I trust my instincts, and I know 'e done it'.

Keen rose from his chair, walked round to the front of the table and placed the flats of his hands on its roughly-planed and knotted surface. 'Done what?' he asked. 'Did what, I mean? There's no evidence of a crime. No body. No motive. Who's your witness? An informant I suppose. Care to share him with your superior officer? No, I thought not'.

'But the pearls, sir. Surely they're motive?'

'And how do you know about them? From the man you accuse of stealing them. How much easier police work would be if every criminal gave us all the evidence we needed to convict him'.

'I'm not sure I follow, sir ...'

'Todd wouldn't have told us about the pearls, if he'd stolen them. If he murdered Thornhill and stole the jewels, nobody else would have known they existed. So why volunteer the information?'

'Aye, but he's a rum-looking cove, ain't he guvnor? A wrong un if ever I saw one'.

Keen leaned forward across the table towards Blunt.

'Yes, he's an unusual-looking man. Unfortunate in his physiognomy. Maybe even some gigantism there – look at the size of his hands. One of nature's victims, you might say. And he has a definite disability'.

'You mean the squinty eye?'

'Yes, I mean the pronounced optical obliquity. But squinting is not a crime. And you can't charge a man with looking odd. It would violate his human rights. If we held him, he could sue us under the Habeas Corpus Act for wrongful arrest'.

'But what about the dog?'

'Ah, yes, the dog. How could I forget? Pull him in, and question him. One bark for yes, two for no. Have him dictate a statement. Get his paw-print on an affidavit. Let's see how that stands up in court. Look, there's no evidence against Todd. To all intents and purposes he's an honest London tradesman, who provides a necessary service to his customers. Salt of the earth. Backbone of the country. Not the criminal type, Blunt. Trust me. Now get someone looking for this Oakley. Red Lion Court. And send someone down to Hatton Garden. Ask around about these pearls. And leave Sweeney Todd alone'.

2

Inspector Keen was a new broom at Great Scotland Yard. The detective branch of the Metropolitan Police, established immediately after the execution of Daniel Goode in 1842, had yet to make a name for itself, and was in need of strong and capable leadership.[7]

On 3 April 1842, in the stables of a large house in Roehampton, Daniel Goode took an axe to his common-law wife, Jane Jones, slaughtered her like an animal, and proceeded to dismember her corpse. He then tried to burn the remains, along with his bloodstained clothes. Leaving the murdered woman cooking, Goode went off to Wandsworth, and stole a pair of trousers from a pawnbroker.

The police followed him to Roehampton, entered the premises, and found what was left of a charred female torso. Goode had slipped round the back, and managed to lock the bobbies inside, thus making his escape. He avoided detection for some weeks by travelling to Kent, beyond the reach of what was then the very short arm of the law. Eventually he was identified by a railway manager, who invited him into the Angel Inn in Tonbridge for a drink, and simultaneously alerted the police. Goode was arrested, tried and publicly executed outside Newgate, alongside Smithfield Market, on 23 May 1842.

You can see his story pictorially immortalised in a Penny Dreadful of 1842: the frenzied homicide swinging his axe; the macabre butcher holding up his wife's severed head; the police flinching from their grim discovery; Goode's arrest in the streets of Tonbridge. And finally the condemned man in irons, sitting in his cell at Newgate, awaiting execution.

The Goode case had demonstrated the crying need for a new kind of policing. London needed officers capable of acting on intelligence and information; of pursuing inquiries persistently after a trail had gone cold; of following a criminal wherever he went, far beyond the Met's territorial jurisdiction. It was Keen who, as a young constable, had led the search for the elusive Goode, tracing him to Tonbridge, and finally apprehended him. It was Keen who had obtained Goode's confession. It was Keen who stood beneath the scaffold outside Newgate to watch Goode perform his final vanishing act. He had demonstrated a capability for exactly the kind of intelligence-led investigation and pursuit that the Met so badly needed. This, together with his determination in tracking and seizing the murderer, recommended him for a leadership role in the new detective branch. Which is how, in the summer of 1847, Inspector Keen came to be interrogating Sweeney Todd.

The detective branch, initially consisting of two Inspectors, six sergeants and a number of constables, had been assembled from among the most promising of the Met's officers, some of whom, like Keen, had been involved in the pursuit of Daniel Goode. But they were still, in most respects, fairly ordinary policemen. Keen found his colleagues and officers to be in general lazy, too familiar with the criminal class, and easily tempted to corruption. They were often to be found, even inside the station, rowdy, half drunk, and enjoying the company of whores. They lacked the kind of focus and concentration essential to this new kind of police work. And so Inspector Keen set out on a crusade to reform the detective branch.

He compelled his officers to clear their desks of accumulated debris, and tidy up their personal appearance. All eating and drinking inside the station were banned. Suspects were to be held in the cells below until ready for questioning, so the station was no longer full of shouting drunks and screeching prostitutes. Proper records were kept and maintained, though the staff moaned unceasingly about unnecessary paperwork. Keen encouraged his officers to address their inquiries with focus and concentration, sifting evidence for its true value, and pursuing productive lines of inquiry.

Progress was being made, and there were notable successes, such as the apprehension of James Greenacre for the murder of Hannah Brown, whose torso was found in Edgware Road, her head in a canal at Stepney, and her legs in Camberwell.[8] The traditional police method was to try to apprehend the murderer immediately after the crime, usually via the hue and cry, the old procedure of the Bow Street Runners. To catch the villain literally red-handed, his clothes still wet with the victim's blood, the smoking knife still clutched in his trembling hand. Or better still, to seize the criminal, with a great display of moral authority and legal triumph, when he wandered hopelessly into a police station to give himself up; a scenario which enabled them to take full public credit without even leaving the station. The Brown case was different. The initial manhunt went nowhere, and found nobody. It was only by persisting , under Inspector Keen's orders, in diligent and painstaking inquiries, over the following weeks, that the Detective Branch eventually found their suspect, James Greenacre, an acquaintance identified by the dead girl's brother.

Other murders, however, remained unsolved, such as the throat-cuttings of barmaid Eliza Davies, and pretty prostitute Eliza Grimwood.[9] The vanishing of Thornhill had been Keen's first case as a detective, and all his inquiries led nowhere. They found no trace of the mysterious Mr Oakley, or of the string of pearls. Even the dog disappeared. For a while Thornhill's name was displayed in white chalk on a blackboard on the station wall, under the heading 'Mispers'. After a month of fruitless investigation, Keen surreptitiously wiped the board clean.

Shortly after Sweeney Todd first came to Keen's attention, he became intensively occupied in investigating the murder of a prominent Whig Member of Parliament, Lord William Russel.[10] One morning the housemaid had come downstairs to find the ground floor rooms a shambles of furniture-strewn disarray. Assuming there had been a robbery, she rushed to the room of Lord William's French valet, Courvoisier, and found him already up and dressed. Together they ascended to Lord William's bedchamber, threw open the shutters, and found his throat cut from ear to ear.

The police were called. Courvoisier helped them in their search, pointing out marks of violence on a back door where, he suggested, the intruders must have entered. The murder was classified as a robbery gone wrong. So the search immediately began for a gang of burglars who had broken in, stolen money and jewellery, and when disturbed, slit Lord William's throat to dispose of a witness. The Met sent their informants in pursuit, rounded up the usual suspects for questioning, and waited for stolen goods to surface. They found nothing. And so the Detective Branch was called in, and Keen took over the case.

Instinctively Keen knew that something didn't add up. An exhaustive search of the underworld had produced nothing – not a word, not a tip-off, not a ten-pound note. Was it really the work of professional cracksmen? Keen insisted, against the prevailing conventions, that the house be searched again. Immediately some of the missing jewellery turned up, hidden behind a cupboard.

'Dropped on the way out', suggested Blunt.

'And carefully concealed behind a cupboard?' replied Keen. 'I don't think so'.

The search was extended to the servant's quarters, and in Courvoisier's room, Keen discovered a screwdriver with paint-marks on the blade. The implement matched up to the scratches on the back door, indicating that Courvoisier had made them himself.

Courvoisier was put on trial. The case was not going well, owing to the lack of hard evidence. The jury would rather have had Courvoisier surprised by the bedside, bloodstained razor in his hand. Forensics was in its infancy: they found abstruse arguments about hidden jewellery, and the matching of a screwdriver to marks on a door, relatively hard to follow. But then came Keen's decisive breakthrough: some of the household silver was found in the lodgings of a French family known to Courvoisier. Being told of this, the murderer confessed to the robbery, but continued to protest his innocence of the murder. Notwithstanding, the uncovering of the loot was enough to hang him. He was convicted and executed outside Newgate Prison.[11]

Returning from the execution, Keen found his station pervaded by an air of quiet celebration. His methods had been validated: the murderer found, identified and brought to justice. A new era of policing was dawning: one ruled by an open mind, and a respect for evidence. Discard all conventional assumptions; be prepared to look in the most unlikely places; follow the evidence wherever it leads. As he strolled through the neat, unencumbered aisles between his officers' scrupulously tidy desks, Keen noticed a pile of debris pushed to the back of sergeant Blunt's workstation. As this resembled nothing so much as the kind of detritus Keen had declared anathema, he paused to see what it contained.

And was surprised to uncover its contents. Scraps of paper, posters, newspaper cuttings: not organised into any kind of order or sequence, but randomly piled in a chaotic and meaningless jumble. Rifling through the papers, he was taken aback by the inconsequential and incoherent miscellany of documents, none of which seemed to have anything to do with one another. Here was a record of Sweeney Todd's interrogation, with an advertisement for his barber's shop: 'A Clean Shave. Teeth pulled. Bloodletting'. Next to it was a poster advertising 'Mrs Lovett's HOT MEAT PIES, available Every Day from the Bakery in Smithfield Market'. An article clipped from a newspaper told of a terrible smell emanating from below the floor of the church of St Bartholomew the Great.[12] What did it all mean? Another newspaper clipping: 'Mysterious poisoning of a dog'.[13] A plan of Smithfield Market. What was Blunt thinking of? This was no serious criminal investigation, starting from a self-evident crime, pursuing a trail of evidence and apprehending a guilty suspect. This was more like the methods of the old school: heap information into piles, and hope that something significant falls off the top. Blunt seemed to be still harping on Sweeney Todd, the barber questioned about the disappearance of Thornhill. But Keen had closed that case months before. A foul smell from the crypt of a church? A poisoned dog? A cattle-market? 'A clean shave'? 'Hot meat pies'?

'Where's Blunt', asked Keen.

'Interrogation Room no.1, Sir'.

'Right'.

4

'Don't make me do it sir, I beg you. 'E'll kill me for sure. Don't make me do it'.

The speaker was a boy, aged about thirteen or fourteen, who faced Blunt across the table with an expression of unmitigated terror on his drawn white face.

'Take it easy, son', said Blunt soothingly. 'We'll protect you'.

'A word, Blunt', said Keen peremptorily, and preceded Blunt into the corridor.

'We got 'im, Sir', Blunt began.

'Got who?'

'Todd, of course'.

'Todd? I thought I told you …'

'That', said Blunt decisively, stabbing his index finger towards the cell, 'is Todd's apprentice. Tobias Wragg. Cheerful little fellow he was, when I first met him. Now look at him. Afraid of his own shadow'.

'And he is here … why?'

'Oh, I thought you'd heard. We've arrested Todd. There he was this morning, walking down Fleet Street, sporting a pair of diamond shoe-buckles.[14] Rich footwear for a barber, you'll say. Anyway this woman screams at the top of her lungs, points at his feet, and swears they belong to her husband. Mr Jeffries. Last seen wearing them, leaving his house in Fetter Lane, and off to get himself – guess what – a *shave*. Never seen again. Registered missing a month ago. She yells for the police, and Todd's arrested. Here's her statement. She made a positive ID on the shoe buckles'.

'Impressive. And the boy?'

'Indentured to Todd, lives in the shop. He's been helping me with my inquiries, so to speak. He sees everything. Knows everything. But he's not talking just yet. Terrified of his master'.

'Todd's story?'

'Bought the buckles in Smithfield market from a man with one eye. Didn't know they were stolen'.

'Very well', said Keen. 'Charge him'.

'With murder, sir?'

'With receiving. A buckle's not a body. There's no evidence of foul play'.

5

Todd stood in the dock, truculent and saturnine. His unfocused eyes roamed unpredictably and alarmingly around the court, disconcerting anyone they lighted on. The magistrate was elderly, confused and impenetrably deaf. Everything had to be explained to him by an usher. British justice, thought Keen. Envy of the world.

Mrs Jeffries, appearing for the prosecution, affirmed that the buckles had belonged to her husband, but could testify nothing as to his whereabouts, or produce evidence of any contact with Todd. Todd, defending himself, cross-examined, and easily confused her on places, dates and times. Toby was then placed in the witness-box, and presented a pitiable spectacle, snivelling and wiping his nose on his sleeve. When Todd fixed him with a glaring eye, his terror was tremblingly manifested. He seemed incapable of answering any questions. 'Tell 'im to stop staring at me!' was all he could say. The old magistrate leaned over and struggled to hear what the boy was saying. An usher interpreted, speaking loudly into the old man's ear. 'The prisoner will refrain from staring at the witness', the magistrate pronounced in a querulous voice. Todd's eyes executed a panoramic sweep of the court, and he vented his short barking laugh. The usher spoke into the old man's ear again, to the effect that the man was walleyed, and couldn't help where he was looking. The magistrate wrote something down. Keen sighed. This was not going well.

Having got little out of Mrs Jeffries, and even less out of Toby, Blunt summed up his case. Todd then called a witness, and all eyes turned towards the door. In came a woman, young and vivacious, provoking a flutter of excitement in the public gallery. Not exactly pretty, there was a kind of voluptuous magnetism about her, a stirring and effusive warmth that attracted a hungry kind of attention. A faint dew of animal sweat coloured her cheeks and made them glow. Her breasts, abundantly on show, quivered like translucent jelly under the crust of a warm pork pie.[15]

Keen was alone in his immunity to her bestial charm. He thought her smile fixed, like the humourless smile on the face of a ballerina; and her slanting eyebrows seemed to harbour a shadow of menace. A lurking devil in her eye.[16] But every other man in the court-room, even the senescent magistrate himself, gazed at her with an expression of yearning like that of a starving man drawn to the smell of gravy. Their hungry eyes perceived her as something literally edible.

The witness was introduced as Mrs Lovett, who ran the hot meat pie stall in Smithfield Market. She swore she had seen Sweeney Todd buy the buckles from a one-eyed man right in front of her stall. The magistrate wrote something down. The witness's corroboration of the man with one eye seemed decisive. Keen watched with a kind of awed fascination the rapid and irreversible collapsing of the case.

And that was it. Case dismissed. Sweeney Todd was once again a free man.

As Todd was leaving the court, his swivelling eye fixed on Toby, who whimpered in fear and crouched under Blunt's protective arm, and then lighted on Sergeant Blunt himself. 'Bad luck, copper', he sneered, and barked his short mirthless laugh. Blunt's face flushed scarlet, and before Keen could hold him he threw himself at Sweeney, grabbed him by the throat and pinioned him to the wall. 'Help, help!' the barber shouted. 'Police brutality! Get 'im off me! 'E'll murder me! I know my rights!'

With the help of a court officer, Keen dragged Blunt away and outside, followed by the mocking sound of Sweeney's laugh.

'Get a grip on yourself, man', hissed Keen. 'You're suspended from duty. With immediate effect. Go home'.

Blunt composed himself, straightened his jacket and walked stiffly away, the thin white shadow of Toby dogging him at heels.

7

Blunt's outburst outside the court brought disgrace to the force, and was completely unacceptable. But aspects of the Todd case continued to trouble Keen. Blunt was a good officer, and his instincts were usually right. Why had the boy been too afraid to testify? Who was the mysterious pie-seller who had appeared for Todd? Keen remembered that Mrs Lovett's pie stall had featured in the miscellany of evidence on Blunt's desk. More than coincidence? And the woman herself had looked untrustworthy. There was something he couldn't put his finger on about the case.

So in a mixture of curiosity and respect for his absent colleague, Keen tried to discover everything he could about the barber from local church registers and civic records as well as his own criminal archive. Todd had been abandoned by his mother, he discovered, left as a baby on the doorstep of the Foundling Hospital in Coram Fields. The name Todd had been given to him. A rough, unmanageable boy, he had ended up in the workhouse, where he was badly and regularly beaten by a bullying beadle of the name of Bamford.[17] Although clearly gifted with a natural intelligence, he seemed unamenable to formal education, and prone to violent attacks on teachers who tried to force learning on him. Since his only enthusiasm seemed to be for knives and razors, objects he was continually stealing and hiding, he was apprenticed to an elderly barber in Fleet Street, where he learned the trade. After a few years the old man disappeared. Todd affirmed that he'd decided to abandon the business and go abroad. He produced a document, signed with the old man's seal, leaving the shop to his apprentice. As there was no-one to contest this covenant, Sweeney inherited the shop, and began to build up the business.

Slowly Keen built up a psychological profile of Sweeny Todd. Born with no advantages, and no place in the world, Todd had yet managed to grow a successful business. This indicated strength of character, industry and a dedication to duty. As a child he had been subjected to violent abuse at the hands of municipal officials like Beadle Bamford. This explained his marked propensity for bullying, and his intimidation of young Toby. The abused becomes the abuser. As a foundling and workhouse boy, Todd would have possessed none of the finer things of life, and must have looked with understandable envy on those who had. Perhaps there was something shady in his acquisition of the buckles, a valuable commodity bought for a song on a street-corner. But a man who had grown up knowing what it is to have nothing could be forgiven for letting his appetites occasionally overshadow his respect for the law.

All in all there was nothing Keen could find in Todd's behaviour that could not be explained by the circumstances of his birth, upbringing and education. If there was violence in his character, he was the product of a violent society, and there was still no evidence he had harmed anyone. He had turned his obsession with sharp instruments into a professional skill, and established himself in a respectable trade. He may be a bully and a petty criminal, but these traits were peccadillos compared to the grave charges of which Blunt clearly suspected him. Perhaps some wise and sympathetic clergyman could be enjoined to talk to Todd, with the aim of persuading the barber to see the error of his ways, and to learn techniques for managing his anger.[18]

Keen also checked the background of Todd's key witness, Mrs Lovett. She too appeared to be a respectable tradesperson, running a highly successful enterprise in Smithfield. Her pies had the reputation of being 'the best pies in London', and attracted every morning long queues of eager and hungry customers.[19] He could find no criminal record for her, no contact with any criminal acquaintance, and no undisclosed connection to Todd. If there were some kind of conspiracy between them, then the evidence was buried deep underground, like the noxious cadavers in the crypt of St Bartholomew the Great.

He put the case from his mind. But it continued to trouble him. Strange images of death rose to haunt him in unaccustomed nightmares. A madman swinging a razor; rotting cadavers piled in a dusty vault; a huge brick oven whose door he dared not open. Blunt's suspicions flowed through his dreams like the dark current of an underground river.

8

While Keen was making his peace with Sweeney Todd, Blunt was busy declaring war. From the court-room he made his way home, stopping only to collect the contents of his desk from the station. Toby, who had continued to follow him, slinking along the edges of the street, was soon engaged as an assistant to help carry Blunt's things.

Blunt wasted no time in setting up an incident room in his rented apartment in Farringdon Road. Two of the four whitewashed walls were devoted to Todd and Mrs Lovett, while the longer wall at the back provided space for a big map of the City, with certain points flagged for emphasis: the barber's shop in Fleet Street, adjoining St Dunstan's Church; the Church of St Bartholomew the Great; Mrs Lovett's pie stall in Smithfield Market. Here light from the dusty windows fell strongly on what Blunt hoped would be the lineaments of truth, charting what he knew in his heart to be a map of evil.

Blunt was convinced that Sweeney had murdered Thornhill, disposed of his body and kept the string of pearls. If he had done it once and got away with it, he had probably done it over and over again. There were several persons listed as missing from, or last seen in, the area of Todd's Fleet Street shop, all men, mostly visitors from out of town. Blunt had engaged young Toby as an informant, and through him gained covert and illegal access to the shop: but his search produced nothing incriminating.

Blunt was also convinced that Sweeney must have an accomplice, but he seemed to have no friends or even acquaintances beyond his circle of customers. His suspicions towards Mrs Lovett arose from something Toby had said, to the effect that Todd sent him frequently to Smithfield to buy one of Mrs Lovett's hot meat pies. Though perpetually racked with hunger, Toby didn't dare touch it, and presented it to his master with the crust immaculately unbroken. Sweeney would then shut himself in a back room, alone with the pie. But then there was something intriguing about the boy's account. After a while Sweeney would re-emerge, and call Toby to finish off the remainder. What the boy found strange was that although Sweeney had obviously broken the crust and forked around among the pie's contents, he never seemed to eat any of it. As Toby would gorge greedily on the tasty fragments, he had little motivation for objecting to his master's apparent frugality in relation to Mrs Lovett's hot meat pies.

Blunt was convinced that some kind of message was being transmitted inside the pies; and when Mrs Lovett appeared as a witness at Todd's trial, he found the corroboration decisive. The two of them were up to something, and concerned to keep their contacts secret. There must be another channel of communication between them, invisible to the light of day.

After a few days Toby's confidence was restored, together with the colour in his face. After his abuse at the hands of Sweeney Todd, Blunt's protective kindness was like sunshine to a wilted plant. Capitalising on this trust, Blunt began to draw out of Toby crucial information as to Todd's *modus operandi*.

The barber's method with customers, Toby informed him, was always the same. As soon as the client was seated in the chair, Sweeney would lock the front door and display the 'CLOSED' sign. Toby would assist him in his preparations, mixing the lather to a creamy white foam, honing the razor to cut-throat sharpness on a leather strop. There were two rooms at the rear of the premises, each with its own door, one kept always locked. Once the barber was ready, he would dismiss Toby to one of the back rooms, ostensibly to fetch something, but actually to keep out of sight if he valued his life. A skilled craftsman needed absolute privacy, Todd would explain to the customer: any minor distraction, like a boy sniffing or fidgeting, could lead to a catastrophic slip of the razor. And so Toby would shut himself in an inner room, from whence he could hear Todd exchanging everyday pleasantries with the customer as he worked. After a short interval Toby would hear Todd making some excuse for leaving the customer alone for a few moments; then the barber would withdraw into the other back room, the one that was always locked. Shortly afterwards Toby would hear strange sounds, the rapid drawing of a heavy bolt, a rushing noise and the sound of a heavy blow. He would hear Sweeney go back into the shop, talking apparently to himself. After a while Toby would be let out of his temporary prison, to observe the barber's chair where the customer had been seated standing vacant. Sweeny would be cheerfully standing in the open doorway, looking expectantly for the next client.[20]

On the day Sweeney shaved Mr Thornhill, Toby, on returning to the shop, had noticed that the customer had left behind a silver-headed cane, and pointed this dereliction out to his employer. Sweeney took the cane and dealt Toby a massive blow on the head with the heavy end. 'That will help you remember', said the barber, 'not to notice things that don't concern you'.[20]

9

Toby's dislike of the barber, and his appreciation of Blunt's protective custody, were motivations strong enough to enlist him in the detective's service. With so short-handed a team, Blunt decided, he would have to entrust Toby with some aspect of the operation. So he got him into a disguise, consisting of a blonde wig and the uniform of a charity boy. Toby's job was to stake out Mrs Lovett's pie stall, to watch and listen as unobtrusively as he could. Having dispatched the boy on this errand Blunt took himself off to the church of St Bartholomew the Great alongside Smithfield Market.

Earlier in his inquiries he had picked up reports of a terrible smell troubling the worshippers at the old church. An abominable stench had begun to pervade the sacred precincts, disturbing the parishioners and interfering with the services. Old ladies were obliged to arm themselves with bottles of smelling salts every time they went to church. The vicar would officiate and preach with a vinegar-soaked handkerchief clasped to his mouth and nose. A visiting bishop had refused to conduct a service of confirmation until the problem of the terrible charnel-house smell had been rectified. A builder had been called in to re-point the tombstones in the flagged floor; but there was no discernible improvement. Worshippers had been so overcome with nausea that following service they had repaired to the nearby market and refreshed themselves on the invigorating flavour of a pork or veal pie from Mrs Lovett's stall.[22]

Blunt identified himself to the curate, and asked to be shown down into the crypt. He was led through the nave, past the Chapel of the Holy

Icon, the tombs of illustrious parishioners, the banner of the Worshipful Company of Butchers, the tomb of Prior Rahere, the church's founder, and down some stone steps to the space beneath the Lady Chapel. The stench immediately assailed him, forcing him to retch and cough. The curate seemed unperturbed, evidently being blessed with a deficient sense of smell. But Blunt recognised the unmistakable odour of putrefaction, the stink of recently decomposed human or animal flesh. Covering his mouth and nose with a handkerchief, he borrowed the curate's lantern and began to search the vault. The distinctive stench could not be emanating from these ancient tombs, which contained only desiccated skeletons long since crumbled to ashes and dust. The smell seemed to seep up from below the floor, but there was no indication of a lower level, no trap door, no stairs leading down.

Without additional resources Blunt had to give up the search as fruitless. He would need men to excavate the floor and dig down into the church's foundations to locate the source of the dreadful stink. Nonetheless, as he stood in the dark vault, surrounded by the horrible effluvia of recent death, the flame of his lantern burning blue from the gaseous products of putrefaction, he was as sure in his own mind as he could be that a dark secret lay beneath the antique stones of St Bartholomew's crypt; and that it had something to do with Sweeney Todd.

On his way home Blunt reflected ruefully on the paucity of his evidence, and guessed at how Keen would receive it. He could hear the cutting irony of his superior's cold intelligence. 'Well done, Blunt', he would say: 'I can see the headlines now: "Dead body found in cemetery". "Corpse discovered hiding out in coffin"'.

So Blunt pondered on his next step. The old church with its stench of violent death and secret interment lay directly between Sweeney's shop and Mrs Lovett's pie stall. Was it possible that Sweeny had found some way of disposing of his victims there? And what of Mrs Lovett and the pies? Was there some foul play entailed in their manufacture? Unthinkable ideas began to form themselves in Blunt's uneasy mind, and horrible ideas forced themselves on his consideration. He recoiled from the hideous possibilities, but felt duty bound to continue his investigation.

Toby was back shortly after Blunt arrived home, to report that Mrs Lovett's stall had closed and that nothing of any significance had happened. At Smithfield Toby had concealed himself behind some hides left drying in the sun close to the stall, from which point of vantage he was able to see and hear everything that occurred. But there was nothing to disturb the normal operation of the business: pies delivered, customers buying, money handed over, customers eating. When her stock was running low Mrs. Lovett would crawl underneath her table, pull up some kind of trap-door and disappear below ground. Soon she would re-emerge with another batch of hot pies, indicating that the bakery must lie beneath the stones of Smithfield.

'Are you sure there was nothing out of the ordinary?' Blunt insisted. 'Think now. Any tiny detail that didn't seem quite normal'.

'Well there was one thing', Toby said thoughtfully. 'But it was nothing really'.

'Tell me about it', said Blunt, his interest growing.

'Well there was this man bought a pie – pork, I think it was – or maybe veal – I'm not sure …'

'The content of the pie don't matter', said Blunt. 'What did he say?'

'He said he found something in the pie. He thought it looked like a fingernail'.

'A fingernail? Go on'.

'So he showed it to Mrs Lovett. Wanted his money back. Said it must be one of her fingernails. Said he nearly broke his tooth on it'.

'And what did she say?'

'She said' – Toby paused to sort his recollections and give an exact account. 'She said: "that's a bit of 'oof, that is. We uses real animals in our pies, dearie. And I makes 'em myself. None of my fingernails is broken"'.

'Then what?'

'Well the man said he wanted to have a look at her fingers. See if he could match up the nail. Other fellows was eggin' 'im on: you know, saying rude things about Mrs Lovett's fingers, what they'd like her to do with them … you know'.

'I know', said Blunt. 'But then?'

'Well then Mrs Lovett picks up a big hammer, like the ones they uses in the market to stun the beasts. Big heavy iron thing, it was. She says the only way he was going to get any closer to her fingers was if she 'it 'im with it. So o'course 'e scarpered quick'.

10

The next morning a well-to-do farmer in muddy top-boots was to be seen walking along Fleet Street from the direction of Smithfield, accompanied by a boy in a country smock and chewing a straw.[23] The pair paused at the Bull's Head tavern, where the farmer left the boy sitting outside with a glass of ale, while he crossed the road to a shop that displayed the red-and-white, blood-and-bandage emblem of the barber. He entered the shop, the bell ringing cheerfully above the door. And was welcome by a pair of large hands and a twisted smile.

'Good morning, sir', said Sweeney unctuously. 'And what can I do for you this fine morning?'

''Ee can give me a shave', the farmer replied in a rich country burr, and sat himself comfortably in the barber's chair.

Sweeney took a white sheet and furled it around him, tying the tapes around his neck. 'Up from the country, I see?'

'Come up from Braintree with beasts on commission. Stoppin' at the Bull's Head. A matter of 200 cattle I brung up, I did, d'ye see, and sold 'em all yesterday in Smithfield, for 550 pund'.

'You sold them all?' said Sweeney, with intense interest, as he mixed lather in a white china bowl.

'That I did. And have the money here in my pocket, all in bank-notes. Safe bind, safe find. I carries it always with me, I does, d'ye see'.

'£550?' said the barber reflectively, as he stropped his razor. 'A tidy sum'.

'So it be. And 'ee will see some of it, if 'ee gives me a close shave'.

'As you wish', said Sweeney mysteriously. 'Now this razor ain't sharp enough for the cheek of a country gentleman. I'll just slip into the back room and fetch another'.

The barber disappeared into the back of the shop, softly closing a key in the lock of the door. No sooner had he done so than the farmer sprung from the chair, divested himself of both the sheet and his rural smock, and drew a pistol from inside his coat. He watched in horror as the chair he had sat on rose from the floor on a turning board, tipped over and swivelled downwards, disappearing into darkness before swinging back and righting itself again. Had he remained seated, he would have been tipped headlong into the cellar, no doubt dashing his brains out on the stone floor some twenty feet below.[25]

Sweeney did not re-emerge from the back room. Blunt – for it was he – heard heavy steps going downwards, then the sound below of an uttered curse. Pausing only to open the front door and blow his whistle, a signal to young Toby to come to his aid, Blunt tried the back-room door, but found it locked. He shot off the lock with his pistol, and forced his way into the room. In the corner a cupboard door stood open, and from inside the recess stone steps wound down into darkness. Toby hurried in behind him, handing Blunt a lantern. The detective bounded down the stairs and emerged into a cellar under the shop. There on the flagged floor, directly beneath the barber's chair, a gruesome pattern of dark stains told the grim tale of Sweeney Todd's true business. In the fitful light of the lantern, which cast grotesque shadows on the walls, Blunt could clearly see fragments of bone and brain matter lodged among the blood-stains.

But there was no sign of Todd. Glancing around the cellar, Blunt took in rows of shelves, stacked from floor to ceiling with shoes, hats, walking sticks, umbrellas, folded coats, the looted spoil from slaughtered victims. But where was Sweeney? There must be another way out. Bloodstained tracks on the floor pointed out the direction in which the corpses had been dragged. Blunt trained the light of the lantern on the corner of the room, and at last found what he was looking for: an open trap-door through which the barber had obviously descended. He dropped to his knees and stared down into darkness. Below he could see movement, and from beneath hear a strange sound as of rushing water.

He held the lantern down into the trap. Sure enough, directly beneath them ran the dark waves of an underground river. Of course! The Fleet. Why had he not realised it before? One of the old rivers of London, become in the last century an open sewer, now bricked over and built on. This was the shadowy channel that linked Sweeney to the charnel-house beneath the church, and to Mrs Lovett's stall. Whatever their grotesque business was, it was trafficked and transacted under here along the ancient city waterway.

Dropping quickly down through the open hatch, he found himself standing on the brick-paved towpath of the subterranean stream, hearing from further down the river the splashing sounds of Todd making his escape in some boat he was rapidly paddling. Moored to the bank was another craft, a kind of raft that had obviously been used to transport corpses, its waterlogged timbers stained with blood. Blunt leapt aboard and seized a paddle, while Toby slipped the knot on the mooring-rope. Soon they were sliding through the brick tunnels of the Fleet, borne on the river's rapid current towards the Thames. As they reached what Blunt knew were the foundations of St Bartholomew's church, he scented once again the dreadful stench of rotting corpses. There they were, Todd's mutilated victims, lined along the banks of the river deep below the crypt, piled on top of one another like cadavers in a plague pit, the meat stripped from their bones, their putrefying skeletons gnawed by rats. The empty eyes of their skulls lit up with an unnatural glow as the rays of his lamp travelled rapidly past.

The little raft bowled on along the stream, until up ahead Blunt could see a dim light showing through the open end of a tunnel. Lodging the paddle against the brickwork, he managed to stop the onward passage of the raft just before it emerged into the light. Peering round the end of the tunnel, what he saw struck him to the very soul with horror.

The river flowed through a large subterranean cellar, lit with the shadowy illumination of lanterns. The space was vast, but of a dim and sepulchral aspect. The floor was of rough red tiles, and large jagged stones were hammered into the earthen walls to strengthen them, while here and there huge pillars made by beams of timber rose perpendicularly from the floor, propping large flat pieces of wood to support the ceiling. Here and there gleaming lights seemed to be peering out from furnaces, and there was a strange, hissing, simmering sound, while the air was impregnated with a rich and savoury vapour.[26]

The smell came from huge brick industrial oven, such as is used for mass baking. Around the room there were shelves laden with bags of flour, lard, and cuts of white meat – leg, shoulder, haunch – that Blunt knew instinctively had not come from any slaughtered pig or calf. A big iron mincing-machine stood ready to convert the raw meat into the anonymous pulp used to fill pies. A tray of pie-crusts stood on a tray waiting to be filled with their dreadful freight of murdered human flesh.[27]

Blunt took all this in at a glance. But it was the tableau of horror at the centre of the room that grabbed his attention. There stood a butcher's block, littered with the knives and saws used to cut and trim meat, and stained with blood. Next to the table was an open safe, gold coins and banknotes piled untidily within, some strewn around the floor as if just taken out. And there was Todd, standing over the table, a bloodstained razor in his hand. Below him, spread-eagled on the table, was what was left of Mrs Lovett, her throat slit from ear to ear and her heart's blood cascading down over the lip of the table: while her abdomen was slit from sternum to pubis, entrails bulging out from the keen incision. Her face still showed the final agonising sensations of violent death. Sweeney was in the act of inserting his free hand into her insides, touching with a kind of tenderness the still warm offal of her organs. What could possess a man to do such a thing; to commit such a nameless, unspeakable act?[28]

Blunt stood paralysed at the horror of the scene. He drew his pistol, but it was already discharged and useless. Behind him little Toby instinctively crouched in terror. Todd glanced towards them, then immediately turned with his razor brandished aloft, and charged towards Blunt.

The violent percussion of a pistol shot echoed through the cellar, and Todd stopped in mid-charge, arrested by the impact. The razor fell from his hand, and tinkled down onto the stone floor. Blood began to run from his smashed shoulder where the ball had hit. His arm dropped to his side, and he fell to his knees. Behind him Blunt could see the figure of Inspector Keen, holding the smoking pistol, and backed by a team of officers, who quickly ran to seize Todd and secure the scene. There was no hope for Mrs Lovett, who lay slaughtered like an animal on the butcher's block. But Sweeney would live long enough to face the hangman's rope. Even in this exigency his dark, caustic humour never left him. 'I deny it all', he shouted with his short, barking laugh, as the officers roughly pinioned his broken arm. 'Ouch, get off me. You've got the wrong barber. I want a lawyer. I wasn't even here'.

11

The customer who found a fingernail in his pie had been sufficiently concerned about apparent violations of environmental and food safety regulations to report the matter to the police, and by the next day Keen had caught wind of it at Great Scotland Yard. Recalling Blunt's suspicions and his own uneasiness about the case, he had sent to Blunt's apartment and found him already out. Instinctively worried, and putting two and two together, he gathered a team and went straight to Smithfield, where he found the trap door under Mrs Lovett's stall open, and clearly heard scream of agony from below.

Todd and Mrs Lovett had for years colluded together in their murderous business. Todd had dispatched the victims with his mechanical chair, and shipped the corpses down the Fleet River, despoiling them of their possessions, and roughly butchering the carcasses of their flesh. Stopping underneath the church, he had disposed of the remains there, and voyaged onwards with his raft laden with prime meat. In the cellar underneath Smithfield, the meat had been processed and baked into pies. The hungry citizens of London had for years been feasting on the flesh of their fellows.

Keen thought it best to keep the mystery of the pies a secret, since the discovery of a plague of involuntary cannibalism would be liable to cause civil disorder and unrest. Sweeney would hang just as securely for the murder of his partner, and the missing victims would remain safely and innocuously missing. Better to believe that your lost loved one was drowned or disappeared, than to think of seeing him again under the crust of a hot veal-and-ham pie. The trial was brief and uneventful, the press was kept out of it, and Sweeney was sentenced for execution at Newgate the day after tomorrow.

Blunt and Keen visited Sweeney in his cell, and Keen did his best to elicit from the murderer some credible motivation or cause. He asked him about his abuse at the hands of Beadle Bamford, who Sweeney scarcely seemed to remember. Then about the old barber to whom the young Sweeny was apprenticed. Did he abuse the boy? Was he cruel, harsh, violent? Did he interfere with him in any way?

'Him?' asked Sweeney scornfully. 'That silly old sod? He was too timid to swat a fly. I had ideas for building up the business. But he weren't interested. He was – how should I put it? – in my way, he was. So I tipped him down the cellar stairs. Cracked 'is skull wide open'.

Keen gave Blunt a significant glance. 'You murdered your employer?'

'Murder's such an ugly word, Gov'nor. Gives you the wrong idea. He were an old man, nobody would miss him. I helped him on his way'.

Looking for somewhere to dispose of the body, Sweeney had found his way down through the cellar to the underground river. At first he thought of just hurling the body in and letting the river take it, but realised it would float downstream, emerge into the Thames under Blackfriars Bridge and likely be discovered. So he stowed it in a recess of the old brick-work, and never looked back.

'And your partner in crime, Mrs Lovett. Do you regret what happened to her?'

'Oh she were a game one, she was', said Sweeney, rolling his eyes salaciously. 'Enjoyed every minute of it. We stashed the money under her bakery, planning to run off together. So she thought, anyway. Women get these ideas in their heads. I would have split it with her, fair do's. But when she sees me with the safe open, she jumps to conclusions, and goes for me with a hammer. I would have cut her in. But the way things went, I had to cut her out. And ...' here he chuckled grimly to himself, 'cut her up as well'.

Sweeney and Mrs Lovett had met in the Bull's Head in Smithfield. He was immediately smitten by her animal charms, and she was drawn by a dark sexual perversity to the monstrous potency in him. Their sex life was a chronicle of violent and reciprocal perversity, since she lusted after pain, and he enjoyed inflicting it. Soon they plotted together to find ways of synergising their respective businesses for mutual profit. Every day he held beneath his razor the exposed throats of a dozen potential victims. Every day she baked pies filled with increasingly expensive animal meat. Supposed they merged their enterprises? When Sweeney told her about the Fleet River running underneath the shop, their dreadful demonic plan was hatched. The barber would produce the meat by murder, the baker would provide the public with pies.

12

At eight o' clock the next morning, Sweeney was taken to Newgate for execution. Only a small crowd gathered to see him off, since Keen had managed to keep the lid on the grisly details of the case. Todd mocked the hangman, spat at the spectators, and gave the impression of a man enjoying hugely the spectacle of his own violent death. As the executioner slipped the rope around his neck, Sweeny fixed him with one baleful eye, and the hangman, veteran of a hundred executions, literally flinched. The trap was sprung, the rope tightened, and Sweeney was dancing on air. His carcase dangled from the rope like that of a beast outside a butcher's shop, swinging gently in the early morning breeze.[29]

Blunt and Keen had joined the crowd to see Sweeney hang. Keen regretted that he had been unable to reach out to the murderer to unlock the secrets of his personality. Somewhere inside that grotesque and malformed body, he was convinced, now swinging limply from the gallows, lay a sensitive soul crushed by childhood abuse and cruelty into a shape of malevolence. We are all victims, if the truth were known; every killer has his own story. *Nil mihi humanum alienum puto:*[30] to understand all is to forgive all.

To Blunt the dead man was a monster, possessed by evil, and utterly indifferent to the fate of his helpless and innocent victims. In a terrible complicity with the partner of his crimes, he had subjected good people to unimaginable cruelty, robbed them of their hard-earned valuables, and subjected their pitiable slaughtered corpses to unthinkable atrocity. Such evil was beyond the human: incomprehensible, bewildering, sickening to behold. A demon he was, this barber; a demon of a barber.[31]

Sweeney Todd. The Demon Barber of Fleet Street.

Butcher at work, Smithfield Market

AARON KOSMINSKI
(JACK THE RIPPER)
PREFACE

For my story about Jack the Ripper I have shifted a little to the east from my primary psycho-geographic territory, to Whitechapel. But the familiar connections between the Ripper atrocities and animal slaughter are too tempting to resist. I have chosen a genuine Ripper suspect (i.e. one named, investigated and placed under surveillance by the police), a Polish Jewish butcher, Aaron Kosminski, who may have been a *shochet* or kosher slaughterman. Kosminski was admitted to Colney Hatch asylum in 1891, and died in captivity.[1]

His story is imagined through the invented case notes of the real medical attendant at the asylum, Dr Kouchin (converted here into a progressive psychoanalyst). The fictional narrative is collated with extracts from historical documents – police reports and memoirs, coroners' inquests, medical reports, sociological descriptions of Whitechapel – all of which are easily accessible due to an overwhelming curiosity about the Ripper murders. I have also added details on Jewish ritual slaughter, the laws of the Torah, Old Testament poetry and the history of the Jewish diaspora in Poland.

Dr Kouchin tries to treat Kosminski, and gradually discovers his true identity. Finally the doctor resorts to an extreme medical procedure in order to cure the incurable, to eradicate evil from one of the most evil characters in history.

The documentary method of the story owes something to Bram Stoker's *Dracula* (London: Archibald Constable and Company, 1897), which in turn has connections to Jack the Ripper, and Dr Kouchin bears some resemblance to Stoker's Dr Seward. Other books consulted include Stewart P. Evans and Keith Skinner, *Jack the Ripper: Letters from Hell*

(London: the History Press, 2001); Philip Sugden, *The Complete History of Jack the Ripper* (1994, revised London: Robinson, 2002); Paul Beg, *Jack the Ripper: the Facts* (London: Portico Press, 2004); Fiona Rule, *The Worst Street in London* (London: Ian Allen, 2008). The website *Casebook: Jack the Ripper*, compiled by amateur historians, is full of primary source transcriptions and insightful discussions, so I have cited it extensively. The leading authority on Aaron Kosminski is Robert House, hence his book *Jack the Ripper and the Case for Scotland Yard's Prime Suspect* (NJ: John Wiley and Sons, 2011) is indispensable.

Aaron Kosminsky
(Jack the Ripper)

1

Colney Hatch Lunatic Asylum, 7 February 1891[2]

Patient Admission, 11190

Date of Admission: 7 February 1891

Name: Aaron Kosminski

Age: 26

Address: Sion Square, Commercial Road, Whitechapel

Occupation: Butcher

Place of Work: Aldgate Meat Market, Smithfield Market

Religion: Hebrew

Time insane: 2 years

Physical symptoms: Self-abuse

Form of Disorder: Mania

2

Casebook of Dr Eli Kouchin, Medical Officer attending at Colney Hatch Asylum. 10 February 1891

The manner of admission for this patient, Aaron Kosminsky,[3] two days since, was unusual. He was brought here by an elderly gentleman, Mr. Jacob Cohen, who gave a full account of his symptoms. Mr Cohen is not a relative, but a man of some authority in the Jewish community of Whitechapel. In addition, escorting Kosminski in handcuffs, were two policemen, and a senior police Inspector, who did not wish his name to be recorded. The Inspector made a point of insisting that Kosminski be restrained, though his quiet behaviour here would not normally warrant such a procedure. We have been given to understand he is capable of violence.

Mr Cohen informed the receiving medical officer that Kosminski was in the habit of going about the streets picking up bits of bread out of the gutter and eating them. He would also drink water from the tap, and refuse food at the hands of others. The occasion of his admittance was a domestic dispute in which he took a knife, and threatened the life of his sister.[4]

Today I examined the patient myself, and corroborated Mr. Cohen's opinion. Patient declares that he is guided and his movements altogether controlled by an instinct that informs his mind. He says that he knows the movements of all mankind. He refuses food from others because he is told to do so, and he eats out of the gutters for the same reason. He admits that he is ill, but does not know what it is that afflicts him. The orderlies on night duty advise that he practices self-abuse, attended by such violent motion and noise that he was alarming the other patients, and so he was restrained in the strait-waistcoat.

The view of my colleagues is that Kosminski suffers from a form of mania, probably caused by years of uncontrolled auto-erotic stimulation.[5] They are old-fashioned in their opinions, always ready to seek the causes of mental illness in vicious behaviour. They know nothing of the new teachings on the science of the mind that are gaining ground in Germany and America. Their recommendation for treatment of the patient is restraint of the hands to prevent further self-abuse, and to be kept under observation.

3

Whitechapel, 1889 [6]

On the right, as we leave the Minories, is the Aldgate Meat Market, a row of shops used by butchers from time immemorial. Hundreds of carcases hang here in rows, and dozens of waggons loaded with hides stand in the roadway.

Shirt-making in buried basements, packing-case, or, perhaps, cardboard box-making, on the ground-floor; and glimpses of very dirty bald heads, bending over cobbling, or the sorting of 'old clo',' through the cracked and rag-stuffed upper windows. Jewish names – Isaacs, Levy, Israel,

Jacobs, Rubinsky, Moses, Aaron – wherever names appear, and frequent inscriptions in the homologous letters of Hebrew.

Fashion Street, Flower and Dean Street, Thrawl Street, Wentworth Street. Through which shall we go to Brick Lane? Black and noisome, the road sticky with slime, and palsied houses, rotten from chimney to cellar, leaning together, apparently by the mere coherence of their ingrained corruption. Dark, silent, uneasy shadows passing and crossing – human vermin in this reeking sink, like goblin exhalations from all that is noxious around. Women with sunken, black-rimmed eyes, whose pallid faces appear and vanish by the light of an occasional gas-lamp, and look so like ill-covered skulls that we start at their stare. Horrible London? Yes.

4

Dr Kouchin's Journal, 15 February 1891

My interest in the patient Aaron Kosminski having grown over the few days since his admission, I have begun this journal to preserve a detailed record of my examinations, the behavioural traits of the patient, and the success or failure of my recommended treatments.

Kosminski is a most unusual and intriguing subject. When admitted less than a week ago, he exhibited all the symptoms of advanced mania. He appeared morose and melancholy, and confused in his speech. My initial conversations with him suggested a serious form of insanity: he told me that all his actions were guided by some external force, and that like God he knew the secrets of all hearts.[7] Such delusions are clearly causing his abnormal behaviour, since it is in response to inner voices that he refuses to accept food from others, scavenges from the gutters and so forth. Through his incoherence and profound sadness, I could glimpse a faint glimmering of reason: he acknowledged that he is ill, without knowing the cause.

Now, less than a week later, Kosminski seems a changed man, and to all intents and purposes a rational creature. He apologises to me for his behaviour, saying he has no idea what came over him. He understands that such conduct must be punished, and begs my forgiveness for any offence caused. I asked him to explain the self-abuse, and though he was at first circumspect in his replies, he eventually admitted that the practice is a gross and repellent perversion, and expresses gratitude to my colleagues for preventing his further indulgence in the solitary vice by restraining of his hands.

Changing the subject, I sought to distract him from brooding on his mental state by asking about his life. He lives in a large Jewish community in Whitechapel, speaks Yiddish as well as English, and I think instinctively trusts me more than other doctors on account of my own Jewish inheritance. Though I can hardly claim to be the most pious or observant of my race, my Jewishness is sufficiently obvious to encourage some tribal solidarity. I know a little Hebrew, and still feel the pull of those bonds of race, religion and family that bind the people of the covenant so closely together.

I asked him to describe Whitechapel for me. Was it not a very poor place?

- Yes, he replied, there is poverty, but plenty of employment for those willing to work hard.

- And for those who do not?

- They must face the consequences of their own actions.

-You work as a butcher, I believe?

- Yes, doctor, a butcher's man. My uncle owns the business. I drive the cart. Taking meat to Smithfield for the early morning market.

- So you work through the night?

- Yes, all night sometimes.

- A messy business? (He did not seem immediately to understand). Messy? Oh, you mean the blood? No, no. For as it is written: 'the blood is the life'. And I have my leather apron to protect me. Yes: my leather apron.[8] (He spoke of his apron with a kind of fondness, as a cherished possession).

- Do you work at the slaughtering?

- Yes, I assist.

- is it not cruel work?

- No, no, not cruel. The beasts are slaughtered cleanly, by the code of *shechita*. We use the *chalaf* – the very sharp knife – to slit the throat, according to the law of Moses. One quick transverse incision to sever the major structures and vessels (he listed them as something he had learned by rote): the trachea, the oesophagus, the carotid arteries, the jugular veins – all cut quickly, in one uninterrupted action. Without hesitation, you understand, or turning.

-So you are a *shochet*?[10]

- I am trained in the craft.

- You ensure that the slaughtered animal is *kosher*?

- Yes. Also the *shochet* must examine the organs and vessels immediately after severance by the *shechita* incision. By sight, you understand and by touch. We must examine the lungs, the *b'dikath hareyah*, to ensure there are no defects, and the animal is *kosher*. This is required by *Halacha*.

- So you know where the internal organs are? (he did not seem to hear the question). And what are your feelings towards the animals you kill?

- (Here he glanced at me quickly, his dark eyes suspicious). Feelings? It is the commandment of God. For it is written in the Torah: 'Thou shalt slaughter of thy herd and of thy flock'.[11] The beast is there to serve us. And we are there to serve God.

After this evasive answer Kosminski retreated into silence, and would answer no more questions. He fixed his gaze on the light that filtered through a small barred window high up on the wall of his room. Clearly he does not wish to talk about his feelings.

5

Post-mortem on Catherine Eddowes performed by Dr. Frederick Gordon Brown, Golden Lane Mortuary, 30 September 1888 [12]

The body was on its back. The abdomen was exposed. The throat cut across.

The intestines were drawn out to a large extent and placed over the right shoulder. The throat was cut across to the extent of about six or seven inches. The big muscle across the throat was divided through on the left side. The large vessels on the left side of the neck were severed. The larynx was severed below the vocal cord. All the deep structures were severed to the bone.

The throat was cut across to the extent of about six or seven inches. All the deep structures were severed to the bone, the knife marking intervertebral cartilages. All these injuries were performed by a sharp instrument like a knife, and pointed.

The peritoneal lining was cut through on the left side and the left kidney carefully taken out and removed. The left renal artery was cut through. I would say that someone who knew the position of the kidney must have done it.

The lining membrane over the uterus was cut through. The womb was cut through horizontally, leaving a stump of three quarters of an inch. The rest of the womb had been taken away with some of the ligaments.

I believe the perpetrator of the act must have had considerable knowledge of the position of the organs in the abdominal cavity and the way of removing them. It required a great deal of medical knowledge to have removed the kidney and to know where it was placed.

6

The Laws of Shehitah[13]

1. It is a positive commandment of the Torah that whoever wishes to eat meat must first slaughter the animal, as it is written, 'Thou shalt slaughter of thy herd and of thy flock, which the Lord hath given thee, as I have commanded thee, and thou shalt eat within thy gates, after all the desire of thy soul' (Deuteronomy 12:21).

2. Only one who is knowledgeable in the laws of *shehitah* and proficient in its practice, and who is a believing, pious Jew, may act as a *shohet* in performance of the commandment.

3. *Shehitah* must be done by means of a swift, smooth cut of a sharp knife whose blade is free of any dent or imperfection.

4. *Shehitah* entails severing the trachea and the oesophagus in accordance with the oral tradition, which requires that five improper procedures be avoided, lest they invalidate the *shehitah* and render the animal unfit to be eaten.

7

Inquest on Catherine Eddowes. Coroner's Court, Golden Lane, 4 October 1888 [14]

Dr. Frederick Gordon Brown was then called, and deposed: I am surgeon to the City of London Police. (Witness here described in detail the terrible mutilation of the deceased's body.)

Mr. Crawford: I understand that you found certain portions of the body removed? – Yes. The uterus was cut away with the exception of a small portion, and the left kidney was also cut out. Both these organs were absent, and have not been found.

[Coroner] Have you any opinion as to what position the woman was in when the wounds were inflicted? – In my opinion the woman must have been lying down. The way in which the kidney was cut out showed that it was done by somebody who knew what he was about.

[Coroner] Does the nature of the wounds lead you to any conclusion as to the instrument that was used? – It must have been a sharp-pointed knife, and I should say at least 6 in. long.

[Coroner] Would you consider that the person who inflicted the wounds possessed anatomical skill? – He must have had a good deal of knowledge as to the position of the abdominal organs, and the way to remove them.

[Coroner] Would the parts removed be of any use for professional purposes? – None whatever.

[Coroner] Would the removal of the kidney, for example, require special knowledge? – It would require a good deal of knowledge as to its position, because it is apt to be overlooked, being covered by a membrane.

[Coroner] Would such a knowledge be likely to be possessed by someone accustomed to cutting up animals? – Yes.

8

Dr Kouchin's Journal, 17 February 1891

Kosminski is a most unusual specimen of maniac. Never, before in all my years of practice with the mentally disturbed have I come across a man whose manifest delusions are accompanied by such a clear intelligence and such a capability of reason. He has talked to me expansively about his employment, his professional training, his religion. But any attempt to turn his mind inwards to reflect on his own emotional life – his unconscious, as Dr Freud would put it – is met with stubborn resistance. He is determined not to give himself away. Which means he has something to hide. Today I have every intention of discovering what that is.

First I asked him to tell me about his family. He came to England from Poland as a boy of about sixteen.[15] His mother remained there, though he believes she is still alive. He knows nothing of his father. He arrived here in the company of his sisters, Betsy and Matilda, and with other members of a large Polish family, who settled in Whitechapel, where his uncle established a business in butchery. Aaron lives with his sisters, at least one of whom, Betsy, is married and has children. The extended family appear to live together in a crowded tenement house, typical of the living conditions of such immigrant people.

I asked Aaron if he had any memory of his father. He says he has none. I asked him if he missed his mother, and if she might one day travel from Poland to re-join her children. He says he barely remembers his mother, which seems incredible if he parted from her a teenager. I asked him if he has good relations with his sisters. He loves his sisters, he said, who have always cared for him. It seems that Betsy is his favourite.

- You love your sister Betsy?

- I love Betsy, yes.

- Then why (I asked him, with an attempt at disarming innocence), did you threaten your sister with a knife?

My interrogation had been too abrupt. Aaron shook his head, as if in disappointment, and again turned his attention to the window. He would answer no more questions.

- Enough for today, doctor. I'm tired now. Please leave me alone.

9

Statement by Harry Cox, Detective Inspector, London City Police. 10 February 1881 [16]

We must first of all understand the motive of the Whitechapel crimes. The motive was, there cannot be the slightest doubt, revenge. Not merely revenge on the few poor unfortunate victims of the knife, but revenge on womankind. It was not a lust for blood, as many people have imagined.

The murderer was a misogynist, who at some time or another had been wronged by a woman. And the fact that his victims were of the lowest class proves, I think, that he was not, as has been stated, an educated man who had suddenly gone mad. He belonged to their own class.

The man we suspected was about five feet six inches in height, with short, black, curly hair, and he had a habit of taking late walks abroad. While the Whitechapel murders were being perpetrated his place of business was in Butcher's Row, Aldgate, and after the last murder I was on duty in this street for nearly three months … You can imagine that never once did we allow him to quit our sight.

It is indeed very strange that as soon as this madman was put under observation, the mysterious crimes ceased, and that very soon he removed from his usual haunts and gave up his nightly prowls. He was never arrested for the reason that not the slightest scrap of evidence could be found to connect him with the crimes.

10

Dr Kouchin's Journal, 20 February 1891

I am now certain that Aaron, whatever his mental condition, has sufficient intelligence to hide his true nature. In order to arrive at an explanation for his illness, I am obliged to find some means of breaking into his mind. But he resists me with every possible strategy of evasion and distraction. Whenever I come close to an interrogation of his emotions, he closes up and seals himself in some distant mental place where I can no longer reach him.

I have resolved therefore to hypnotise him, and to enter his subconscious mind while his defences are down. If I can compel him to revisit the scenes of his childhood, and to describe his true feelings about his parents and siblings, I may yet begin to grasp at the root of whatever it is that ails him.

Saying nothing to Aaron, I begin to make passes in front of him, from over the top of his head downwards, with each hand in turn. Aaron gazed at me fixedly for a few minutes, and then his eyes closed. He remained completely still, his breathing and heartbeat so relaxed that the hypnosis had obviously taken effect. I signalled to the orderly to remove the leather restraints from his wrists.

- Aaron, I said, can you hear me?

- Yes, doctor, I can hear you.

- I want you to travel back in time to when you were a child, a little boy of five or six. Can you do that for me?

- Yes, I can do that.

- Where are you Aaron?

- In the *stetl*.[17]

- Where is the *stetl*?

- A hundred miles from Kiev.
- What do you remember?
- It's very cold outside. The stove is warm. Mama is cooking soup.
- Is your father there?
- Abraham Kosminski. He went out into the snow. A long time ago.
He never came back.
- And your sisters?
- Betsy and Matilda. They are sewing. It's nice and warm inside. Ice on
the windows.
- Very good, Aaron, very good. Now I want you to tell me about
something that happened to you, here in this house. Something you
remember.
- No I don't want to.
- There is something, Aaron, I know there is. Something that happened.
You must remember.

(For a moment he struggled in the chair, as if resisting the spell. Then
his breathing slowed again, and he relaxed into the trance).

- Noises outside. Horses tramping. Men shouting. Mama looks out of
the window. She's frightened. I don't know what to do.
- Go on, Aaron. Remember.
- They're banging on the door. Ugly voices, shouting. Russians. They're
going to break the door down. Quick, Aaron, Mama says, hide under the
bed. I don't want to, Mama. I'm frightened. Do it now, she says, hide, and
don't make a sound. Betsy, Matilda, into the cellar. Through the trapdoor.
Quickly, now, do as I say.
- Did you hide under the bed, Aaron?
- I'm under the bed now. The door breaks open. A terrible noise. Cold
blows in. I hear men tramping in, I see their fur boots. I don't understand
what they are saying. They're shouting at Mama. Then something bounces
on the bed above me. Mama says no, please, no. The bed starts to move,
up and down, the springs creak. A loud snorting sound from one of the
men. Then quiet. Mama sobs. Another weight bounces on the bed. The
bed moves again, up and down. A bellowing sound like a bull. Then quiet.
And again, a bounce on the bed, the bed moves up and down, a strange
strangled cry like someone dying. Then quiet. An awful quiet. I see the
boots of the men move across the floor, towards the door. No sound
now, only a soft whimpering from Mama. I don't want to stay under the

bed. I creep out and see Mama, her shoulders hunched, her face to the wall. Betsy and Matilda come up from the cellar. Matilda sits on the bed and puts her arms around Mama. Betsy shuts the door against the cold. The men are gone now.

- Aaron, I said carefully: tell me, how did you feel when you were under the bed? When the men were doing that to your mother? How did it affect you?

- I don't want to go under the bed. Don't make me.

- You're there, Aaron. You're under the bed. It's not time to come out yet. Tell me how you feel.

- I don't want to go under the bed. Mama makes me. Why does she do that? She doesn't want me anymore.

- You think Mama doesn't love you?

- She doesn't love me. She put me under the bed.

-The men have gone now, Aaron. You are safe. How do you feel now?

- Cold. Betsy and Matilda are whispering to Mama. They've forgotten me. Betsy, Betsy, I'm here. And he began to chant, softly, some ancient, strangely familiar yet forgotten words of Hebrew: הָעֹרָה, זֹל יְנָאוּ יֹל יְדוֹד סִיֹנַשׁוֹשֵׁב. Betsy says nothing. My sisters are cuddling Mama. No-one is cuddling me. Mama loves my sisters. She doesn't love me.

- You feel abandoned?

- Abandoned, yes.

Then a strange smile came over Aaron's face, a smile the like of which I pray never to see again. His hands, freed from the restraints, reached down and opened the front of his trousers. His penis was erect. With a slow, luxuriating motion, he stroked the shaft. Then he grabbed it by the base and violently thrashed it to orgasm. At the moment of release he cried out one word:

- Mama.

11

Inquest on 'Polly' Nicholls. Coroner's Court, Working-lads Institute, Whitechapel Road, 22 September 1888 [19]

Coming to a consideration of the perpetrator of the murder, the Coroner said: It seems astonishing at first thought that the culprit should have escaped detection, for there must surely have been marks of blood about his person. If, however, blood was principally on his hands, the presence of so many slaughter-houses in the neighbourhood would make the frequenters of this spot familiar with blood-stained clothes and hands, and his appearance might in that way have failed to attract attention while he passed from Buck's-row in the twilight into Whitechapel-road, and was lost sight of in the morning's market traffic.

12
Dr Kouchin's Journal, 25 February 1891

I have spent the last few days between my rounds reviewing my notes from the sessions with Kosminski, researching the social conditions of his past, and thinking about his case. Because he is so adept at emotional concealment, what I learned from hypnotising him has proved invaluable. His psychiatric condition can clearly be traced back to the trauma of his childhood.

I knew something of the persecution of the Jews in Russia, but Aaron's story is overwhelming in its violence and brutality. The date of the Kosminksi family's emigration coincides with the pogroms of 1881, when the Russian Jews were blamed for the assassination of Tsar Alexander II. Already condemned to live in the Pale of Settlement, they were attacked, many killed or wounded, and hundreds of women raped. This history of assault, looting, arson, rape and murder had been going on for decades, justified by Slav nationalism and an irrational hatred of Jews. But in 1881 a flood of barbaric anti-Semitism flowed across Russia and engulfed Aaron's family in its blood-dimmed tide.[20]

Aaron's traumatic memory concerns the violent rape of his mother by at least three men, an attack he witnessed at close quarters from under the bed. As a child he was too young to understand that his mother had no doubt surrendered to the assault in order to save her children. He recalls only an experience of abandonment as he was made to stay under the bed, and the sensation of love withheld when his sisters returned to comfort his mother. Who can measure the emotional damage sustained in the developing mind of a child at the witnessing of such an appalling atrocity?

Such events may well have been commonplace for Jews at that time. In Aaron's case, the damage has clearly been both permanent and profound. The effect of this trauma on his sexuality has been destructive in the extreme, since he identifies not with the victim of the assault, his mother, but with the perpetrators, the rapists. Under hypnotism he actually became sexually excited when reliving the scene of the rape. His sense of abandonment at the hands of his mother is compounded by the memory of her sexual congress with the rapists. In an extremity of perversion he sees the rape of his mother as an enviable intimacy from which he was excluded.

There is one further detail in Kosminski's case history that continues to intrigue me, and might prove to be one of the keys to unlocking his mind. That is that he threatened his sister with a knife. By all accounts his sister Betsy is his favourite, and has always been good to him. But there is something strange about his feelings towards her. When my questioning probed his relationship with his sister he avoided the issue. And there was that mysterious Hebrew poetry he seemed to associate with her. I took the trouble to note down what he recited, and looked it up. Aaron was quoting from the *Song of Songs, which is Solomon's*: יִתְשֶׁקב, תּוֹלִיֵלֽב יְבָכְשׁמ-לַע, וִיתְאָצֽמ אֹלְו, וִיתְשֶׁקב ;יִשֽׁפַנ הֽבָהֽאֶש תֽא. 'By night on my bed I sought him whom my soul loveth: I sought him, but I found him not'.[21]

Once Aaron is safely under the hypnotic spell, I ask him about Betsy.

- Aaron, can you hear me?
- Yes, doctor, I can hear you.
- Tell me about Betsy.
- My sister.
-Yes, your sister.
- דְיָנָֽהֽרֶנֽצֽמ קֽנֽע הֽחֽאֽב ,דְיֽנֽיֽעֽמ (תֽחֽאֽב) דחאב יֽנֽתֽבֽבֽל ;הֽלֽכ יֽתֽחֽא ,יֽנֽתֽבֽבֽל[22] *(again the Hebrew words).*

- Can you say that in English, Aaron?
- You have taken my heart, my sister, my bride.
- Were you very close?
- Oh yes, doctor, very close.
- (A thought occurred to me). Did you sleep together, Aaron?
- Yes, we slept together.
-Where is Matilda?
- Matilda sleeps with Mama. Betsy sleeps with me.
- Aaron, I want you to go back in time again to your childhood. It's night. You're in bed with Betsy. How do you feel?

- Warm. Warm and comfortable. Betsy is beside me. She puts her arms around me and kisses me goodnight. She keeps me warm.

- Are you wearing clothes, Aaron?

- No clothes. Both naked. Betsy is asleep. I can see her in the moonlight from the window. I can see her breasts.

- How do you feel, Aaron?

- I want to touch her. 'How fair is thy love, my sister, my spouse?' I want to touch her breasts. So soft under my hands. Her nipples are firm. I can feel them in my palms.

- Then what happens, Aaron? What do you do now?

- The bedclothes are round her waist. I can't see. I put my hand down between her legs to feel what's inside her. So soft. So warm. 'Open to me, my sister, my love'.

- And now?

- I want to see. Push the bedclothes down. Betsy's legs are open. Soft and warm. (Here Aaron began to struggle against the memories, twisting his head from side to side as if trying to break free from the hold of his own imagination). No, he cried, no! 'A garden enclosed is my sister, my spouse'. (Then suddenly he uttered a terrible scream). No! No! Blood. Black in the moonlight. White sheets. Blood. Wet and warm. Betsy is hurt. She's bleeding. Must wake Mama.

So! Another traumatic memory dislodged by hypnosis. This time an incestuous fantasy of intimacy with his sister, violated by the shock of observing her menstruation. Sleeping with his sister, Aaron experiences a premature and unnatural sexual awakening, touching her breasts, putting his hand between her legs. But then he uncovers the bedclothes, soaked in her blood, and the sight fills him with horror. His emotional memories also seem to be permeated by the poetry of the *Song of Songs*, which repeatedly calls the female lover both sister and spouse.

And so there is yet another dimension to Aaron's twisted sexuality. I have already diagnosed a perverse attachment to the mother, prompted by his childhood witnessing of her violent rape. Now it appears he also has a traumatic memory of intimacy with his sister, that sexual awakening breached by the onset of her menstrual cycle. It must have seemed to him that as he tried to penetrate his sister's body, that 'garden enclosed' as he put it, quoting from the *Song of Songs,* he wanted to open to him, had literally opened up to disclose its deepest and most abhorrent secrets.

'A garden enclosed is my sister, my bride; a spring shut up, a fountain sealed'.[23] His incestuous desire was from that moment contaminated with a violent fascination to explore the innermost secrets of the female body, to reach inside her and feel her nethermost parts.

All this traumatic background gives context and cause of the action that precipitated Aaron's admission to this facility: *he took a knife, and threatened the life of his sister.* The adult is still possessed by the horror and fascination that afflicted the child. Aaron still wants to get inside his sister, if not by sexual intercourse, then by violent penetration. And who knows what dreadful harm he might visit on his sister, or another woman, if the child's sick and perverse desire to enter the female body is combined with the adult's proficiency as a slaughterman?

13

Post-mortem on Mary Jane Kelly, performed by Dr. Bond, 10 November 1888 [24]

The whole of the surface of the abdomen & thighs was removed & the abdominal Cavity emptied of its viscera. The breasts were cut off, the arms mutilated by several jagged wounds & the face hacked beyond recognition of the features. The tissues of the neck were severed all round down to the bone.

The neck was cut through the skin & other tissues right down to the vertebrae the 5th & 6th being deeply notched.

The air passage was cut at the lower part of the larynx through the cricoid cartilage.

The Pericardium was open below & the Heart absent.

13

Dr Kouchin's Journal, 27 February 1891

I grow increasingly concerned about Kosminski. Not about his behaviour, which continues to be quiet and unassuming, giving the orderlies no trouble, and rendering the persistent application of restraint somewhat superfluous: but about the psychological profile I have gradually assembled from the evidence of his background, the results of my examinations, and the sessions of hypnosis. There is evidence to suggest, and reason for believing, that notwithstanding his gentle and compliant demeanour, Kosminski may in fact be an extremely dangerous individual.

First there is Kosminski's childhood experience of racial persecution, and his witnessing of horrific sexual violence against his mother.

Next there is the absence of a father-figure, which clearly hampered his psychological development. He grew up surrounded only by women, who must have seemed to the child there solely to do his bidding. His only encounters with men were as brutal persecutors and bestial rapists. As a child he began to identify with the male aggressor rather than with his female victims. Once he realised that these women might choose to exclude, or even abandon him, a painful anger began to grow in his young mind.

Thirdly there is the intimacy with his sister, a premature and unnatural sexual awakening disrupted by the onset of her menstruation. Her marriage and giving birth to children must have seemed a further betrayal, and was perhaps the occasion of his violence against her.

Fourthly there is the compulsive masturbation, apparently conducted in public. At some point the hyperarousal of his sexual fantasies became uncontrollable, and compelled him to stimulate himself in the sight of others.

All these factors seem to have contributed to a condition of negative attachment to other human beings, especially to those nearest to him. His refusal to accept food from others is evidence of this condition. Those traumatic childhood emotions of powerlessness, abandonment, the apparent withholding of love, have produced an individual who cannot distinguish between reality and fantasy, who tries to control and manipulate others to compensate for a debilitating sense of impotence, and who adeptly conceals beneath a docile exterior a maelstrom of hatred and rage, especially against women. When first admitted, he exhibited a kind of megalomania, saying that he knew the secrets of all hearts, and obeyed the commands of mysterious inner voices.

I have compared Aaron's profile to some work done by a medical colleague on the criminally insane. Everything in his mental state points towards the character of a homicide, exemplified in the potentially murderous threat to his sister.

It is time to get to the bottom of all this, and to pluck out the heart of Aaron's mystery.

I intend to hypnotise him and force him to tell me, not about his childhood, but about his recent experiences. If he truly is a dangerous homicide, then any crimes he has committed must lie just under the surface of his mind. If Aaron's behaviour has been consistent with his profile, then he may have attacked or even killed other women before threatening his sister. If he has killed in the past, then he will, by the twisted logic of his personality, kill again in the future. That being the case, it is my duty to establish exactly how dangerous he is; to inform the authorities of my opinion; to adjust Aaron's treatment accordingly, and even to reconsider whether or not this facility – which is a hospital, not a prison; a place of refuge, not of confinement – is the right place for him.

14

Written in chalk on a wall in Goulston Street, Whitechapel, 29 September 1888

The Jewes are
The men that
Will not
be Blamed
for nothing.[25]

15

Dr Kouchin's Journal, 28 February 1891

Horror! horror! horror! As the poet says, tongue nor heart cannot conceive nor name thee.[26] Today I have, by the power of hypnotism, penetrated deep into Aaron's psyche, and uncovered there such spectres of abomination as I had never dreamed could exist. The things he claims to have done – Oh God – no, I cannot speak of them here. Even if they are merely a madman's fantasies, they remain in the extremity of their violence impossible to describe or even contemplate. If Aaron has in fact put his dreadful dreams into practice, and inflicted such atrocities on poor, innocent creatures, then he is not a man at all, but a monster.

I have sent an urgent message to the Inspector who brought Kosminski to me, requesting an immediate conference. If the police, Kosminski's family and the Jewish elders of Whitechapel know anything of these dreadful secrets, then they must be obliged to share them with me. I cannot endure the searing flames of such knowledge alone.

16

Inquest on Catherine Eddowes, Coroner's Court, Golden Lane, 4 October 1888 [27]

Daniel Halse, detective officer, City police: On Saturday, Sept. 29, pursuant to instructions received at the central office in Old Jewry, I directed a number of police in plain clothes to patrol the streets of the City all night. At two minutes to two o'clock on the Sunday morning, when near Aldgate Church, in company with Detectives Outram and Marriott, I heard that a woman had been found murdered in Mitre-square.

After visiting Leman-street police-station, I proceeded to Goulston-street, where I saw some chalk-writing on the black fascia of the wall. Instructions were given to have the writing photographed, but before it could be done the Metropolitan police stated that they thought the writing might cause a riot or outbreak against the Jews, and it was decided to have it rubbed out, as the people were already bringing out their stalls into the street.

[Coroner] As to the writing on the wall, did you hear anybody suggest that the word 'Jews' should be rubbed out and the other words left? – I did. The fear on the part of the Metropolitan police that the writing might cause riot was the sole reason why it was rubbed out. I took a copy of it, and what I wrote down was as follows: 'The Juwes are not the men who will be blamed for nothing.'

17

Dr Kouchin's Journal, 3 March 1891

So it is true. This strange, quiet, clever man, with his inscrutable mental disorders; this professional Jewish butcher of Aldgate and Smithfield; is none other than the infamous sexual maniac and multiple murderer, Jack the Ripper. He is safely under lock and key now, restrained in the strait-waistcoat, confined to the padded room. I am now in possession of the full story, which I will set out here as well as I can understand and express it.

Severely as I remonstrated against the Inspector for leaving me in the dark, and entrusting to the care of a mere doctor one of the most dangerous criminals ever to have walked the earth, I am now finally convinced that everyone involved in this subterfuge has acted throughout with the best possible intentions, conducive to the best possible outcome in the interests of public safety.

Evidently the police investigating the Ripper murders were as sure as they possibly could be that Kosminski was their man. But they could not assemble anything like sufficient evidence with which to charge him. The criminal genius who managed to commit such atrocities, in open public spaces, and consistently evade capture, was not to be so easily apprehended or convicted. Once Kosminski became aware that the police were onto him, the murders ceased. I have no doubt that the attack on Aaron's sister occurred because his blood-lust was in this way frustrated by the constant surveillance. The police, operating under cover, even saw him assessing potential victims, but knowing he was being watched Aaron could take no action. In this respect at least the methods used by the police have proved to be justified: by keeping him under close observation, they stopped him from killing again. Under hypnosis Aaron revealed to me certain details never made public, and known only to the investigating officers. The Inspector's corroboration of this evidence proves beyond a shadow of a doubt that Kosminski is indeed Jack the Ripper.

Several other factors, aside from the lack of evidence, inhibited the police from arresting and charging Kosminski. The fact that he was a man of some standing in his community, a *shochet* trained in ritual slaughter, provided circumstantial evidence of his ability to commit the crimes, but at the same time made the police reluctant to apprehend him. To arrest a well-known member of the Jewish community in Whitechapel on suspicion of such notorious crimes would inevitably have inflamed public feeling against the Jews, stirring into white heat the always simmering furnace of racial hatred and resentment. Desirable as it was to bring to justice the perpetrator of such horrors, justice would not have been served by encouraging an angry and excited population to irrationally blame the crimes of an individual on an already persecuted race. Instead the police used Kosminski's attack on his sister as a means of persuading his family that he should be committed to a place of safety, and taking into their confidence the Jewish authorities of the local community, took steps to confine Aaron to a place where he could do no further harm, safely caged in an asylum.[28]

It may seem a grotesque injustice that Jack the Ripper, his identity known, should thus be allowed to escape the penalty of the law. But as a Jew myself, I can well understand the motives of those who felt that, in this peculiar case, subterfuge and concealment would better serve the cause of justice than an open accusation against a member of our unfortunate community. The sins of one man, though as grave as any offences ever committed by one human being, cannot be allowed to justify revenge against an innocent people.

18

Report of Sir Charles Warren, Commissioner Metropolitan Police, to the Home Secretary. 6 November 1888 [29]

4 Whitehall Place, S.W.
6th November 1888

Confidential
The Under Secretary of State
The Home Office

Sir,

In reply to your letter of the 5th instant, I enclose a report of the circumstances of the Mitre Square Murder so far as they have come under the notice of the Metropolitan Police, and I now give an account regarding the erasing of the writing on the wall in Goulston Street

The most pressing question at that moment was some writing on the wall in Goulston Street evidently written with the intention of inflaming the public mind against the Jews, and which Mr. Arnold with a view to prevent serious disorder proposed to obliterate, and had sent down an Inspector with a sponge for that purpose, telling him to await his arrival.

A discussion took place whether the writing could be left covered up or otherwise or whether any portion of it could be left for an hour until it could be photographed; but after taking into consideration the excited state of the population in London generally at the time, the strong feeling which had been excited against the Jews, and the fact that in a short time there would be a large concourse of the people in the streets, and having before me the Report that if it was left there the house was likely to be wrecked (in which from my own observation I entirely concurred) I considered it desirable to obliterate the writing at once, having taken a copy of which I enclose a duplicate.

I am, Sir,

Your most obedient Servant,
(signed) C. Warren

19

Dr Kouchin's Journal, 10 March 1891

There he sits, here in my asylum, his arms in a strait-waistcoat, confined to the padded cell, with one small barred window high up on the wall, the infamous Jack the Ripper. He will never be brought to trial, or publicly answer for his crimes. He will never be forced to confess his guilt, explain his motives, or receive the appropriate penalty of the law.

There he sits, an inscrutable smile on his face, for all I know re-living again and again, in the poisoned cauldron of his memory, the abominable perversion of his crimes.

What should be done with him? The Inspector made it clear I was to have *carte blanche*, and could impose upon him any treatment I think fit. I have revolved in my mind a number of possible options, sought advice in confidence from a number of respected colleagues, and decided on a course of action.

There is a new experimental procedure, known as psychosurgery, so far very rarely performed, aimed at the modification of the mind to remove criminal tendencies and impulses of violence.[30] The operation is simple: we insert a sharp implement through the skull and into the brain, and rotate it in order to separate the frontal from the parietal, occipital and temporal lobes. The results have been mixed: most of the patients operated on have certainly lost their desire to commit crime, but some have also lost other vital brain functions, and been reduced to living vegetables. The operation is clearly very delicate. The stakes are high, but since I am treating a patient so depraved and vicious as Kosminski; one who ought, by due process of law, to have been executed for his crimes – there seems little to lose.

As a scientist and a liberal thinker I am out of step with many of the opinions of my age. I believe we have only scratched the surface of what is possible in understanding and treating the human psyche. Execution seems to me a crude and barbaric means of dealing with criminality: we achieve nothing by abruptly extinguishing the flame of a diseased mind. Since our ideas of an afterlife seem to me little more than childish dreams, I see no prospect of divine punishment beyond the grave for one such as Kosminski. Death would be for him merely a release from the torment that is his life.

Better, surely, to study the diseases of the mind in so perfect an exemplar? And for punishment, is it not better to keep the murderer safely confined, and to find some way of forcing him to contemplate, throughout his remaining years, the enormity of his crimes? If we can, in some way, remove from the mind the capacity and the desire for evil, can we not compel the criminal to confront the reality of his actions, to see his crimes as we see them? If we can shut down the strident, clamorous voices that bawl their gospel of evil into Kosminski's ears, may it not be possible for him to hear, beyond that deafening diabolical roar, the still small, voice of conscience?

And so I am resolved. The patient is on the table, etherised into unconsciousness. I have borrowed from one of my surgical colleagues a tool, rather like a small ice-pick, specially designed for the conduct of this operation. Two small holes drilled into Kosminski's skull, a gentle insertion of the pick into each in turn, a few motions of the device, and – let us hope – the corrupted mind of Jack the Ripper will be no more.

20

DI Robert Sagar, London City Police [31]

We had good reason to suspect a man who worked in Butcher's Row, Aldgate. We watched him carefully. There was no doubt that this man was insane, and after a time his friends thought it advisable to have him removed to a private asylum. After he was removed there were no more Ripper atrocities.

21

Dr Kouchin's Journal, 15 March 1891

Well, Kosminski survived the operation, and after a few days recovery seems in reasonable health. He no longer makes any objection to being fed, though he seems so far incapable of feeding himself. He has not yet spoken, or moved, though he is not physically restrained and would be free to do so. He simply lies back in his chair and stares, with eyes that have become strangely glassy and unfocused, at the meagre light filtering in through his high window.

Jack the Ripper addressed one of his famous letters to the authorities 'From Hell'. I had hoped to send him back there. Not to the imaginary Hell of the rabbis and priests, where souls howl in torment for eternity, but to a real place of mental punishment created by modern science, where rational contemplation of wrong would supersede the violent delights of crime.

Aaron, or Jack as I have unconsciously become habituated to call him, may be in Hell, surveying the physical wreckage of the lives he cut short, examining the mutilated bodies of the women he butchered so cruelly, and feeling the kind of painful compassion the rest of us feel when we call to mind the Ripper's crimes.

I hope so. But I cannot tell. My surgical intervention has removed Jack to a place where I can no longer reach him, no longer open up his mind to decipher his thoughts and feelings. And that obscene, inscrutable smile that now and then creeps across his blank features causes me to wonder if I have not instead sent him to a kind of Heaven, or a Hell in which he still can reign, the prince of demons. Behind those opaque illegible eyes he may be systematically recalling, with appalling relish, the gruesome details of all his slaughters: feeling again the touch of his keen knife against a soft throat, the grating of its edge as he reached the vertebrae, the sucking sound of an abdominal incision, the warm wet touch of exposed internal organs. He even claimed, in that same terrible epistle from Hell, that he had cooked and eaten the flesh of one of his victims, a piece of kidney, as if it were the meat of an animal. 'It tasted nise'. Perhaps that pungent, rancid taste lies in his mouth still.[32]

I have done my duty as required by authority and law: as long as he lives, Jack will never harm another human being. But I had hoped to achieve more, to uproot the flowers of evil from the toxic soil of the Ripper's mind. Instead I fear I may have confirmed his delusion of sovereignty over all humanity, leaving him with nothing but the perverse pleasure of his poisonous memories.

The mind is its own place, and in itself can make a Heaven of Hell, a Hell of Heaven.[33]

'Newgate cell', basement of The Viaduct Tavern, Newgate Street.

Amelia Dyer:

Preface

Amelia Dyer was a notorious 'baby farmer' and serial killer who murdered hundreds of young children, at first by deliberate neglect and later by strangulation. She was briefly held in Newgate Prison, tried at the Old Bailey and convicted of the murder of a child, Doris Harmon, in June 1896. Her execution took place in Newgate. While on remand in Reading Goal in the spring of that year, her incarceration coincided with that of Oscar Wilde, serving two years with hard labour for sexual offences. Wilde had also been held in Newgate for his trial at the Old Bailey in 1895.

The following play imagines an encounter between the two prisoners in April 1896. The encounter with Amelia provokes Oscar to reconsider his views on morality and social conceptions of wickedness. The third character, Thomas Martin, was a Warder who befriended Wilde and smuggled newspapers and treats to him. In 1897 Martin was dismissed from his job for giving a sweet biscuit to a distressed child prisoner.

Wilde's conversation is of course invented, but draws on his writings, especially *The Picture of Dorian Gray*, *De Profundis* and *The House of Pomegranates*. Material is also taken from the two letters he wrote to the *Daily Chronicle* in 1897 to protest against cruelty to children in prisons, and against the dismissal of Warder Martin. I have also used the records of his trials. Richard Ellman's *Oscar Wilde* (London: Hamish Hamilton, 1987) remains for me the definitive biography, which may be supplemented by Matthew Sturgis, *Oscar : a Life* (London: Hodder and Stoughton, 2018).

Most of the detail concerning Amelia Dyer's crimes is drawn from the record of her trial at the Old Bailey, from *The Whole Proceedings of the Queen's Commission of Oyer and Terminer and goal delivery for the City of London, etc., of the Central Criminal Court, held on Monday January 7th, 1895, and following days*, Eighth Session,725-747, supplemented by Alison Rattle and Allison Vale, *The Woman who Murdered Babies for Money* (London: Andre Deutsch, 2011), which cites documents and correspondence preserved in the archives of the Thames Valley Police Museum, the Crime Museum at New Scotland yard, and local record offices.

Amelia Dyer

Oscar and Amelia: A Play in Two Acts

Act One. 4 April 1896.

SCENE. Reading Gaol.
CURTAIN

Two adjacent cells, separated by a central wall running upstage to downstage. Each cell contains a stool, table with a copper wash-basin, a narrow plank-bed against the dividing wall. A small barred grating high up on the central wall allows communication between the two cells.

Stage right, sitting on the bed with back to the wall and head in hands, dressed in prison clothes, is OSCAR WILDE. Stage left, also sitting on the bed, back to the wall, dressed in black civilian clothes, handbag on knees, staring straight ahead, is AMELIA DYER.

AMELIA: (begins to sing softly).

> 'Tis the last rose of summer,
> Left blooming alone …

(Wilde sits up and listens).

> All her lovely companions
> Are faded and gone …[1]

OSCAR: Who's there?

AMELIA: I beg your pardon, sir. I was only singing to myself.

OSCAR: I'm not a warder, madam. I'm a prisoner, like yourself. In the next cell.

(AMELIA looks up at the grating).

AMELIA: I thought the rule here was silence.

OSCAR: It is. But we can hear the warders coming along the landing, when they do their rounds. In the meantime you and I can speak. You don't know how wonderful it is to hear the sound of another human voice.

AMELIA: Likewise, I'm sure. You're very well-spoken, sir. Are you a gentleman?

OSCAR: There are differences of opinion on that subject. My name is Oscar Wilde.

AMELIA: Mr Wilde? The literary gentleman? Why, I've read about you in the papers. Is it really you?

OSCAR: The very same, dear lady. And what is your name?

AMELIA: My name is Amelia Dyer.

OSCAR: And what is your trespass, Mrs Dyer?

AMELIA: I'm sorry, sir?

OSCAR: What are you in for?

AMELIA: I don't really know, sir. I don't know anything about it. It's a mystery to me.[2]

OSCAR: I envy you. The heart of my mystery has been long since plucked out, and thrown to the dogs. My crimes are tossed on the wind, like horrid deeds blown in every eye. The very stains of my sheets have been held aloft, and shown to the people.

AMELIA: I'm sure you were only doing what everyone else does, sir. It's a vicious world out there. Best not to get caught, I say.

OSCAR: My dear lady, if only I'd had the benefit of your counsel, things might have turned out differently. What do you do a for a living, Mrs Dyer?

AMELIA: I'm a nurse, sir. Nurse and midwife. I help mothers with their lying-in, and bring them back to health. I've brought many little babbies into the world. Mostly ones who are not wanted, if you know what I mean.

OSCAR: The basis of every scandal is an immoral certainty.[3]

AMELIA: Very true. It happens more than you'd think. Unmarried girls. Mothers giving birth to children that don't resemble their husbands. Or do resemble their brothers. You understand, don't you sir? You're not one to be narrow-minded.

OSCAR: Good God, no. A high moral tone can hardly be said to conduce very much to either one's health or one's happiness.[4] What happens to the babies?

AMELIA: When the mothers can't look after them, I take them in. They pay me what they can, and I take care of them. They call such as me 'baby farmers'.

OSCAR: You must have a sizeable family. Or should I say farm?

AMELIA: Quite large, yes. I have help from my daughter Polly. Of course some of the little mites don't last long, not having a good start in life. Some are reclaimed by their mothers. If I have too many, I can pass them on to friends in the same business. But surely you're not interested in such things, are you sir?

OSCAR: To the contrary. My plays owe their plots entirely to the popular pastimes of adultery, fornication and bearing children out of wedlock. One of my heroes is abandoned as a baby, and found in a handbag at Victoria station.

AMELIA: A handbag?

OSCAR: With leather handles.

AMELIA: Oh … How curious. I'm sorry to say I've never seen one of your plays, Mr Wilde. I'm not one for the theatre. I love to read, though. That's my passion.

OSCAR: Poetry?

AMELIA: Not really. Lord Tennyson, now I like some of his poems.

OSCAR: (*sighs*) He has not allowed himself to be part of the living world.

AMELIA: But it's stories I read mostly. Mr Dickens, now: would you regard him as a great writer?

OSCAR: Yes, a very great writer. He must be, as he is no longer alive.

AMELIA: I like *Barnaby Rudge*. And Maria Corelli.[5] What do you think of her?

OSCAR: I have no objection to Mrs Corelli on moral grounds. But judging by the way she writes, she should be in here rather than me.[6]

AMELIA: Now you're making fun. And Mrs Henry Wood? Is she good? I thought *East Lynne* was wonderful.[7]

OSCAR: Ah yes, *East Lynne*. A fallen woman, a long-kept secret, a sudden revelation ... I do believe that if Mrs Wood had the gift of writing, she might have penned *A Woman of No Importance*.

AMELIA: I suppose that's one of yours. I'm sorry I don't know it. But *East Lynne* is a beautiful book. I cried my eyes out over the death of Little Willie.[8] He saw Jesus coming for him.

OSCAR: I once said that one would have to have a heart of stone to read the death of Little Nell without dissolving into tears ... of laughter. But you have a tender heart, madam.

AMELIA: Oh yes. Especially for the babbies. Little angels. Angels in the making.

OSCAR: I miss my children.[9] (*sobs*)

AMELIA: That's a shame, sir. But you will see them again, won't you? One day?

OSCAR: I hope so. I do hope so. (*wipes his eyes*)

AMELIA: You mustn't get depressed now. You have to keep your spirits up in places such as these.

OSCAR: You've been in prison before?

AMELIA: Not in prison, so to speak. In the asylum. For my nerves, you understand. And in the workhouse. There's not much difference. But you can't let them get you down. Here now (*draws a bottle from her bag*): would you like a little drink to cheer you up?

OSCAR: You have something? (*AMELIA stands on the bed and passes the bottle thought the grating. OSCAR takes it from her*). Laudanum! Good God, how did you come by this?

AMELIA: I'm only on remand here, sir. I have my own clothes, my own things. They don't take everything from you. Only your bootlaces.

OSCAR: (*drinks*) Ah. Give me to drink mandragora. You seem conveniently furnished with opioids, Mrs Dyer.

AMELIA: It's medicinal, sir. 'Godfrey's Cordial', from the druggist. I use it all the time. We give it to the little ones. To still their crying. Give them peace. We call it 'The Quietness'. Five drops on the end of a spoon at bed-time, and they go off as quiet as anything. Stops their hunger, too.[10]

OSCAR: (*drinks*) I had no idea.

AMELIA: You wouldn't, would you sir? I expect your wife had a bottle handy when your babbies were small.

OSCAR: Well, I have to say, I don't recall them crying much. Laudanum is like absinthe. After the first glass, you see things as you wish they were. After the second, you see things as they are not. After the third, you see things as they really are.[11] And that is the most horrible of all. But here, I have almost drained this. Take it back, before I reach the third stage. Let me see things as they are not.

AMELIA: You keep it, Mr Wilde. I've another bottle. I'll join you from here. (*drains bottle and slumps forward. After a few seconds she rouses and begins to sing*).

When true hearts lie withered,
And fond ones are flown,
Oh! who would inhabit
This bleak world alone?[12]

OSCAR: Tom Moore. Authentic Irish insincerity. A sentimentalist is one who wants the luxury of an emotion without paying for it.

AMELIA: (*a little drunk, speaks shyly*) You did pay for it though, sir, didn't you? With the rent boys? Isn't that why you're in here?

OSCAR: (*slightly taken aback*). Yes: I am one who loved not wisely, but too well. I bought the bodies of boys as one would buy horse-flesh from Tatersall's. They needed the money. I needed love.

AMELIA: We're not so different, you and I. You exchanged money for pleasure. I take away the fruits of pleasure for a fee. You rent young men. I farm babies. We're both in the meat trade.

OSCAR: (*hurt*) But I was in love with youth. And surely you have the instincts of a mother. People are not animals. They can't be bought and sold.

AMELIA: People are animals. Look at the way they carry on. They fuck like foxes. Drop their babbies in the dirt. Pay me to get rid of them. Look at you. Sheets stained with semen and shit.[13] 'In love with youth?' The beast with two backs. Worse than a beast, they called you. I remember. I remember. (*sings*)

Jesus calls the children dear,
'Come to me and never fear,
For I love the little children of the world;
I will take you by the hand,
Lead you to the better land,
For I love the little children of the world'.[14]

OSCAR: What do you mean 'Get rid of them'?

AMELIA: (*extracts another bottle from her bag and uncorks it. Her speech is harsh and slurred*). They say I done her in. Little Doris. I know nothing about it. Her mother called herself 'Evelina'. Fancy name for a slut barmaid from Cheltenham. She advertised in the *Bristol Times*: female child for adoption. I wrote to her saying I'd take the dear little baby girl. Rest assured, I said, I will bring her up just the same as my own child. Every care will be taken. 31 March 1896. She gave me the babby with a box of clothes. And £10. It was cold. The babby had a pelisse, fawn-coloured, to keep her warm. The mother wouldn't leave, took me to the station, carried my carpet-bag. I wrote to her a few days later: 'The dear little girl is a traveller. She slept all the way'.[15] (*drinks and sings*)

I'm a long time travelling here below ...[16]

OSCAR: What happened to the baby?

AMELIA: I don't know anything about it. It's a mystery to me.[17]

OSCAR: I wrote a story called *The Star Child*. Two woodcutters were making their way home through a great pine-forest. It was winter, and a night of bitter cold … as they were bewailing their misery to each other this strange thing happened. There fell from heaven a very bright and beautiful star. They thought they would find a crock of gold. And lo! there was indeed a thing of gold lying on the white snow. But it was a cloak of golden tissue, curiously wrought with stars, and wrapped in many folds. They thought they had found treasure. But, alas! no gold was in it, nor silver, nor, indeed, treasure of any kind, but only a little child who was asleep. One was disappointed, seeing no profit in a child. But the other said it were an evil thing to leave the child to perish here in the snow. So very tenderly he took up the child, and wrapped the cloak around it to shield it from the harsh cold, and made his way down the hill to the village. His companion asked if he could at least have the cloak. But he answered him, saying, 'Nay, for the cloak is neither mine nor thine, but the child's only'.[18]

AMELIA: (*drinking deeply from the second bottle*) There was another babby. Jessie Goulding. From Gloucester. She had a box of clothes, too. JG. Three pinafores, two shirts, two bibs, a napkin, a nightdress, two pairs of socks, a brush and a child's red wool hat. Polly wrote her mother a letter: 'gave her a nice warm bath, fed her and put her to bed at half past eight. *We never heard a sound from her*'. The mother sent more clothes. How is the little girl? She wanted to know. We wrote again: 'the slippers fit the baby nicely'. Such a dear little thing, we said. '*She is not a bit of trouble now*'. We put the clothes in the cupboard.[19] (*sings*)

I'll not leave thee, thou lone one

To pine on the stem …'

OSCAR: Children are a blessing. Mine are called Cyril and Vyvyan.

AMELIA: Little angels. Jesus wants them more than their mothers. You know what one of them wrote in a letter? 'I'll see you in hell before I own the child or pay any more. You can do what you like with it for all I care'. So I did what she told me. Little Harry, now, he was a devil if ever I saw one. Harry Simmons. From Ealing. His mother brought him down to Reading. He did nothing but cry, cry for food, cry for his mother. We plugged the rubber titty in his mouth, but it didn't shut him up. Little Devil, I said, if it keeps this up, I shan't stick it for long.[20]

OSCAR: And where is little Doris now? And where is Harry?

AMELIA: *(laughs malevolently)* In a hand-bag! Like your play. Victoria Station. I'd like to see it. Can you get me a ticket? *(drinks, and talks increasingly to herself)*. 9.15 from Paddington. Fast train. Particularly dark, that night. Got to Reading at 10.05. Down to the Clappers footbridge. Who's there? Someone in the bushes. Pouring with rain. Fifteen minutes till he was gone. Dark the river, fast-flowing. A handbag. Through the railings with it, an almighty splash. But down it went. Hurry home, now. Hurry. In the dark. Past the railway arches. 'Goodnight', someone said. Did he see anything? My heart beat fast. He was so close. We might have touched one another as he passed.[21]

OSCAR: Madam, what are you saying? Speak more clearly. I cannot understand you.

AMELIA: *(speaking more and more quietly, to herself, so OSCAR can't hear)* At first I used to let them starve, little pinched faces growing pale and blue, only the laudanum colouring their cheeks. But it took them so long! Then the voices told me to strangle them with tape. White tape from my work-box. A few turns around the neck, and tie the knot tight, tie it in a bow, underneath the ear. Over in a few minutes. An end to all suffering. An angel with Jesus. I wish the world could understand what it is to have someone saying to you. 'Get rid of them, get rid of them'. I used to like to watch them with the tape round their neck, but it was soon all over with them. When I had thrown them in the water, then I felt easier in my mind. Before I die I want to tell the mothers of the little babbies that I pray for them every night to forgive me in their hearts.[22] *(sings)*

Since the lovely are sleeping

Go sleep thou with them.

(AMELIA'S head slumps onto her chest and she sleeps. OSCAR kneels by his bed, crosses himself reverentially and clasps his hands in prayer).

CURTAIN

CURTAIN

Act Two. 11 June 1896.

SCENE: Reading Gaol.

CURTAIN

Scene as before, AMELIA's cell empty. OSCAR in his cell, seated on the bed. Standing before him, Prison Warder THOMAS MARTIN.

OSCAR: Thomas, it's been so long!

THOMAS: Yes, Mr Wilde. But it was nice to be out of the old place for a while.

OSCAR: Travelling?

THOMAS: In a manner of speaking. Escorting prisoners. Only travelling from one gaol to another.

OSCAR: I've so missed our conversations. I have no-one else to talk to. No-one to bring me the *Daily Chronicle*. Or ginger biscuits. The other Warders are not like you.[23]

THOMAS: Oh, they're not such a bad lot. It's more than their job's worth to be seen making a prisoner happy.

OSCAR: I quite understand your feelings. I would not for worlds get such a friend as you are into any danger.[24]

THOMAS: Me! I'm too soft for this job. I don't see the point of unnecessary suffering. Especially with children. There were three of them brought in last week. Little nippers. Convicted of snaring rabbits. Court imposed a fine. How the hell can they pay a fine? So they bring them to us. Terrified they were, standing there with their sheets under their arms. One of them, so small he was, they couldn't find clothes to fit him. Poor little mite. I give him a sweet biscuit. Stop him crying. I don't care.[25]

OSCAR: I remember seeing such a child, in the cell opposite. A warder was talking to him, kindly enough. Just telling him to be a good boy and stay out of trouble. But the child's face was a white wedge of sheer terror. In his eyes the terror of a hunted animal.[26]

THOMAS: They shouldn't be in prison at all. What's the point? But at least in here they're alive. Not like the poor little brats your friend Mrs Dyer took care of.

OSCAR: My friend? Mrs Dyer?

THOMAS: You can't have forgotten her! She spent the night in the cell next door, two months back. She said she'd talked with you. I didn't inquire too closely as to how.

OSCAR: Yes. I remember her. The baby farmer. We conversed for several hours. Through the grating (*glancing upwards*).

THOMAS: Did you, indeed? You have been a naughty boy. How did you two get along?

OSCAR: An interesting woman, though common of course. She seemed knowledgeable, cultured even. Had a sweet singing voice. Polite and courteous. Up to a point. But then rather too free with the laudanum. She lapsed into a kind of rambling, then babbling, then raving: terrible, mad fancies. She sounded like a drunken sleepwalking Lady Macbeth. She got round to insulting me, I seem to recall. Then I think she passed out, as I heard no more from her. What happened to her?

THOMAS: (*pause*) You haven't been getting the paper, so you won't know anything about it. Amelia Dyer was hanged for murder in Newgate Prison at 9 o' clock yesterday morning.

OSCAR: Murder! Good God. Murdered whom?

THOMAS: A child. Or rather children. Supposed to be a nurse, she was. Took unwanted children into care for money. Began by letting them die of neglect, then graduated to killing them outright. Tried at the Old Bailey. They charged her with just one murder, but they think she killed hundreds.

OSCAR: The name of the child? The victim? Was it Doris?

THOMAS: That's right. Did she talk to you about it?

OSCAR: Indirectly. And incoherently. She spoke of two children, Doris and Harry. Took them into her baby farm. Talked about their clothes, I remember. And, something odd: I mentioned the handbag in my play, *The Importance of Being Earnest*. The hero's a foundling, left in handbag at Victoria Station. It seemed to affect her: she kept harping on the bag.

THOMAS: Really? How remarkable.

OSCAR: Why so?

THOMAS: Because the corpses of Doris and Harry were found in exactly such a handbag. In twelve feet of Thames water, under the Clappers footbridge at Reading. Weighted down with a brick.[27]

OSCAR: Merciful Jesus! Then what she was saying was no hallucination! She must have told me the whole story! A confession!

THOMAS: A rehearsal, apparently. They moved her from here to where she could see them arresting her daughter Polly. Straight away Amelia sat down and wrote out a full confession, to get her daughter off the hook. 'I must ease my mind', she wrote. 'I do most solemnly declare that my daughter had nothing at all to do with it: she never knew I contemplated doing such a wicked thing until it was too late'. 'I have done this dreadful crime', she said. 'God Almighty is my judge'.[28]

OSCAR: She confessed to save her daughter?

THOMAS: It seems so. Polly was the key witness at her mother's trial.

OSCAR: Some good she meant to do, in spite of her own nature.[29]

THOMAS: What's that, sir?

OSCAR: Nothing. Shakespeare. But tell me about the trial, Thomas. Were you there?

THOMAS: I was, Mr Wilde. I had to take a chap up to Newgate, and managed to get into the Old Court to hear the whole thing.

OSCAR: The Old Court! I remember it well. So she stood in the dock where I stood to receive my sentence! What did she look like?

THOMAS: A stout woman, big-bosomed, red-faced, country-looking. We heard from Doris's mother, Evelina, about how the baby was handed over for £10, with a box of clothes. Evelina read out Amelia's letter: 'I don't want the child for money's sake, but for company and comfort'. 'Bring a warm shawl', she told the mother, 'to wrap around baby on the train'. We heard all about the carpet-bag Amelia carried with her, and a joint of bacon wrapped in brown paper. Amelia took the train to her daughter's house in Willesden, and killed the baby there. Wrapped a length of sewing tape around its little neck, and tied it tight with a bow. Next day Amelia collected another nipper, Harry. From his aunt, Amelia Sergeant. Killed him too, same method. That was her signature, the tape round the neck. Stuffed them both in the handbag with the brick. Over the top she put the brown paper that had held the bacon, and tied the whole lot up with string. Took the late train back to Reading, and dumped them in the river. Police dragged the river, a couple of days after you spoke with her. Found the poor little mites in the handbag. And pulled out half a dozen more little bodies from the same stretch. Hard to imagine what that mother must have felt, Evelina, taken by the police to that cold mortuary, and shown – her little Doris. Lying on a slab under a rough blanket, head on a pillow of brown paper. 'There I saw the body of my child'.[30]

OSCAR: A monster! How did Amelia take these women in?

THOMAS: Well some of the mothers knew what was going on. But others really wanted the best for the kid. And she was quite a charmer, Amelia. Not good-looking, you understand, but she came across as motherly, kindly, caring. 'She appeared a kind person', one of the mothers said at the trial: 'I took her to be a kind, homely, motherly woman'. 'I should not have thought her capable of committing the crime she is charged with'. And yet she could do such things! Take a baby, a few months old, from its mother, wind a tape round its little neck, pull it tight and stop its breath. For a few pounds! She kept all those baby clothes, and pawned them when she needed more money. It took the jury four and half minutes to declare her guilty. I expect you think capital punishment brutal and cruel, Mr Wilde. Well I tell you, I've known no-one to deserve so well that sentence of death. What she did to those bairns! But they wound the rope around her neck too, and tied it tight, right under her ear. The hangman told me he used only a short drop, on account of her weight and the softness of the textures. Meaning she was flabby, you know. 'It proved', he said 'to be quite sufficient'.[31]

OSCAR: I once wrote that 'One is absolutely sickened, not by the crimes that the wicked have committed, but by the punishments that the good have inflicted; and a community is infinitely more brutalized by the habitual employment of punishment than it is by the occasional occurrence of crime'.[32] But I fear I may have to revise that opinion, along with many others. You see I don't think I have ever before met anyone truly evil. Should I have said something? Should I have reported her? Was it my duty to speak out?

THOMAS: Now, Mr Wilde, sir, don't go down that road. You're a convict. C.33. A famous convict; a celebrity convict; a very unusual convict. But a convict nonetheless. It's not your job to inform. You're under no obligation to repeat what you hear in this place. Leave it to the authorities. They know what they're doing. They brought her to trial with one of the best-made cases I've ever seen. And that was on top of her confession, and her daughter's collusion. They worked it out between them.

OSCAR: What of the daughter?

THOMAS: She was in on it, no doubt. Impossible to say how deep and how far. In any event, her case will collapse any day now, and she'll go free. They wanted a stay of execution on Amelia so she could testify at her own daughter's trial. Tit for tat, you might say. But – this is a good one – the court ruled that being under sentence of death, Amelia was already legally dead. So she couldn't be called as a witness.[33]

OSCAR: *Non mortui testimonium.* The dead cannot bear witness.[34] She fooled me utterly. Made me think of my own children. She seemed truly affectionate, spoke so kindly of the babies, of stilling their crying, of putting them to sleep – oh good God, is that really what she meant?

THOMAS: Without a doubt.

OSCAR: And even sentimental: she said she cried on reading of a child's death in a novel. Little Willie. And I joked about the death of Little Nell in *The Old Curiosity Shop*. God forgive me.

THOMAS: You know what sticks in my mind is the fact that she was such a fat woman. Nothing wrong with that in itself, of course: my wife's a big girl. A handful, I call her. But Amelia starved those poor kids to death, while feeding herself fat on the proceeds. You know before she got on the train for Reading, she went into a pastrycook's, and bought herself something for the journey.[35] There she sat, in that railway carriage, gorging on pastries, with that handbag, with its dreadful load, stowed under her feet. Those murdered bairns, wrapped in greasy paper like joints of meat. Licking her fingers. How could anyone do that?

OSCAR: How would you know, Thomas? You're the man who risked his employment to give a sweet biscuit to a crying child. 'For I was anhungered, and ye gave me meat; I was thirsty, and ye gave me drink … Inasmuch as ye have done it unto one of the least of these my brethren, ye have done it unto me'.[36]

THOMAS: Matthew. The sheep and the goats. At least one person pays attention in chapel. And what happens to those who don't feed the hungry?

OSCAR: 'Depart from me, ye cursed, into everlasting fire, prepared for the devil and his angels'.[37]

THOMAS: Justice. It was the weight of her own body that killed her, like the hangman said: the softness of the textures. A short drop. It proved to be quite sufficient. Do you think she's in Hell?

OSCAR: Perhaps she always was. I only heard her voice, you see: a sweet voice, singing old songs and sentimental hymns. If only I'd been able to see her, look into her face. Surely her wickedness would have been written there.

THOMAS: Evelina Harmon didn't see it. Amelia Sargeant didn't see it. I tell you who did though: little Doris and little Harry, they saw it. It was the last thing they ever saw. In a darkening vision, as she choked the life out of them. They saw her face: the face of evil.

OSCAR: Malice and cruelty, they must be revealed in the face at last. Not in the face we see, in the street or in the salon. But somewhere, perhaps on the face in a painting, locked away at the top of the house in a mildewed mouldering room. Or the face inside us, the one that's visible only to God. I never really believed in evil and eternal punishment. To me evil was always material for a paradox, an aphorism, a *bon mot*. 'Wickedness is a myth invented by good people to account for the curious attractiveness of others'.[38] That was one of things I said. I played with ideas; tossed them in the air and transformed them; made them iridescent with fancy, winged with paradox. I wrote poems and essays in praise of crime: made sin marvellous, and evil full of subtlety.[39] But here, in this tiny cell, for the first time, I have come close to the heart and mind of someone really wicked, a true enemy of God and man. We are each of us our own devil, and make this world our Hell.[40]

THOMAS: I know you've found your time here very hard, Mr Wilde. And I know terrible things have been said about you. But the strictness here, the discipline, the punishment for the slightest offence, what seems to you arbitrary cruelty: it's just the system. The rules. We impose them because that's our job. It's not what we really think or feel. Those poor little kids now, the ones who are in here, when we see them in the exercise yard: there's not a single man here, warder or prisoner, who wouldn't gladly take their punishment for them, to set them free. You can see it in their faces. And the kids are in here for stealing nuts off a tree, or snaring a rabbit: just looking for something to eat. Should those be treated as offences at all? You know there's plenty of people, ordinary fellows as well as gentlefolk, who see you as the victim of an unjust law. Doing what everyone does. In fifty years time what you were convicted for won't even be a crime.

OSCAR: I called it the love that dare not speak its name.

THOMAS: But its name will be spoken, in days to come. Broadcast, loud and clear.

OSCAR: I'll never live to see it. The governor told my friend I'd be dead in two years.

THOMAS: Let's hope not. But your name will outlive you. Not as a badge of shame, but as a flag of liberty. Oscar Wilde, a great writer, and a martyr in the cause of freedom. Freedom to live, freedom to love. But Amelia Dyer, now: her crime is the worst of the worst. Always has been, always will be.

OSCAR: The primal eldest curse.[41]

THOMAS: What's that?

OSCAR: Cain and Abel. The blood of those children cries from the ground, like sacrificing Abel's, to us for justice and rough chastisement.[42]

THOMAS: That's where we need the law, that's where we need punishment, that's where we need execution. She's there to make us all look virtuous. You know when her daughter was a little girl, she asked Amelia what happened to all those babies who came to the house and then disappeared. They've become angels, her mother told her; Jesus wants them more than their mothers. I'm making angels. I'm an angel-maker.

OSCAR: God forgive her. God forgive me.

THOMAS; I doubt that God will trouble himself about you when he has the likes of Amelia Dyer to deal with.

OSCAR: I don't know. We have so much in common. Both held in Newgate. Both tried in the same court at the Old Bailey. Both imprisoned here. We must share something. What were her last words?

THOMAS: The hangman told me. She was asked to make a final statement on the scaffold. Her reply? 'I have nothing to say'.[43]

OSCAR: In that respect at least Amelia and I are singularly different. She had nothing to say, and I lack words only when silenced. I had much to say after my sentence, and was not permitted to say anything. 'And I?' I remember shouting over the cries of 'Shame' that rang around the court. 'May I say nothing?'

THOMAS: I'm sure you still have much to say, Mr Wilde. You could write about your time in here, for a start. There must be some fine writing you can salvage, even out of these depths.

OSCAR: 'Depths'? I must write that down. 'De Profundis'. I only hope I live long enough to complete it. Thomas: would you be so kind as to fetch me some paper and a fresh bottle of ink?

CURTAIN

Tauroctony from the Temple of Mithras, Walbrook

HEINRICH HIMMLER

PREFACE

In 1954, in the course of clearing bomb damage for reconstruction, a Roman temple of Mithras was uncovered in Walbrook, less than a mile from Smithfield. The cult of this Indo-European god, always displayed in the act of slaying a bull, was popular among the Roman military, and extensively practised in Britain. The London Mithraeum has now been restored as a museum beneath the Bloomberg Building at 12 Walbrook, while some of its artefacts can be seen in the Museum of London.

In the 'alternative history' narrative that follows it is 1942, and Britain has been conquered and occupied by the Nazis. *Reichsbevollmachtiger* Heinrich Himmler appropriates the Temple of Mithras with a view to harnessing its esoteric power to convert the British to National Socialism. Nazi investment in the occult, as featured fantastically in the Indian Jones films, was genuine and enthusiastic. In the underground crypt of the castle of Wewelsburg in Westphalia, now a museum focused on the history of the SS, Himmler hoped to indoctrinate the Nazi leadership with occult knowledge. In this tale he tries to adopt the underground temple of Mithras to similar ends.

The national spirit of Britain, personified in the sacrificial bull, has other ideas.

My main source for Himmler's ideas is Peter Longerich, *Heinrich Himmler: a Life* (Oxford: Oxford University Press, 2011). I have also drawn on Christopher Hale, *Himmler's Crusade: The Nazi Expedition to Find the Origins of the Aryan Race* (Secaucus: Castle Books, 2007); Heather Pringle, *The Master Plan: Himmler's Scholars and the Holocaust* (New York: Hyperion, 2006); and Nicholas Goodrick-Clarke, *The Occult Roots of Nazism: Secret Aryan Cults and Their Influence on Nazi Ideology* (London: Tauris Park, 2005).

For the Mithraeum I have used John D. Shepherd, *The Temple of Mithras, London: excavations by W.F. Grimes and A. Williams at the Walbrook*

(London: English Heritage, 1998), and W.F. Grimes, *The Excavation of Roman and Medieval London* (London: Routledge and Kegan Paul, 1998). For Mithraism generally I have consulted David Ulansey, *The Origins of the Mithraic Mysteries: Cosmology and Salvation in the Ancient World* (Oxford: Oxford University Press, 1991), and Manfred Claus, *The Roman Cult of Mithras: the God and his Mysteries* (London: Routledge, 2001).

HEINRICH HIMMLER

1

With a soft, discreet, unobtrusive click of the heels, Heinrich Himmler bent to kiss the extended hand of King Edward VIII, monarch of the Third Reich protectorate of *Grossbritannien*. The year was 1942, the date 14 June.

'Your majesty'.

'Thank you, Herr *Reichsbevollmachtiger*.[1] What can I do for you?'

Himmler could overhear in Edward's tone, as he retreated behind his desk, a strain of that plaintive dependency that always seemed to dog the King, a barely submerged consciousness that his authority derived only from the National Socialists who had restored him to power following the conquest of Britain, the execution of Churchill and the hasty flight of his brother and family to America. The *Restauration* had been plotted largely by von Ribbentrop, and agreed at a secret meeting in Spain.[2] In the event of Britain falling to the invading forces of the Third Reich, Edward would resume the throne from which he been deposed in 1937, with his wife Wallis as Queen, as a conditional monarch subject only to the plenipotentiary authority of the *Reichsbevollmachtiger*, which derived in turn directly from the *Fuhrer*.

On those few sunny days in 1940, when the Spitfires and Hurricanes of the RAF had been blasted out of the skies by the invincible might of the *Luftwaffe*, leaving their wreckage strewn for miles across the green fields of the Home Counties, the German forces had landed from the sea and advanced inexorably on London. Pounded by relentless bombing, the air force destroyed and the Navy captured, the army overwhelmed and the civilian population in flight, the British government had had no choice but to capitulate, and hand over Winston Churchill to the occupying power. After a brief show trial in which he was convicted of war crimes against the Third Reich, Churchill had been shot in Parliament Square. Sir Oswald Mosely was released from Holloway Prison,[3] nominated as

Prime Minister and instructed to form a government, and Edward VIII was restored to his vacated throne. The red, white and black Swastika flag flew proudly outside Parliament, Buckingham Palace and all other state and government buildings.

Himmler sat down opposite Edward. 'Your majesty has heard of the archaeological excavations taking place in the City of London?'

'Well, yes', replied Edward uncertainly. 'What of them?'

'As you know some of the buildings destroyed by our glorious Luftwaffe are being demolished and rebuilt. In the process of those demolitions, some ancient monuments have been uncovered, the remains of Roman civilisation'.

'Yes, of course. London has been a human settlement for over 2,000 years'.

'I am particularly interested in one such excavation, currently taking place in Walbrook, at the end of Queen Victoria Street. Your archaeologists have unearthed the remains of a Roman temple. Your builders are standing by to fill the foundations and begin new construction. But the excavation will need more time'.[4]

'I see', said the king, who was still wondering where the conversation was going, and why Himmler was interested. Walbrook? Roman temples? Archaeologists?

'In brief', said Himmler, sensing the royal vacancy and anxious to conclude, 'I will be taking personal control of the excavation. I request that you sign this order to dismiss the Excavation Council archaeologists, halt the building work and give my team access to the ruins'. And he pushed a paper across the desk to the king.

'Why of course, if that's what you want', replied Edward obligingly. He took a Mont Blanc fountain-pen from the pocket of his silk suit, and signed the paper.

'Thank you, your Majesty', said Himmler, rising to his feet and extending his right arm in the Nazi salute. 'Heil Hitler'.

Raising his hand somewhat limply, the king nonchalantly replied: 'Heil Hitler'.

2

Himmler wasted no time in returning to his official car, which swiftly took him eastwards through the devastated city. As he watched from the window of the fast-moving Mercedes the ruins of the once elegant and beautiful buildings of Westminster and Victoria, they spoke to him of German achievement in bringing a proud and ancient nation to its knees. The heavy responsibility of rebuilding London seemed to him only an opportunity to secure renewal and impose change: the Nazification of everything in London that was not already Germanic.

Reaching a heavily-bombed site near the junction of Cannon Street and Queen Victoria Street, he left the car, closely surrounded by a small group of SS officers, and entered the ruins. A few men and women in dust-covered overalls were on their way out, looking disconsolate, and muttering resentfully among themselves. These were the archaeologists of the Roman and Mediaeval London Excavation Council, already dismissed from their duties and ordered to leave. As they caught sight of Himmler, the conversation froze on their lips, and they passed him with averted faces and downcast eyes.

Himmler had to duck down to pass through a low doorway leading into an ancient stone building, where a small group of German scientists and technicians stood waiting for him. They were standing beneath the domed brick ceiling of an underground Roman temple. The dig had already uncovered long, low brick pediments that ran the length of the space, creating three aisles, divided by seven stone columns. The stumps of wooden posts suggested that long benches had originally surmounted the low walls. At the west end a raised platform indicated the position of the altar.

'Let me see it', said Himmler impatiently, addressing the tallest man of the group, who wore the swastika armband and insignia of the SS.

'This way, Herr *Reichsbevollmachtiger*' was the reply, and the scientist led Himmler over to a small bench littered with archaeological tools, in the centre of which stood an object covered with a cloth, which with a flourish of demonstration he plucked aside. 'Here he is. Mithras'.

Himmler gazed at the bas-relief with awe. The Roman sculpture depicted the god Mithras bestriding the bull, with his left hand violently tugging at the animal's nostrils to lift and pull back its head, and with his right plunging the sacred dagger deep into its shoulder. The *Tauroctony*.[5] Two torch-bearers attended the god. At the four corners of the tablet were the heads of Sol the sun and Luna the moon, and two gods of the wind, the whole tableau encircled by the signs of the zodiac. His distinctive Phrygian cap on his head, cloak blowing out behind him, Mithras was the very embodiment of youth, energy and strength, legs securely gripping the great muscled flank of the bull, hand firmly planting the sacerdotal knife into the sacrificial victim's vitals. The mystery was a symbiosis: the man took on the power of the bull, and the bull became partly human, like the Cretan Minotaur.

'We have found him', said Himmler reverentially. 'At last. Mithras. He is ours'.

3

Himmler knew that the population of Great Britain would never submit to mere brute military force. They were a proud, independent-minded people, who had not experienced occupation since 1066. Their original bloodstock was Aryan, formed from the merging of Danes and Saxons with the Normans, the Northmen, who had invaded from across the Channel and defeated the English at Hastings. Over the centuries the Aryan bloodline had become polluted and contaminated by immigration and miscegenation, but was still dominant, and the British remained, for the most part, a white race, needing only a little cleansing and segregation.

The offer of German friendship and alliance had been refused, and the islanders had fought for their freedom against insuperable odds. Now they were subjugated but not defeated, bloody yet unbowed. Himmler saw it in their faces, heard it in their voices: an elusive expression of defiance, a covert refusal to yield in the spirit. Although there was very little sign, at this stage, of a strong and organised resistance, he had to contend every day with a slow, ponderous inertia that betokened an intractable non-co-operation. *Man kann die Pferde zur Tränke führen, saufen müssen sie selbst.* You can take a horse to water, but you have to drink it yourself.

He knew that the British spirit, the *Nationalgeist*, had somehow to be subdued and commanded, in a realm beyond the reach of compulsion and repression. And in order to achieve this, he as plenipotentiary leader had to seek for a lost wisdom buried deep in the nation's soil. He had to find the symbols, unlock the mysteries, discover the keys that would unlock the true Aryan soul of the land, interred as it was under centuries of Christianity and democracy.

Even in Germany it had not been an easy matter to decrypt and translate the mysteries of *Blut und Boden*, blood and soil.[6] Even the Germans had lost contact with their spiritual birthright. Which was why he had had to found the *Ahnenerbe*, the 'ancestral heritage' project with Wirth and Darre in 1935, and later incorporate it into the *Schutzstaffel*.[7] The *Ahnenerbe* had conclusively proved that the Aryan race, displaced from Atlantis by a cosmic catastrophe, was the origin of humankind, and that its runic language pre-dated all others. Prehistoric Runic inscriptions had been found in Italy, showing that the Aryans had founded ancient Rome. His scholars had proved beyond doubt that Jesus was of the Aryan race, which explained how he had managed to achieve the impossible, replacing the power of Judaism with a new religion of heroism and sacrifice.

But Christianity in turn had been Judaized, and turned into a religion of victimhood and submission, the greatest of plagues, that had almost mortally weakened the Aryan race. Now those twenty centuries of stony sleep, the twilight world of the Nazarene, had given way to a new world order and a new religion, the worship of Waralda, the Ancient One of the old Frisians. Waralda, who created all things. Waralda, omnipresent but invisible, a spirit. All things proceed and return to Waralda. Waralda is the beginning and the end. He alone is the creator, and nothing exists without him. The communists had replaced Christianity with atheism, but Himmler's world-vision had no room for unbelief: there were no atheists in the SS.[8] He had taught them a new scale of values: the scale of the macrocosm and the microcosm, the starry sky above us and the world in us. Man is nothing special at all. He must once again look with deep reverence into this world. Then he will acquire the right sense of proportion about what is above us, about how we are woven into the cycle of the universe.[9]

But mankind must look back to these ancient origins not directly, as individuals, but through the prism of the race Waralda had created, in all its invincible strength and incomparable beauty. 'We must once again', he had said in a speech to the SS leaders in Berlin, 'be rooted in our ancestors and grandchildren, in the eternal chain and eternal sequence. Only thus can the German people overcome Christianity and create the Germanic Reich which will be a blessing for the earth. For thousands of years it has been the mission of this blond race to rule the earth, and again and again to bring it happiness and culture. This is the destiny of the German nation'.[10]

Britain presented him with a particular problem. Wherever the Reich had extended its territory across continental Europe, it had been a relatively straightforward matter to apply the principles of *Blut und Boden*, blood and soil. The blood of the race could be purified by segregation and extermination, by ethnic cleansing and breeding programmes. And the land, the soil, could always be incorporated into the single land-mass of a greater Germany. The old Teutonic gods lay dormant everywhere in the soil of Europe, in Norway and Denmark, in Hungary and Poland, even in Italy and France and Spain. His Hyperborean ancestors had struck out from their ancient northern kingdom of Thule to colonise every European country, leaving the traces of their history for later ages to find. Fragments of Aryan civilisation littered Europe, turned up by the plough, uncovered by the archaeologist's trowel.

Some of the most potent symbols of the Teutonic race were to be found outside Germany. In Spain Himmler had personally sought for the Holy Grail in vain in the castle of Montserrat.[11] At some time it had rested in France, where the Templars had preserved its true secrets, mysteries pre-dating Christian mythology by thousands of years.[12] In Italy the Nazis had found the Spear of Destiny, and taken it home to Nuremberg.[13] He was confident that the Hammer of Thor, not a symbol but a futuristic weapon, lay buried somewhere beneath the ice-mountains of Norway.[14] Very soon his archaeologists would discover the location of the Ark of the Covenant, hidden on Mount Ararat.[15]

These artefacts testified to a lost unity of country, people and hero. The *Volk* and the land were one, and were at one, *Blut und Boden*, with the supreme leader, the *Führer*. With the eventual conquest of Russia, the Nazis would have succeeded in restoring unity to the whole continent of Europe, an expanded *Ultima Thule*, creating a *Reich* that would stretch from the Pacific to the Atlantic, from the Arctic Circle to the Equator: one land, occupied by one master race, led by one *Führer*. *Heil Hitler; Sieg Heil.*

But Britain was different. This stubborn little island, a ragged rock set in a salt-sour sea, could be over-run but not overcome, made to kneel but not to yield. They were Northmen, but of a different kin, as dogged and intractable in their own way as the Germans. It was Himmler's mission to bring them back to the ancient ways, back to the mysteries that lay buried deep in the fertile black soil of the land, back to a knowledge of Waralda. Only then, when as *Reichsbevollmachtiger* he would be able to stand before them and hold aloft the symbols of their own deep past, re-induct them into the secret wisdom of their own race, unleash the awesome power of the occult substratum of their own land, would the British kneel before him in fealty, and willingly accept the leadership of the *Reich*.

This new religion, a pagan monotheism, lay at the heart of Himmler's political project. At the castle of Wewelsburg[16] in Westphalia, he had established a temple of National Socialism. He took over the beautiful triangular Renaissance palace, built for the Prince Bishops of Paderborn, and converted it into a training and indoctrination centre, a *Reichsführerschule* or leadership college for the SS. What he taught there was not military strategy or political ideology, but esoteric wisdom. In the round North Tower he designed a circular *Obergruppenführersaal*, a meeting room for the supreme leadership of the SS, modelled on the legends of Camelot. Twelve pillars supported the ceiling, and at its centre was the symbol of the Black Sun. A round oak table was installed where the SS leaders gathered around Himmler in a mystic circle, like the Arthurian knights of old. Below the hall, in a crypt known as the *Graf*, he designed a circular temple, with a domed ceiling and a circular sunken floor. Around the circle were twelve black stone blocks, plinths on which the SS leaders could stand and observe the rituals. In the middle of the circle there burnt a perpetual flame, its smoke rising to alternately obscure and reveal the swastika motif at the centre of the ceiling. Here in this subterranean pagan temple, abhorrent mysteries of torture and sacrifice, of animals and humans, were regularly conducted by Himmler himself, until his sudden departure for Britain in 1940.

It was Himmler's intention that after the expected National Socialist conquest of the globe, Wewelsburg would become the *Zentrum den Neues Welt*.[17] The castle would become the spiritual heart of the new world order, the thousand-year Reich, as the Vatican had been for two millennia of Christianity. There in Wewelsburg the elite of the SS would come to have their faith strengthened, and their devotion renewed; to be initiated into arcane and secret knowledge, uncovered by men who feared nothing save the Maker of all things.

Though Himmler knew that other senior Nazi leaders were sceptical about his interest in the occult and esoteric, even to some degree the *Fuhrer* himself, he was absolutely convinced that Germany owed its phenomenal military and political success not only to generalship and charisma, but also to the secret mysteries practised in Wewelsburg. The dark, invisible waves of power that throbbed and pulsed from the crypt of the castle formed a tidal wave that swept the German armies to victory after victory. The SS was invincible not only because of its racial purity and indissoluble Aryan brotherhood, but because its leaders were initiates, inducted in the *Graf* at Wewelsburg into the secret wisdom of the ages, men who had made their oblations and offered themselves to the ancient Teutonic power, the creator and destroyer of all living things.

Now it was time to embark on the spiritual conquest of Britain. And now he had discovered the place from which that mission could begin: the Temple of Mithras.

4

Himmler gave strict orders to secure the perimeter of the temple site and allow no-one but SS staff to enter. He then gave detailed instructions as to how the site was to be developed, the oak benches restored, the altarpiece replaced. The space was to be illuminated at all times, with burning torches installed around the walls. All preparations must be completed within one week, ready for the Summer Solstice of 21 June.

The god Mithras was widely worshipped in the Roman Empire, especially by soldiers.[18] He was of Indo-European, therefore Aryan, origin, arriving in Rome via Zoroastrian Persia. The worshippers of Mithras, exclusively male, would meet in underground temples, drink and feast together, and perform secret rituals. Like the SS they were a brotherhood, known to one another as *syndexioi*,[19] united by a handshake. The brothers would pass through seven grades of initiation, each finding his proper level: the Crow, the Bridegroom, the Soldier, the Lion, the Persian, the Sun-runner. Only the greatest of devotees would reach the final grade, that of the Father. Ascent to this level entailed a mystic entry into the persona of the god himself, by the mastery and slaughter of a bull.[20]

The sacrifice of the sacred bull, the *Tauroctony*, always appeared as the centre of the Mithraic religion. In Vienna Himmler had seen a Roman relief from Aquilia, showing Mithras in a cave, killing the bull, and looking over his shoulder at the figure of Sol, the sun, in the sky above. The blood of sacrifice was being offered to the sun, and through it Mithras, the dark god, would gain equality with *Sol Invictus*, the unconquered sun. After the sacrifice, according to the legends, the bull would be skinned, and Mithras and Sol would banquet together on its hide.

This was Himmler's dream. The *Fuhrer* himself was Sol, indomitable like the sun. Himmler could see him now, standing on the terrace of the *Berghof*, his aquiline profile sharp against the blue Bavarian sky, clothed like an eagle in the rays of the sun. Once the initiation was complete, he, Himmler would emerge from a sacred subterranean darkness, illuminated only by the invisible beams of the *Schwarze Sonne*, the black sun, and join the *Fuhrer* in a mystic brotherhood on the astral plane, completing the fraternal union of Sol and Mithras. Thus linked together, hand in hand, *syndexioi*, between them they would command unprecedented and unconquerable power.

Himmler slipped a watch out of the pocket of his black *Allgemeine* uniform, and glanced at its face. The watch was the Junghans model, specially designed and engraved for Hitler's 47th birthday on 20 April 1936, bearing the eagle and swastika on the reverse, and linked by a chain to a medallion of the Fuhrer's head.[21] One week to the Solstice. He must prepare.

5

On the night of 20th June 1942, Heinrich Himmler had a dream.

He had spent much time exploring the Smithfield area of London, believing it to be in some ways the true heart of the city, one of the chief wellsprings of the nation's blood. From earliest times English men and women had gathered on the 'smooth field' to trade livestock, to slaughter animals for food, and to eat and drink and dance in boisterous popular festivities such as the annual Bartholomew Fair. Smithfield had become the premier site for public executions, a custom Himmler had enthusiastically revived, giving orders for looters and thieves, dissidents and deviants to be summarily shot against the wall of the hospital, the very spot where William Wallace had bled, where Wat Tyler had been struck down, where Christian martyrs of every denomination had been boiled and burned. Over the centuries the soil under Smithfield had been enriched and fertilised with the dung and urine of beasts, with the blood of animals and humans.

Though there was much bomb damage in the surrounding area, the beautiful Victorian meat-market building still stood. On the east side Himmler had hoped to find traces of the old Priory of the Knights Hospitaller, the crusader cousins of the Templars and the Teutonic

Knights, but hardly anything had been left after the cruel ravages of the Peasants' Revolt. He requisitioned the great hospital of St Bartholomew, establishing in the private wing exclusive medical services for the SS, general wards for the British people, and research laboratories for experiments in eugenics and racial purification. He ordered the Church to be temporarily closed, and dispatched an expedition to Rome to recover the skin of St Bartholomew. He believed that the legend of the flayed saint had been appropriated from a pagan source, and that Bartholomew was in fact an Aryan animal god. Once the skin was recovered the Church could be re-dedicated as a pagan temple. The Old Bailey was commandeered for the distribution of National Socialist justice, and public executions were once again conducted on the site of old Newgate.

In his dream, Smithfield was empty of people, the broad market square strangely vacant and quiet. At its centre was an empty catafalque, draped in black silk.[22] He heard a sound of solemn music, a low Wagnerian pulse of horns, a beating of muffled drums, keeping the rhythm of a funeral march. A squadron of SS officers slowly and gracefully goose-stepped their way from the direction of the church, and spread out to encircle the catafalque, followed by a procession of soldiers carrying banners, and lastly by an open black coffin borne on a gun carriage. In his dream Himmler craned his neck to observe who was in the coffin, but he could not see. The soft mournful plangency of the music expanded with a rising arpeggio of bass strings: Siegfried's funeral march from *Gotterdamerung*. In keeping with its rhythm, the coffin was lifted onto the shoulders of six tall SS officers, and lowered gently onto the bier.

Hundreds of mourners filed past, right arms extended in salute. Women laid wreaths, or threw white flowers onto the catafalque. Children cried.

He saw the handsome Karl Wolf, his own Chief of Personal Staff *Reichsfuhrer-SS,* come forward and stand at the head of the coffin to deliver the eulogy. 'The death of this martyr will remind all Germans that Britain is a Reich domain, and will remain so for ever'.

They were adapted from the very words Himmler had spoken at Heydrich's funeral in Prague.[23] But who was in the casket? He craned to see.

Suddenly in the dream he could look down, as if floating in the air above the bier. The corpse in the coffin was dressed in full SS uniform: highly-polished black leather riding boots, black flared knee-breeches,

Allgemeine tunic and visored cap. The sun glinted on the *Totenkopf*[24] badge, and on the silver honour ring on the finger of one of the white, clasped hands. And the face … the face was unmistakable. His spirit quailed. The face of one who had died in pain. Thin lips puckered together; small eyes sunk deeply into their sockets behind round, rimless spectacles; a scrubby moustache under the finely-chiselled nose.[25]

It was his own face. This was Himmler's funeral. He stared wildly, and with disbelief, around the square. The SS guards had vanished, their places taken by a crowd of local people, still emerging from the surrounding buildings, gathering in a circle around the bier. There were butchers from the market, in their white caps and blood-stained aprons, long knives and sharp cleavers in their hands. There were doctors and nurses from the hospital, in their dark suits and white uniforms. There were priests from the church, in long black cassocks and white surplices. There were lawyers from the Old Bailey, in their gowns and powdered wigs. He could see no pity, only a kind of grim satisfaction, on their pale faces. Behind these figures he thought he could see, tremulous in the heat-driven air, prisoners, some wearing handcuffs and leg irons, seemingly released from the long-demolished prison, and spectral figures in chain mail and surcoats, ghosts of the old Knights of St John, coming from the ruins of the Clerkenwell Priory. All around there was a terrible loud bellowing, as of beasts brought to the slaughter.

As he stared down in horror, ignited flames began to lap upwards around the sides of the coffin, and black smoke plumed into the air. The flames flickered and forked, catching the silk drapery, flaring swiftly and hungrily through the dry wood of the casket. The cadaver's head was haloed in fire. The music reached a climax: an immensely loud stentorian clamour of brass and percussion to hymn the hero's burning.

But Himmler was no Siegfried, and there was no Brunnhilde to ride her horse into the fire and join her husband in death. His disembodied spirit was suddenly incarnated again, this time fused with the corpse in the coffin. Helplessly he watched the flames flare around his boots, leap up his body, blister his skin and burn through to his entrails. Hopelessly he endured the agony of imaginary immolation.

And then he woke, sweating and gasping for breath, leapt from his bed and flung wide the curtains to assure himself he was back in the real world. A nightmare. Thank the gods. A symptom of the fear he must overcome. No matter: soon he would be beyond fear. Tonight was the night of his ascension, when he and Mithras would at last become one.

6

'Where are you?'[26]
  'I am here'.
  'Is it day or night?'
  'Night'.
Himmler stood before the altar of Mithras, facing a man in priestly garb, and wearing a ritual mask. A softly-beaten drum kept time. They were performing the litany of initiation, as reconstructed from a fragmentary Egyptian papyrus. Himmler himself was dressed in the short tunic, leggings and Phrygian cap common in representations of Mithras. Around one shoulder he wore a red linen sash with four dangling tassels.

The temple was bright, hot, full of sweating bodies. Thirty of Himmler's elite SS sat on the benches, stripped to the waist, wearing only their black *Allgemeine* trousers, finishing wooden bowls of food, and draining beakers of strong red wine. Finely-muscled torsos gleamed in the flaring torchlight. Two torch-bearers stood alongside the leader as he faced the priest and solemnly repeated the words of initiation. Behind the priest the *Tauroctony* glowed and flickered with a mystic physical energy.

  'Is the night black?
  'The night is black'.
  'You are the Crow. Are you prepared?'
  'I am prepared'.
  'You are the Bridegroom. Do you have courage?'
  'I have courage'.
  'You are the Soldier. Where is your courage?'
  'In the Leonteion'.
  'You are the Lion. Do you wear the cap?'
  'I wear the cap'.
  'You are the Persian. Have you received the fiery ones?'
  'I have'.
  'You are the Sun-runner. Where do you dwell?'
  'In a pit'.

'It is good. Who made you all these things?'

'The Father'.

'Who is the Father?'

'The Maker of All Things'.

'Are you girded in the red linen with the four tassels? Have you drunk of the sacred drink, and eaten of the sacred food? Are you ready to assume the mantle of the Father, the Maker of All Things?'

'I am ready'.

The priest turned around and made obeisance to the icon of Mithras, sprinkling the stone tablet with a libation of wine. The torch-bearers held their blazing brands aloft to illuminate the altar. The worshippers on the benches were hushed in a silence of expectation.

'Bring in the bull'.

All eyes turned to the door of the Mithraeum. Two muscled officers came first, holding the ends of iron chains. Behind them, reluctant, powerful legs pushing backwards against the ground, came a magnificent black bull, its immense polished horns spreading outwards in a long flat arc. The chains encircled its neck and ran along its ribs. Two more strong men brought up the rear, hauling on the chains to guide the huge animal into place. There was scarcely room in the narrow temple for its massive withers and great barrel flanks. The beast was uneasy, a foam of sweat coating its black dewlap, great eyes rolling in its head. Nervously it tossed its horns from side to side, scattering some of the seated officers from their benches as they sought to avoid the deadly points.

Himmler stared the bull directly in the eyes, seeking to master it with his superior spirit. The animal flinched from his direct gaze, moaned quietly in fear, and shook the irksome chains that held it fast. The priest handed to Himmler a short sword similar to the Roman *gladius*, its blade sharpened to razor keenness. The bull kept its head low, avoiding the man's gaze, seeing him askance from the rolling eyes, hooves anxiously pawing the ground. He sensed danger, but did not know where it would come from. But he would be ready.

It would have been an easy matter to kill the bull from where Himmler stood, leaning over the boss and plunging the sword into its shoulder, severing the aorta, as a matador slides in his blade for the *estocada*. But he knew this would not satisfy the requirements of the ritual. Everything must be done as it was written, as it was once performed, here in this very temple some two centuries ago. Giving the horn a wide berth, Himmler moved warily around the bull's left flank, set his foot onto one of the chains, and hoisted himself onto the beast's back. The bull suddenly became quiet, sensing the man on his back. The muscles of his withers tensed, his head dropped low, and his eyes took on a cautious and crafty look.

Himmler threw back his head and uttered a long loud bellowing sound, straining his belly to excite the five senses, as prescribed in the Mithras Liturgy, bellowing until he was out of breath.[27] He felt the lightning bolts gathering behind his eyes, the stars ready to issue from his body. Soon the chthonic power of the bull would enter him, merge with the harnessed energies of light and air, and he would achieve *apathanatismos*.[28] He raised the sword in his right hand, point downwards, and thrust it deep into the bull's vitals.

But the bull had other ideas. Even as the sword sought his heart, in one deft movement he tilted his head to thrust the left horn upwards, and flicked the muscles of his withers, causing the man to jolt sideways, and slide helplessly onto the waiting point. The bull's horn passed easily into Himmler's abdomen and through his body, its point emerging from his back. For a moment the animal held him there, dandling him like a rag doll, and then with a contemptuous toss of the head, cast him off. Himmler fell face down, clutching in agony at the perforated rent in his body, through which his torn bowels began to protrude, and his life blood to pour. The bull fell to his knees, a long snuffling dying breath flaring out his great black nostrils.

There was nothing Himmler's comrades could do as they looked at his grey, pinched face, and the contorted stricken body lying beside the great collapsed bulk of the bull.[29] Their leader was fallen. Terrified, they fled from the temple.

7

It was the beginning of the end for the Nazi occupation of Britain. Himmler's death in the Mithraeum sparked a chain reaction in which the British resistance sprang to life, and German forces began to retreat towards the coast.

Himmler never did get the hero's funeral foreshadowed in his dream. When resistance fighters found his body in the Mithraeum, they just threw a blanket over him, and left him there.[30]

Interior Smithfield Market

TARIQ SHARMIN

PREFACE

This final story, wholly invented, concerns two Muslim brothers who work in their father's slaughtering business in North London, killing animals by *halal* ritual, and delivering meat to Smithfield. The younger brother Tariq is radicalised by his sibling Yusef, and given a key role in a terrorist plot to bomb Smithfield market.

A story of faith, loyalty, betrayal and revenge, the tale follows Tariq's progress from innocence to disenchantment and enlistment with ISIS in Syria. The method of the story is realistic, providing an authentic London Muslim social and cultural background, permeated by Islamic tradition and the influence of the Quran. The story prominently features the now notorious anti-Semitic mural in Brick Lane, made famous by Jeremy Corbyn's imprudent support of the artist.

In 2015 an ISIS cell in Israel was found practising beheading on animals. It would be easy to relate the widely-perceived cruelty of *halal* slaughter to the vicious atrocity of ritual beheadings, as published by ISIS in the notorious 'execution videos'. This story suggests that to the contrary, there is no necessary connection between the killing of animals for food, and the inhumanity of murdering defenceless captives. The focus of this story is on what happens in the human soul to render such inhumanity possible.

Of all the stories in this volume this one owes least to other sources, and most to unmediated lived experience, and to my own critical and imaginative work on terrorism, evidenced especially in my *Tales from Shakespeare: Creative Collisions* (Cambridge University Press, 2014), Part IV. Works underpinning that study include Sören Kierkegaard, *Fear and Trembling*, translated by Alistair Hannay (1843, London: Penguin, 2003); Jacques Derrida, *The Gift of Death*, translated by David Willis (Chicago: University of Chicago Press, 1995); Jessica Stern, *The Ultimate Terrorists*

(Cambridge, Mass.: Harvard University Press, 2001); Terry Eagleton, *Holy Terror* (Oxford: Oxford University Press, 2005); and in fiction John Updike, *Terrorist* (NY: Knopf, 2006) and Monica Ali, *Brick Lane* (London: Doubleday, 2003).

TARIQ SHARMIN

1

And Cain talked with Abel his brother: and it came to pass, when they were in the field, that Cain rose up against Abel his brother, and slew him. And the LORD said unto Cain, Where is Abel thy brother? And he said, I know not: Am I my brother's keeper? And he said, What hast thou done? the voice of thy brother's blood crieth unto me from the ground. (Genesis 4.8)

2

The conveyor belt was slow that morning, and kept stopping. Tariq was bored. The day was warm, and his fluorescent yellow waterproof heavy on his shoulders. So was the yellow helmet on his head, and the protective goggles over his eyes kept fogging so he could barely see. He badly wanted to slip out for a cigarette, but there was no question of leaving his post. At any minute the belt would start up again, and he would need to be there.

Further up the line stood his big brother Yusef, clad in exactly the same protective gear. Yusef was occupying himself honing the blade of his knife on a whetstone. Tariq didn't know whether Yusef ever did get bored, since he never showed it. His imperturbable self-possession seemed to indicate that he was always, and at all times, focused, alert, and at home inside his own skin. Tariq envied his elder brother's insouciance. He was almost the opposite in every way.

Suddenly there was a clanking and grinding of machinery, and the belt started up again. At first there was nothing on it, but Tariq poised himself in readiness. Then the first animal appeared around the corner, and cleared the dangling strips of thick plastic sheeting. It was a sheep, standing helplessly on the moving rubber, its eyes wide in terror, feet splayed apart to keep its balance. Tariq gave the beast no time to register his presence, but grabbed its neck in the crook of his left arm and pulled it close to his body. His left hand clamped over the animal's mouth, and pulled back its head to expose the neck.

Bismillaahi wallaahu 'Akbar.[1]

Bringing forward in his right hand the knife he had concealed behind his back, with a swift slicing cut, Tariq drew his sharp blade across the sheep's throat. Keenly, so as to sever the windpipe, jugular veins and carotid arteries. But gently, so as to avoid slitting the creature's spinal cord, and killing it prematurely. The sheep gagged and spluttered, its body kicking and heaving in pain and terror, and blood splashed messily from the wound in its neck.

Allaahumma minka wa laka.[2]

Tariq let the belt take the animal from him. Yusef grabbed the sheep's hind legs, and buckled them with the end of a chain attached to a hoist. Immediately the chain was drawn up and the sheep lifted clear of the conveyor belt, its body bucking and spinning, the half-severed head hanging slackly from the twisting neck, and the life-blood quickly ebbing away. No-one should touch the carcase during exsanguination. That would be *Haram.*[3]

Allaahumma taqabbal minnee.[4]

A clean kill. All must be done cleanly, for this is one of the practices of the Prophet (Peace and Blessings Upon Him). Tariq never thought to question the laws he had been taught, and the methods he was trained to use. The animal must reach him alive, and conscious, and capable of hearing the prayers. It must be dispatched by a single cut from a non-serrated knife. *Dabihah.*[5] 'Forbidden for you are carrion, and blood, and flesh of swine, and that which has been slaughtered while proclaiming the name of any other than God'.[6]

All this made perfect sense. Tariq knew that *Halal* slaughter was regarded by the *kafirun*[7] as excessively cruel, violent, the infliction of unnecessary pain. Yet it had been soberly and piously practised for thousands of years by the Jews, and according to his Imam, by the Christians too, before they took the wrong path, and turned their face away from God. What could be more holy than to sacrifice an animal in the name of God, the Compassionate, the Merciful, the Beneficent? (Though these attributes of God were not named in the ritual of slaughter, since it was deemed inappropriate to name the virtues of pity in combination with an act of violence). All things belong to Allah; the animal is a gift from Allah; the ceremony of *Dabibah* reconsecrates the gift back to the Creator from whose generosity it came. Its flesh is not taken selfishly, in greed or mere carnal appetite, but religiously, in the name of God. The Christians stunned their beasts before slaughter, but to a Muslim this was expressly forbidden, for you should never eat an animal that has been killed 'by a violent blow'.[8]

When the belt broke down again, it was near enough to finishing time for the two brothers to quit their bloody, sacramental work. Yusef tossed his knife casually into a corner, and headed for the showers. Tariq picked up his brother's blade as well as his own, knowing that the knives should be cleaned and sharpened before the next day's work, and left them in a sink in the corner.

By the time Tariq reached the showers, Yusef was already half invisible inside a cloud of steam. Tariq stripped off his bloody clothes, dropped them into a laundry basket, and slipped into the showers next to Yusef. The elder boy's broad back and muscular buttocks obtruded through the drifting plumes of steam. Tariq felt acutely conscious of his own more slender frame. If the elder brother was aware of how intimidated his sibling was by his superior bulk and strength, he clearly didn't care, but rather revelled in it, especially in these moments of fraternal proximity. Yusef turned towards Tariq and briskly soaped his circumcised penis, which was as thick as Tariq's wrist; then tossed over the soap and threw back his head to let the hot water stream down over his chest. I could never expose my throat in that way, Tariq thought, not even here in the safety of his father's factory, with his big brother here to protect him. He had seen too many bestial necks presented nakedly to the sacrificial knife. Yusef seemed to feel in himself a kind of invulnerability, and almost dared the universe to attack him, if only to prove his strength. Bring it on, his hard-muscled body seemed to say. Show me what you've got.

After showering the brothers found their day clothes in lockers that stood against the wall opposite the showers. They both dressed in the same way: crisply-laundered white shirts with long sleeves; smart black trousers, with black leather belts; polished black shoes. Side by side they left the building and picked up the family van from the car park. The vehicle was old, but kept spotlessly clean. Emblazoned on the side was the family crest: 'Sharmin Halal Meats'. Tariq drove, while Yusef smoked a cigarette and looked morosely out of the window. Something was preoccupying him. But Tariq knew better than to ask questions when his brother was in that gloomy frame of mind.

3

The slaughterhouse sat among the bleak industrial wastelands around the North Circular; but the boys lived in a block of flats in Camden Road. Originally a council block, most of the flats were now privately owned, with a few still dedicated to social housing. These latter were the most run-down and disreputable, with their unmended broken windows, and bedsteads on the balconies; but the whole block was characterised by a systematic neglect. The gate was propped open against the meagre privet hedge, as its hinges had long since rusted and broken. The doors into the lobby displayed blistered and peeling paint. The door pushed open onto an untidy pile of junk mail, circulars, and letters to tenants who were long gone, or had never existed in the first place: 'Urgent'; 'Final Demand'. The senders' addresses were those of debt collection firms, bailiffs, DWP, DVLA. The boys filed up the echoing concrete stairs to the third floor, and let themselves into their father's flat.

The dark entrance hall was almost blocked with stuff: boxes, cans, plastic tubs of rice, shopping trolleys, bicycle wheels, shoes, tins of paint, sacks of flour, old newspapers. It was a two-bedroomed flat. The brothers had their own rooms at the back, while their father slept on a legless bed in the living room. Each of the two bedrooms was neat, tidy, almost ascetic in appearance. White walls, single bedsteads, a wardrobe, a dressing table with mirror. No posters on the walls, no apparatus for playing music, no books, other than, on each dressing-table, a blue-and-gold copy of the Noble Qu'ran. Both bedrooms spoke of a rigorously simple life, as uncluttered by material possessions as the life of a Bangladeshi villager, or the cell of a prisoner serving life for some criminal or political offence. The rest of the flat – kitchen, living-room, hall – was the chaotic domain of their father, who had mentally retired to his village in the foothills of Rangpur, and had forgotten how to navigate through the detritus of modern western living.

Mahmoud Sharmin had come to Britain many years before with his younger brother, and established a butchering business selling Halal meat in Smithfield Market. The firm prospered, and eventually they were able to buy their own slaughterhouse, where the sons now worked. Once the family was established in London, Mahmoud summoned a wife from his home village, the young daughter of a neighbour whom he had known as a baby. She had grown into a pretty, sweet girl, who expected very little of life. Against all odds, the arranged marriage proved to be a marriage made in heaven. The couple had never seen one another before they wed, but afterwards, such was their devotion, they saw little else apart from one another. Dutifully she delivered him two sons. When his wife died of breast cancer, a light went out in the old man's eyes. He became reclusive, uncommunicative, spending most of his time in the living-room of the flat, watching television with the sound turned off, or peering through thick spectacles in the dim light at the Bangladeshi newspapers. He cooked simple meals for the boys when they returned from work, and exchanged a few words with them, but would then retreat into his den, and leave them to their own devices.

Tonight the old man met them with a pale smile, and put their food on the kitchen table: spicy chicken, boiled rice, parathas. They were an incongruous group: the old man with straggly grey beard, in dirty floor-length white jubba and embroidered jali hat; and the two handsome, clean-cut boys in their smart western clothes. After a while Mahmoud took a bowl of rice into the living room and settled down in front of the silent TV.

It was a Saturday night. After their evening meal the boys would usually wander along the canal to Camden Lock, and meet up with a group of their compatriots. Together they would walk around the streets and estates, smoking cigarettes, looking at girls, or kicking a football around in an empty school playground. There was a certain aimlessness to these activities, and at school Tariq had found himself envying the Saturday nights of his white school-fellows, who would look forward all week with growing excitement to a night of drunkenness and sex. This troubled him a little, but after a while there were no more white kids at the school, so the temptations of alterity were no longer there.

This night was destined to be different.

'Come on', said Yusef, wiping his plate clean with a piece of bread. 'We've got an appointment'.

Together they walked down the road. The fabric shops were closing, the grocers still optimistically staying open. The air was thick with the spices of Indian cooking: hot oil, turmeric, garlic. Tariq paused for a minute by a huge mural that decorated a blank brick wall.[9] He had often studied it, and rarely passed without another admiring glance. Seated in a semi-circle, staring towards the viewer, were six figures, with a large flat board spread before them. The square surface was marked out as a kind of board game, at its centre a pile of green American dollars. Among the counters were miniatures of the Statue of Liberty, the Eiffel Tower, the Gherkin, monuments of western capitalism.

A global game of money and power. The board rested on the painfully bent backs of a circle of bald, brown-skinned men; and the faces of the players displayed the enlarged noses, grey beards and heavy moustaches of cartoon Jews. Above them the artist had depicted, in lurid colours, images of industry: chimneys and cooling-towers venting black smoke, a sky lit by the orange glow of blast-furnaces. Below them, metal cog-wheels intersected to symbolise the global economic system, driven by greed and racial hatred, run over the backs of the prostrate brown masses.

On either side appeared emblems of resistance. 'The New World Order is the Enemy of Humanity' proclaimed a slogan on a placard held up by a shouting figure in paramilitary fatigues, his right hand raised in a clenched fist salute. On the other side was the face of an oriental woman, a dark-eyed and heavy-lipped beauty, holding a baby whose skinny little arm was also raised in clenched defiance. Gazing down at this scene from above was the great all-seeing eye, set in the apex of a pyramid, Tariq had seen on US dollars: the eye of global surveillance.

The New World Order. The godless, materialistic West, allied with the Jews, playing games of money and power on the bent backs of the brown-skinned masses. Tariq took a parting glance at the baby. Weak, vulnerable, yet charged with an indomitable spirit. Suckled on the milk of *jihad;* born into resistance. Then he ran to catch up with his brother, who was already further down the street.

4

They reached the community centre, a low flat building set inside what had once been a municipal park. The playground apparatus had long since been removed, leaving gaping cracks and fissures in the tarmac. Skateboarders had commandeered a concrete basin at the edge of the car-park, from which rose whoops and cries and the running scrape of wheels. The lights were on in the building.

'So where are we going?' Tariq asked his brother.

'A meeting', Yusef replied shortly. 'You'll see'.

The doors to the meeting room were open, and the room already crowded. All of the occupants were men, most under twenty-five. There were not enough seats, so many were already sitting on the floor. Tariq and Yusef stood at the back, and leaned against the wall. Scanning the room, Tariq caught sight of his uncle Sami, who had managed the Halal meat stall in Smithfield Market since their father's retirement, sitting in the front row.

Three men came onto the stage, all dressed in startlingly white jubbas. One introduced the speaker, who stepped forward and took command of the microphone. He was a man of middle age, with a broad face, large dark eyes and a thick grey beard that moved as he spoke. He opened with a few words of Arabic that Tariq barely understood. Some of the young men assumed he was offering prayers, and began to bow their heads and mutter Arabic words under their breath. Then the speaker moved into English, and the atmosphere in the room grew very still.

'My brothers', he began, 'we live in dangerous times. A new law has been passed: the Anti-Terrorism, Crime and Security Act. This law allows the police, and the security services, to arrest anyone without charge. This Act is targeted at Muslims. What happened to individual liberty, equality before the law, Habeas Corpus? For them, brothers, perhaps, but not for us. Have they not broken their so-called covenant of security?'

The preacher glared around the room, projecting his indignation, inviting his listeners to share it with him. 'And now we have the Prevent strategy. The Muslim Council of Britain sent a message to a thousand mosques, demanding that the Imams should help the government to combat terrorism. They want us to be traitors to our own people, or own faith. What should we do? Report to the police any brother who speaks to us of jihad? Denounce a brother who utters words of support for Osama? Betray any brother who urges our young men to travel abroad, and fight the crusaders who tread on our holy grounds in Iraq, or Afghanistan? Mosques are no longer houses of sanctity. They have become call centres for the British secret police. Have they not broken their so-called covenant of security?'

'They force us to take a stand. Do you think we can continue in this anarchy without putting up any resistance? The British government is sitting on a bomb. But brothers, we have the detonator!'

The audience had become possessed with a restless excitement. Heads nodded, lips moved in approbation, hands were raised in *Takbir*.[10] *'Allahu Akbar'*.

The preacher was now confident of his hold over the room. 'Everything changed with the nineteen magnificent terrorists of 9/11', he thundered. *'Allahu Akbar'*, cried the audience in response. 'In the words of our late brother Abu Musab Al-Zaqarwi: if we sting the pig from many different directions, it will die. Muslims in Britain have two choices. We can compromise, or we can follow the true Islam. For too long, we have followed the White House. It's time to follow the Black House of Islam'.

After the speech most of the young men began to file out, some of them looking nervously around as if concerned that some of their companions might be undercover police. Tariq and Yusef walked down to the front to speak to their uncle Sami, but Sami was already deep in conversation with the preacher himself. The boys stood back respectfully and waited. Catching sight of them, Sami introduced them proudly to the preacher.

'My nephews', he said. 'Sons of my brother Mahmoud. Good boys. True sons of Islam'. Then he leaned closer to the preacher's ear and whispered something they could not hear. The preacher looked at the brothers with some curiosity and no little interest, and slowly nodded his head.

To Tariq's surprise Yusef asked him to go outside and wait for him. 'Why?' he asked. 'Business', said Yusef shortly. 'Go on. I won't be long'. So Tariq returned to the back of the hall, He glanced back to see the three men huddled together in close conversation, before leaving to stand outside in the gathering darkness.

5

For a while life proceeded as usual. The brothers went to work, and slaughtered sheep, goats and cattle. Each day they knelt and said their prayers at the five appointed times: *Fajr, Zuhr, Asr, Maghrib, Isha*.[11] After work they went home, ate their evening meal, and exchanged a few words with their father. On Fridays they attended the mosque.

The only variation to this uneventful pattern was that Yusef started to go out on his own in the evenings, leaving Tariq behind to watch the silent TV with their father. He did not tell the younger brother where he was going, or what he was doing. These mysterious disappearances of the elder sibling intensified a consciousness that had in any case been gradually growing in Tariq: that something different was going to happen.

Tariq had never really questioned the fundamentals of his life, since its scope and parameters had been so clearly and manifestly defined. At school he had been taught little but Islam. The curriculum consisted of Islamic scholarship and religious teaching. History was the history of Islam. Science and mathematics were derived from the Holy Qu'ran. Geography was the geography of the Islamic world. There was no music or drama; no sex education; no comparative religion; no hint at all of any explanation of the world other than that embodied in the teachings of the Prophet (Peace and Blessings Upon Him).

Tariq lived his life in a kind of ethnic bubble, separated entirely from the society around him. He knew no white people, had no white friends, had virtually nothing to do with non-Muslims at all. His sense of separateness was reinforced by the xenophobia of his own community: by the continual messages he heard every day from family, school and mosque affirming the superiority of Islam, and the decadence of the West. Non-Muslims were the enemy, to be shunned, hated or even, in more extreme scenarios, destroyed. Tariq did not feel anything like hatred for the strangers he saw all around him. They were simply unreal to him, like so many thin white ghosts incongruously occupying the daylight. Some of the preachers who came to the mosque would depict them as animals, barely human, to be used if they remained docile, or slaughtered if they became dangerous.

So he had grown up to see himself, and to a lesser extent to feel himself, to be simply a good Muslim boy whose place in life was to obey his elders, to live cleanly and in accordance with the sacred teachings, and to put God above everything else. Good Muslim boys left school, got good jobs in the family business, and waited for God to choose a suitable bride. Tariq knew little about women. His school classes were segregated, and he was too self-conscious to associate with the gaggle of giggling, headscarved girls who admired him and tried to get him to talk to them. Somewhere among that crowd, with their pretty faces and long-lashed dark eyes, was his bride-to-be. But he felt no compunction to make her acquaintance before the appointed time.

Of late Tariq had sensed certain changes taking place somewhere within him which he did not understand, and would have found impossible to describe or talk about. The advice received from his elders – represented for him by teachers and religious leaders – was that at his age, young men began to experience carnal desires that had to be repressed until they could be satisfied in the legitimacy of the marriage bed. But that was not really what was troubling him.

For as long as he could remember Tariq had felt a very strong awareness of God within him. In every fibre of his being, in his movements and his thoughts, God was present. *Surely I am very near.*[12] He saw God in the light of the sun as it rose over the roof of the slaughterhouse; in the leaves of the trees as they browned and reddened and slipped from their branches in autumn; in the snow that whitened the streets in winter. *Allah is the light of the heavens and the earth.*[13] And he felt God in his own body, giving him energy for the tasks of the day, guiding his hands in their work, and his feet in their path.

But there was one thought that he struggled with, and could not resolve: and that was what did God intend for him? Where did he fit into the divine plan? Surely there was something more in store for him than this simple routine of work and worship? Surely God wanted more from him than such a life could ever deliver?

He looked for advice from his elders, for wise counsel that would keep him on the straight path. But he heard little from his religious teachers but conventional piety and moral prohibition. From his father, who had become almost a psychological recluse, he acquired nothing of any value. And now his elder brother, the one he had always followed and emulated, was suddenly occupying himself somewhere else, leaving Tariq to while away the long evenings with nothing to do but talk to his father. Under these circumstances there grew inside the boy a kind of restlessness, a powerful energy that seemed to beat with a rhythm inimical to the familiar pulsing of his heart. It compelled him to get up, and go to his bedroom, and stand at the window looking out over the tiled roofs and blinking street lights of Camden. It was a want, a desire, a yearning. But for what? To do something, to be something, other. But who?

6

Every two weeks or so the boys had to make a delivery to Smithfield Market. The market opened at 3 am, so they prepared their deliveries around 5 am, while it was still dark outside. Usually they loaded up the van together, and Yusef drove in by himself, leaving Tariq in charge of the slaughterhouse. This time however Yusef indicated that Tariq was to make the delivery. The load consisted of only one carcase, that of a cow, which was trussed and tightly wrapped in polythene sheeting. Yusef had brought it round from the rear of the building, slung over his shoulder, and thrown it in the back of the van.

'Here you are, little brother', he said, tossing Yusef the car keys. 'Deliver this to Uncle Sami. It's your turn. Don't lose it. And don't smash the van up'. Then hands in his overall pockets, he sauntered back inside.

This was the first time Tariq had been entrusted with a delivery, and the thought of it gave him a quiet satisfaction. Perhaps this was the new road that was destined to open up in his life: greater responsibility, promotion, a higher status. Perhaps one day he would become a supervisor, a foreman, a manager even. He started the van and pulled carefully in between the headlights of the traffic flowing south.

Farringdon Road was blocked with buses, taxis, delivery vans and lorries. Angry drivers honked their horns. The journey took a while. At last he reached Smithfield Market and backed up at the rear. Shouldering the carcase, he entered the small delivery bay and used the hydraulic hoist to sling the carcase over a hook hanging down from the track above. Immediately the mechanism pulled and swung the carcase away from him and into the market hall. From below he followed its progress to the cutting room behind his Uncle Sami's Halal Meat stall. Having seen it safely inside, he made his way through the throng of white-overalled and white-hatted butchers into the great Victorian hall. Above him he could see the colourful cast-iron struts, purple and green, and the ornate blue and gilded clock hanging pendant from the market's cast-iron roof. Sami was standing at the back of his stall, deep in conversation with two men Tariq had never seen before. They did not look like butchers. Both had close-cropped hair and square beards that gave them an aggressive look. They looked very much alike, as though they were brothers, though one had a full-lipped, feminine mouth, while the lips of the other were thin and cruel. Both had dark, deep-set eyes. Both wore nondescript black clothes that looked incongruous among the universal white overalls of the butchers and delivery men.

Sami was laughing at something one of the men had said. When Tariq arrived at the stall, all three stopped talking and turned to look at him. His uncle's face lit up with more than his usual affection, even with something that looked like pride. The two men stared at him in curiosity, and on their faces a shadow of what might have been contempt. Sami took the carcase from Tariq and dropped it onto the counter, thanked him with unnecessary profusion, and indicated that he should leave. As Tariq walked away he glanced back to see his uncle shoulder the meat, and take it into the little office at the back of the stall. The two men followed.

Puzzled and uneasy, Tariq made his way back to the car park. The van was parked up close to the rear of Sami's cutting-room. Unable to repress his curiosity, Tariq stepped up onto the platform of a forklift truck left empty by the wall, and hauled himself up to the green-and-purple steel bars over the window. Within the bars, panes of filthy glass threw a little obscure light onto the shadows of the pavement. Tariq pressed his forehead against the bars, and peeped in.

The three men were standing around a table on which lay the carcase he had delivered. The meat had been unwrapped from its polythene sheeting. Next to it on the table lay a square package, also wrapped in plastic. The covering was stained with blood; the package must have been hidden inside the dead cow. Tariq watched as one of the two men slit open the plastic wrapping with a sharp knife. Inside it Tariq could see thick wads of blue banknotes, bound about with red wrappers. He strained to hear the conversation, but could not make out the words. Then one of the men happened to glance towards the window, and Tariq flinched away to avoid detection. Quickly he slipped back to the van, and drove onto the Farringdon Road.

The journey back was quicker. He was driving against the rush-hour traffic. As he coasted over the Brent Cross Flyover, on his right the rising sun began to break free of its integument of cloud. The road before him began to lighten, but his own thoughts remained cloudy, fogged. Reduced visibility. The realisation that had struck him with the cutting force of a meat cleaver, was that *Yusef had deceived him*. His older brother had not wanted him to know about the money. Why not? What was it for? He had been chosen to make the delivery not, after all, as a privilege, but to balance onto him the burden of risk. Suppose the police had stopped the van and looked inside the carcase? Suppose a health inspector had opened it up to examine the meat? How would he have explained the cash? And above all: why had Yusef not taken him into his confidence?

Tariq resolved to say nothing to Yusef. No-one had seen him peering through the window. As far as anyone else was concerned, he had delivered a carcase to Smithfield. The sharply painful knowledge that he had not only been put in harm's way by the brother who should protect him, but that Yusef had inserted between them a keen sword of mistrust, settled on his heart as a red glow of anger. Secrecy, concealment, betrayal? Two could play at that game.

7

So nothing was said about the mysterious shipment of cash, and business continued as usual. Tariq sensed that Yusef was aware of his suspicions, but it was not in the older brother's character to display concern about another's feelings. And had their relationship ever, Tariq reflected, consisted of intimacy, heart-to-heart, the sharing of confidence? Perhaps after all what held them together was merely the bond of family, community, religion. Perhaps the violent fraternity of animal slaughter was all they truly had in common.

Then one evening as they drove home from work, to Tariq's surprise, Yusef suddenly broke the covenant of silence between them.

'There's someone I want you to meet tonight', he said, looking out of the car window at the dreary procession of flat-roofed warehouses, filling-stations, motor repair workshops that slipped past them along the edge of the grey road. 'You've been kept in the dark, bruv. I know. It's time to switch the light on'.

Later that evening Yusef led the way down an unfamiliar street of Victorian terraced houses, each fronted by a small garden where nothing grew. Concrete steps led down to a basement flat. Yusef rang the bell, and though there was no sound from within the flat, the door opened to admit them.

The brothers entered a dark little room off the hallway. The curtains were drawn, the room lit by an unshaded light-bulb that dangled from a dusty flex. Tariq immediately recognised the grey-bearded preacher from the meeting he had attended a month or so back, sitting on a low settee. Two other men were also in the room, but both remained in the shadows outside the harsh circle of light.

'Welcome, welcome, my son', the preacher said to Tariq. 'You are most welcome'.

Yusef gestured for Tariq to sit down on the floor. The boy squatted cross-legged in front of the preacher, who looked at him for a long time in a kind of rapture from eyes of an unearthly luminosity. Tariq thought he could almost see a halo around the man's head, but it was probably just a trick of the light. A holy man.

'Your brother has told me all about you. That you are a good Muslim, pious and obedient. Do you wish to undertake a task on behalf of Allah?'

So the moment was come! Light hit him with a blinding certainty, like a blow to the head. This was the destiny of his premonitions, the summons he had awaited. A task on behalf of Allah.

Under pressure of this epiphany, he was silent. The preacher glanced up at Yusef, who shrugged slightly. Tariq could feel the restless presence of the other two men, stirring in the darkness.

'What would you do for God?' asked the preacher.

'I would do anything'.

'Would you be prepared to risk your life to destroy unbelievers?'

This time Tariq knew there could be no hesitation. It was the word he had felt, but never brought to mind.

'Yes sir. I would risk my life for Allah'.

'Good, good', said the preacher, with an air of relief. 'We have a plan ready for execution. A scheme that will strike a heavy blow against the infidel. A blow that will clear a space for God to enter. All we need, to bring it to fulfilment, is a hero prepared to risk his life for the *Ummah*'.[14]

Tariq bowed his head. The honour was almost too great for him to bear. Until this moment life had appeared to him as a dark road, obscured by curling fog, leading towards the unknown. Now suddenly his life had shape, and form, and meaning. He would become a hero of the people, a great warrior like the Prophet himself. Then one day, if God willed it, his life would end, in a blaze of glory, and he would wake up in Paradise.

He would accept it. He must accept it. He remembered the words of Ishmael in the Holy Quran, when Abraham his father, confounded by the message of the angel, asked him what they should do. 'Oh my father! Do that which you are commanded. *Insha Allah* you shall find me *As-Sabirun'*.[15]

God spared Ishmael, and a ram was burned in his stead. May it please God, I will be obedient.

8

Everything was ready. Yusef had gone over it all with him, time and time again. The drums of explosive were loaded in the back of a hired vehicle exactly like their delivery van, and covered over with a blood-stained plastic sheet. The drums were wired up to a detonator under the driver's seat. Connected to the detonator was a small electronic device wirelessly linked to a mobile phone.

Tariq knew his instructions by heart. Drive to Smithfield. Park up as close to the Market Hall as you can get. The timing must be exact: three minutes after 7 am. The hall would be filled with workers and with visitors on guided tours. The blast would bring the market hall down on their unbelieving heads.

Drive to Smithfield. Park up as close to the market hall as you can get. Leave the van and walk away, slowly. Don't get out of the van before 7 am. Keep the mobile in your pocket, your hand on it at all times. When you're clear, the other side of the square, three minutes, press the SEND button. Don't look back. Just keep walking. Jump on the tube. Farringdon Station. Circle Line. Don't look at anybody. Keep your face down. Change at Gloucester Road. Piccadilly Line. Get to the airport. Check in. No baggage. Turkish Airlines: Istanbul. Someone will meet you there.

God demands a sacrifice. You are his beloved son. Smithfield will fall and burn, and the smoke of sacrifice will rise to heaven from the carcases of beasts and the bodies of unbelievers. Sting the pig from many different directions, and it will die.

'You OK, with this, bruv? Really?' Yusef put his hands on Tariq's shoulders, and looked into his eyes.

'What's the worst that can happen?' said Tariq with assumed cheerfulness. 'If I go up with it, I'll be a martyr. Allah will embrace me in the garden of Paradise'.

'That's not going to happen. You're too young to be a martyr. I want my little brother in one piece. Got your passport?' Yusef was more nervous than he was. 'Got the money? Don't forget: Istanbul. When you get there, they'll take you over the border into Syria. A holiday in the sun. You'll be in Paradise all right. Leaving us here to pick up the pieces '.

The moment had arrived. It was time to leave. As Tariq opened the van door, Yusef threw his arms around him and held him for a few moments. Clung to him. But Tariq did not want this embrace. Not now, when his body and mind were clean and clear, separate, prepared. Gently he disengaged himself.

'Don't worry', he said to Yusef, 'Everything's going to be all right'.

As he pulled the van gingerly off the forecourt he realised that after this, he would be the younger brother only in years. In terms of experience and achievement, he would have left Yusef a long way behind. Perhaps his brother was saying goodbye to that already superseded state of innocence

Everything went according to plan. He drove slowly and carefully, taking corners with extreme caution so as not to shift the load. He could feel sweat beading inside his leather gloves as they clamped tightly on the steering wheel. There was very little traffic that day, so he arrived at Smithfield too early. He parked up right next to the wall of the building. It was only 6.30. What should he do? Sit in the van next to a huge payload of explosives? Someone would notice him. Ask questions. Maybe even the police. He should get out and walk around a bit, then come back. Gently he eased himself out of the driver's seat and got out. Closed the van door as softly as he could. Felt in his pocket for the mobile. It was there.

There was the usual hubbub of activity around the market. Everyone was too busy to notice him. He strolled around to the front of the hall, watching the delivery men carrying carcases of beasts. He felt a discomfort in his bladder, and realised he need the toilet. Inside he entered a cubicle and sat down to piss. 6.35. He took the phone out of his pocket and examined it. Carefully.

But he should check that the phone was on. He looked at it. His heart stopped. It showed no sign of life. He pressed the power button. Nothing. What was the matter with it? How could he touch off a bomb with a phone that had gone dead? 6.40. There was still time. He took off his gloves and slid open the battery compartment.

It was empty.

The phone's battery had been removed. It could never have worked. Now what? He had no fall-back instructions. He'd better get back to the van and see if he could think of anything.

6.45. The van sat quietly where he had left it. Tariq looked around carefully. No-one was looking. He opened the driver's door, and tipped back the seat. There was the detonator, surrounded by coils of wire. It looked the same as it had when Yusef had shown it to him yesterday. But there was a difference.

Alongside the detonator was a small digital clock, with two displays, one moving, one static. The moving numbers were ticking down, second by second. 6.47. The static display read: 6.58.

The bomb was equipped with a timer device. Set to explode at 6.58. Timed to coincide exactly with the van's being positioned next to the market. And to involve Tariq himself in the common conflagration.

He had been entrusted with nothing. Given a dead cell phone to touch off a bomb that would have already destroyed him. Told to stay in the van until 7 pm, a time he was never destined to see. Used, exploited, betrayed. An unwilling suicide bomber. In a violent spurt of anger, he grabbed the timing device, and tore it way from the detonator.

Then realising what he had done, he shut his eyes tight against the inevitable apocalyptic blast. In a split second he would step off the tarmac and enter heaven. There would be a blinding light, a monstrous noise, a shrieking whirlwind of agony. And then peace.

But nothing happened. He opened his eyes. The detonator sat there quietly, inactive, defused. Looking up, he saw a man in butcher's overalls watching him from a window inside the market. It was over. He had failed, and was detected. Nothing for it but to run. Quickly he stood up, shut the van door, walked across the car park and mingled with the crowds on Farringdon Road.

9

The room was stiflingly hot. The evenings were growing chilly, and the old man had started to turn on his gas fire. Yusef could not stop his eyes from closing, his chin from dropping onto his chest. Then something made him wake up and focus on the TV screen.

A desert. Men dressed in black, with masks over their faces: marching, pointing their Kalshnikovs, raising one finger in salute. A hot desert wind billowed their clothes, and fluttered the black flags streaming above their heads.

Then the video cut to show two men standing on top of a sand dune. One was on his knees, wearing a bright orange Guantanamo-style jumpsuit. His face, lowered, could not be seen. The other stood behind and above him. This was one of the soldiers seen in the previous sequence: black clothes, black scarf and mask. Only his eyes were visible. In his right hand he held a big butcher's knife.

The camera zoomed in on his face. He began to speak, in English, explaining that this prisoner was to be executed according to the laws of *Sharia*, and in retaliation for US airstrikes against *jihadi* positions in Syria. Then with a deft, experienced movement, he drew back the man's head, revealing a face of grey hopelessness, and drew his knife across the exposed throat.

God is great, he said; God is great. The executioner's eyes stared straight at the camera. Yusef knew them, as well as he knew his own face.

The eyes were full of hatred, of anger, of fanatical devotion. But there was something else in them too: hurt, despair, the anguish of betrayal. God is great.

'This is a message', he said, as the body of his victim slumped lifelessly at his feet, 'to the West. We are here. We will never surrender. And we are coming for you'.

Yusef stood up and switched off the TV.

10

And God sent forth a raven, which scratched the earth, to show him how he might conceal the nakedness of his brother's body. He cried out: 'Oh, woe is me! Am I then too weak to do what this raven did, and to conceal the nakedness of my brother's body?' And he was filled with remorse. (Quran, 5.31).

Rahere with St Bartholomew, Church of St Bartholomew the Less, Smithfield

POSTSCRIPT: ST BARTHOLOMEW

PREFACE

The Postscript imagines St Bartholomew telling his own story in an autobiographical memoir. It features a graphic description of flaying, and a legendary history of what happened to his remains. St Bartholomew tells of the monk Rahere who founded St Bartholomew's Hospital in the 12th century, following a life-changing vision of the saint; and introduces Smithfield, the site chosen for the foundation of Bart's, as his own place.

Bartholomew appears in the New Testament in the gospels of Matthew, Mark, Luke, and as a witness to the Ascension in the Acts of the Apostles. His story is told in Eusebius, *The Church History,* trans. Paul L. Maier (Grand Rapids: Kregel, 1999, 2007), Gregory of Tours, *Glory of the Martyrs,* trans. Raymond van Dam (Liverpool: Liverpool University Press, 1998), and Alban Butler, *Lives of the Saints, August,* rev. John Cumming (Tunbridge Wells: Burns and Oates, 1998). For Rahere and the founding of Bart's see E A Webb, 'The founder: To 1123', in *The Records of St. Bartholomew's Priory and St. Bartholomew the Great, West Smithfield: Volume 1* (Oxford: Oxford University Press, 1921), 37-55.

POSTSCRIPT: ST BARTHOLOMEW

Can you imagine what it feels like to be flayed alive?

The skin is the largest organ in the human body. It is embedded, attached, not like a coat that can just be shrugged off.

Before I was flayed I thought of the skin, if I thought of it at all, as an exterior integument, a kind of rind like the skin of an orange, which could be sliced and peeled off in neat identical segments, exposing the raw fruit beneath. If your skin burns, it comes away easily, like peeling paper from a wall. I have seen dead skin cells fall like snow from the heads of grave, white-haired old men.

But the human skin is not like the peel of an orange, or paper pasted to a wall. It must be cut away from the tissue it clings to, sundered by a sharp blade from its firm foundation in the flesh.

As a method of torture and prolonged execution, flaying is an ingenious invention. Remove any other major organ from the body, the heart, the lungs, the liver, the brain, and it dies immediately, becomes a cadaver. Slit the skin from a man's flesh, and he can survive, for hours, even days. Exposed, stripped, the body endures, to feel all the pain the harsh world can deliver. Think of it: every nerve cell screaming in agony at the merest touch of air, yet unable to shut down, incapable of death.

I was lucky. In my case the flaying was merely a prelude to my death by crucifixion. I was saved from further suffering by the greatest suffering of all.

I am able to tell you all this because I am now a saint in Heaven. I could also tell you what it is like to be a saint in Heaven, but that is not part of this story.

I was an apostle of Christ, one of the twelve. Not a prominent apostle such as Peter or John, whose names are household words, but a relatively obscure disciple who left no traces of himself, in word or deed, in the narratives of the Evangelists. Nothing I ever did or said seems to have been worthy of notation. They overlooked me.[1]

But in truth I served the Lord faithfully, to the very end and beyond. After He was taken from us, I travelled to India, and preached the gospel in the shade of beautiful heathen temples, or to eager, dark-eyed people squatting under a burning sun.[2] From there I journeyed into Asia Minor, and brought the word of the Lord to the people of Armenia. Polymius, the King himself, I converted to the faith. But his brother Astyges remained an obdurate pagan, and it was he who encompassed my death.[3]

You may have seen pictures of my execution, my hands trussed above my head, and slung from the branches of a tree, my tormentors making incision at the wrists, and stripping the skin downwards from my forearms. Pink tissue, red blood-vessels, fluttering strips of torn skin.[4]

But that is not how it was. For those who tortured and killed me, at Astyges' behest, were ordered to treat me exactly as a beast brought to the slaughter. I was hung upside down. Incision was made first around my ankles, then in straight lines down the skin of my calves and thighs.

You may have watched the skinning of dead cow, how the skinner with his keen blade slits the hide from the white muscle, at the same time pulling it away from the carcase. The beast is dead, and feels nothing.

Now imagine such sensations visited upon your own percipient body. The skin is cut away, each section requiring the probing of a keen knife to detach the tissue, while the slaughtermen tear the skin away from flesh. Every square inch an acre of agony. Slowly, laboriously, the whole covering of skin ripped down and finally pulled over my head, like the removal of a tight-fitting garment.

So there I was, the hanged man, dangling like a carcase in a butcher's shop. Suspended between life and death: injured beyond recovery, unable to die. What a relief it was, when those cruel pagans cut me down and nailed me, still upside down, to a cross. I followed the example of my Saviour, embraced the rough and knotted wood, and woke into the light of the Heavenly Kingdom.

And God said to Abraham, Abraham ; and he said, behold, here I am. Take thine only son, said the Lord, whom thou lovest, and sacrifice him upon the mountain.[5]

Abraham was obedient, even to the taking of his son's life. But the

Lord is merciful, and sent Abraham a ram, caught in a thicket by the horns, to offer up on the altar of sacrifice. No such mercy from my executioners, no such reprieve. What manner of man will pervert God's compassion, and offer up in sacrifice a man as though he were a brute beast? I was brought as a lamb to the slaughter, and as a sheep before his shearers is dumb.[6]

My earthly body now so much skin and bone, my remains were cast into the sea, drifted unwept upon the watery foam, and washed up on the shores of Sicily. From there they found their way to Rome, and are kept in a marble bath beneath the altar of my church, built over the temple of Aesculapius, god of healing, on the Tiber Island.[7]

There let them rest, for it is of another church I wish to speak. Centuries after my death, a man from England, Rahere, made a pilgrimage to Rome, and fell grievously ill. He prayed to me, I took pity on him, and offered him a vision of dread and sweetness. I took him up, and set him in a high place, and let him peer downwards into the unfathomed pit of his own soul, so cruel a downcast. Then I spoke to him, and put it into his mind that he should return home and build both a church and a hospital in my name.[8]

The site I chose for him was a flat plain in the suburbs of London, known as Smithfield (from 'Smooth-field'), where for as long as anyone can remember horses had been sold, and pigs and cattle slaughtered, and criminals put to death. Here beast were flayed, their hides ripped from their bodies, stripped of their bristles and tanned into leather. Here men and women were disembowelled, and quartered, and burnt to death for their crimes.

You may wonder how a saint in Heaven should be so well acquainted with the topography of mediaeval London. And more particularly why I should have chosen so foul a place, filled with the noises of men and animals dying, the stink of shit and offal, the pungent stench of tanning leather, the gutters running red with bright vermilion blood.

For an answer you must read the stories collected in this book. Or if you have no taste for reading, and prefer to see things with your own eyes, then go to Rome, and enter the Capella Sistina, and find my image painted by the great Buanarroti.[9] See me there, my head still bald from the flaying, my new body restored and whole, my skin draped across my arm like some old overcoat, the skinner's knife held in my hand.

Or go to the Church of St Bartholomew the Great in Smithfield, and see the wonderful statue of me made by artist Damien Hirst.[10] There I stand, flayed, my skin hanging in tatters from my arm. But covered all over with gleaming bright gold.

As you see. Smithfield. My place.

ENDNOTES

Introduction

1. Charles Dickens, *Great Expectations* (NY: Dover, 2001) 128.

2. Graham Swift, *Last Orders* (1996, London: Picador, 2010) 32.

1 William Wallace

1. *Documents Illustrative of Sir William Wallace, His Life and Times*, ed. Joseph Stevenson (London: Maitland Club, 1841) 192 (*my translations*).

2. There is no evidence that Wallace was wrapped in an ox-hide. The detail is appropriated from the execution of Simon Fraser in 1306. See Andrew Fisher, *William Wallace* (Edinburgh: Birlinn, 2007) 244.

3. Both the Earl of Surrey and Hugh de Cressingham were in positions of command at Stirling Bridge.

4. Sir Andrew Moray later died from his wounds.

5. Stevenson 192. *My translation.*

6. Stevenson 192. *My translation.*

7. Stevenson 191. *My translation.*

8. Stevenson 192-3. *My translation.*

9. Liturgy of the Mass from the 11th century *Use of Sarum*. From William Maskell, *The Ancient Liturgy of the Church of England According to the Uses of Sarum Bangor York and Hereford and the Modern Roman Liturgy*, 2nd edition (London: William Pickering, 1846) 56. *My translation.*

10. Stevenson 193. *My translation.*

2 Walter Tyler

1. See Juliet Barker, *England, Arise: the People, the King and the Great Revolt of 1381* (London: Little, Brown, 2014) 218.

2. Revelation 21.2.

3. Adapted from Thomas Walsingham. See David Preest (ed.) and James Gordon Clark (trans.), *The Chronica Majora of Thomas Walsingham* (London: Boydell and Brewer, 2005) 162.

4. Adapted from Froissart. See Geoffrey Brereton (ed. and trans.), *Jean Froissart: Chronicles* (London: Penguin Books, 1978) 212-13.

5. Froissart in Brereton 212-13. John Ball's famous cry for liberty - 'I exhort you to consider that now the time is come, appointed to us by God, in which ye may (if ye will) cast off the yoke of bondage, and recover liberty' - appears in the account of his 'When Adam delved' sermon.

6. R.B. Dobson, *The Peasants' Revolt of 1381* (London: Macmillan, 1970) 130-1.

7. Dobson 130.

8. Dobson 130 and 157.

9. Dobson 139, 142.

10. William Shakespeare, *King Richard II*, 1.1.198.

11. Dobson 161, 209.

12. From the *Anonimalle Chronicle*. Dobson 161.

13. The text is the letter issued by Richard to the men of Hertfordshire, and copied into Walsingham's *Chronica*. See Dobson 180-1.

14. See Barker 256.

15. Richard prayed at the shrine of Edward the Confessor before riding to Smithfield. The prayer is from a mediaeval Commemoration of St Michael the Archangel.

16. Dobson 186.

17. Dobson 164-5, 177.

18. Dobson 165-7, 179, 186, 196, 203-4, 207-8, 211.

19. William Shakespeare, *Henry IV, Part Two*, 3.1.31.

20. William Shakespeare, *King Richard II*, 2.4.18-22.

3 Anne Askew

1. Elaine V. Beilin (ed.), *The Examinations of Anne Askew* (Oxford: Oxford University Press, 1996) 183.

2. The wording is taken from John Foxe's commentary. See Beilin 192.

3. Beilin 121-3.

4. Beilin 93, 96.

5. Beilin 124.

6. This detail was added by Foxe to his 1570 edition. See Beilin *liv.*

7. Beilin 127.

8. Beilin 19.

9. Beilin 20.

10. Beilin 20.

11. Beilin 21.

12. Beilin 27.

13. Beilin 30.

14. Beilin 56.

15. Beilin 23 and 99.

16. Beilin 103-4, 99, 114.

17. Beilin 88-9.

18. Beilin 111.

19. Beilin 112.

20. Beilin 132.

21. Beilin 190-1.

22. Words attributed to Protestant martyr Hugh Latimer by John Foxe in his *Book of Martyrs* (1583 edition). 'Be of good comfort maister Ridley, and play the man: wee shall this day light such a candle by Gods grace in England, as (I trust) shall neuer be put out.' John Foxe, *Acts and Monuments of these Latter and Perilous Days* (London: John Day, 1583) 1770. Like Anne Askew, Latimer and Nicholas Ridley were burnt to death, for heresy, in Oxford on 16 October 1555.

23. Foxe in Beilin 191-2.

24. Foxe in Beilin 192.

25. Foxe in Beilin 192.

4 John Wilmot

1. See Mels F. van Driel, 'Physiology of Penile Erection: A Brief History of the Scientific Understanding up till the Eighties of the 20th Century', *Sexual Medicine* 3(4) (December 2015) 349-357.

2. An analogue to this story is *The Anatomist*, by Federico Andahazi, trans. Alberto Manguel (London: Doubleday, 1998), in which another Paduan doctor, Realdo Colombo, discovers the mysteries of the clitoris.

3. John Wilmot, 'On King Charles', in *Selected Works*, ed. Frank H. Ellis (London: Penguin, 1994, new edition 2004) 17.

4. Wilmot 17.

5. William Shakespeare, *Romeo and Juliet*, 2.4.82.

6. 'The Imperfect Enjoyment', Wilmot 15.

7. The character Dorimant in George Etherege's *The Man of Mode* is based on Rochester. 'I know he is a devil, but he has something of the angel yet undefaced in him'. *The Man of Mode*, ed. John Barnard (London: Bloomsbury, 2007), Act 2 scene 2, ll.15-16.

8. 'A Satyr against Mankind', Wilmot 46.

9. See Antonia Fraser, *King Charles II* (1979, London: Phoenix, 2002) 267-8, and Don Jordan and Michael Walsh, *The King's Bed: Sex, Power and the Court of Charles II* (2015, London: Abacus, 2016) 94. Charles had many children by his mistresses, but Catherine famously remained childless.

10. 'On King Charles', Wilmot 17.

11. 'The Imperfect Enjoyment', Wilmot 16.

12. 'Her face is not so exact as to be called a beauty', Charles told Clarendon, 'though her eyes are excellent good, and not anything in her face that in the least degree can shock one'. Quoted in Fraser 270.

13. 'The Imperfect Enjoyment', Wilmot 16.

14. Harvey's later work focused on reproduction in animals, and his last published work was *Exercitationes de Generatione Animalium* (1651). In the latter he mentions another work on sexual desire and selection: 'But of this elsewhere, in our tract of the *Love, Lust and act of Generation of Animals*, we shall treat at large'. See Geoffrey Keynes, *The Life of William Harvey* (Oxford: Clarendon Press, 1978) 358.

15. According to an anecdote by John Aubrey. See Keynes, *The Life* 287-8.

16. In 1645. Fraser 37-40.

17. Fraser 40.

18. The Grand Tour actually occurred in 1661, when Rochester was only fourteen. See Graham Greene, *Lord Rochester's Monkey* (London: Bodley Head, 1974) 33.

19. Harvey used the colloquial slang term 'yearde' for penis. The Latin here means 'A man's genitals'.

20. Aristotle's typology of causes: material, formal, efficient and final.

21. 'To penetrate the vagina'.

22. To the Greeks *'pneuma'* was both air and spirit. Galen taught that the circulatory system contained a mixture of blood and air.

23. 'To point out from the peculiarities of a particular body, the newly discovered [thing]'. Harvey used this phrase in one of his lectures to justify empirical research in anatomy.

24. Leonardo de Vinci noticed that the penis of a hanged man would contain a large amount of blood.

25. 'Erectile muscles of the penis'.

26. See below n. 27, and for Variolo n. 86.

27. 'Visitor's Book for English Travellers in Italy'. Rochester signed the Book on 26 October 1664. See James William Johnson, *A Profane Wit: The Life of John Wilmot, Earl of Rochester* (NY: University of Rochester Press, 2004) 54.

28. See Johnson 18

29. 'The humour of that time wrought so much upon him that he broke off his course of studies'. Gilbert Burnet, quoted in Greene 32.

30. The details are adapted from Andrew Balfour, *Letters written to a Friend, by the Learned and Judicious Sir Andrew Balfour, M. D., containing excellent Directions and Advices for Travelling thro' France and Italy ... Published from the Author's Original M.S.* (Edinburgh, 1700).

31. *De Omnibus Veneris Schematibus* (1524). See *I Modi: the sixteen pleasures. An erotic album of the Italian renaissance by Giulio Romano,* edited, translated from the Italian and with a commentary by Lynne Lawner (Northwestern University Press, 1988).

32. A predecessor of Harvey at Padua, Fallopio did experiments with a rudimentary prophylactic sheath made from a small linen cap drenched in a solution of salt and herbs, which he tested on 1100 men, none of whom contracted syphilis - as reported in his book *De Morbo Gallico* (1524). Balfour is ahead of his time here: 'Effective condoms, made from materials ranging from silk to animal intestines, would not become readily available until the early eighteenth century'. (Jordan and Walsh 117). Dr Condom is nothing more than a legend.

33. The book was Constantine Varolio, *Anatomiae sive de resolution corporis humani libri III* (Frankfurt: Joannes Wechel and Peter Fifcher, 1591).

34. A case that Harvey recalled having witnessed. See Keynes, *The Life* 32.

35. 'Horny Goat Weed'. An aphrodisiac herb that functions in much the same way as Viagra, though far less effectively. Under its Latin name *'Epimedium'* it features in Giacomo Antonio Cortuso, *L'Horto de Semplici di Padova* (Venice: Giralomo Porro, 1591), a list of plants kept in the Botanical garden of the University of Padua.

36. Rochester's posing as Dr Alexander Bendo is well authenticated. In the Advertisement he had circulated he claims to have been 'a famous Pathologist': 'The knowledge of these secrets I gathered in my travels abroad … in France and Italy'. See Greene 106-113, quotation 108.

37. Stage Direction beginning *Actus Secundus* in John Wilmot, *Sodom: The Quintessence of Debauchery* (1689, Locust Elm Press, 2005). Rochester's authorship of the farce has been disputed, though it is ascribed to him in the British Museum manuscript copy.

5 Tom Nero

1. 'The Legend of St Julien the Hospitaller', in Gustave Flaubert, *Three Tales,* trans. Arthur Macdowall (1924, NY: Dover Publications, 2004) 36.

2. See William Hogarth, *Gin Lane,* in Sean Shesgreen (ed.), *Engravings by Hogarth* (NY: Dover Publications, 1973) Plate 76.

3. See *Gin Lane*, Shesgreen Plate 76.

4. See Flaubert, *Three Tales* 37.

5. See Flaubert, *Three Tales* 39-40.

6. See Flaubert, *Three Tales* 40.

7. See Flaubert, *Three Tales* 42.

8. See Hogarth, *First Stage of Cruelty*, Shesgreen Plate 77.

9. See Hogarth, *First Stage of Cruelty*, Shesgreen Plate 77.

10. Matthew 25.40, via Flaubert, *Three Tales* 45.

11. Hogarth, *Second Stage of Cruelty*, Shesgreen Plate 78.

12. Adapted from Flaubert 52.

13. In my view the church tower represented in *Cruelty in Perfection* is that of

St Nicholas' Church, Chiswick, where Hogarth is buried. Shesgreen Plate 79.

14. See Hogarth, *Cruelty in Perfection*, Shesgreen Plate 79.

15. Drawn from Hogarth's engravings *Before and After*, Shesgreen Plates 37 and 38. In the second plate a book lies on the floor, the author Aristotle, the inscription reading '*Post coito omne animal triste est*', 'After intercourse every animal is sad'.

16. Ann's letter is exposed in the engraving *Cruelty in Perfection*, Shesgreen Plate 79.

17. See Hogarth, *The Reward of Cruelty*, Shesgreen Plate 80.

18. The skeleton of the executed highwayman James McLean stands on a niche high in the wall in the engraving.

19. See Hogarth, *The Reward of Cruelty*, Shesgreen Plate 80.

20. See Flaubert, *Three Tales* 61.

6 Sweeney Todd

1. See *The String of Pearls*, published as *Sweeney Todd: the Demon Barber of Fleet Street,* ed. Robert L. Mack (Oxford: Oxford University Press, 2007) 141. Hereafter cited as *The String of Pearls*.

2. *The String of Pearls* 3.

3. *The String of Pearls* 4-5.

4. *The String of Pearls* 3.

5. *The String of Pearls* 8.

6. *The String of Pearls* 7.

7. Details concerning the murder of Jane Goode by her husband Daniel are taken from the record in the National Archives, MEPO 3/45.

8. The 'Edgware Road Murder' actually took place in 1836. James Greenacre was tried at the Old Bailey and executed on 2 May 1837. See *The Whole Proceedings of the Queen's Commission of Oyer and Terminer and goal delivery for the City of London, etc., of the Central Criminal Court*, Sixth Session, 1837, 856-901.

9. Prostitutes Eliza Davies and Eliza Grimwood were murdered in 1837 and 1838 respectively. The killer or killers were never caught.

10. Yseult Bridges, *Two Studies in Crime: Studies of the Murders of Lord William Russell and Julia Wallace* (London: Macmillan, 1959), and Claire Harman, *Murder*

by the Book: a sensational chapter in Victorian Crime (London: Penguin, 2018).

11. Both Dickens and Thackeray witnessed Courvoisier's execution, which became the subject of Thackeray's famous essay 'On Going to see a Man Hanged' (See Fraser's Magazine 22 (July-December 1840) 150-8.

12. *The String of Pearls* 150-1. I have switched St Dunstan's Church in Fleet Street for St Bartholomew the Great in Smithfield.

13. *The String of Pearls* 42.

14. *The String of Pearls* 217.

15. *The String of Pearls* 30.

16. *The String of Pearls* 31.

17. Beadle Bamford is a prominent character in the Bond and Sondheim versions, not in *The String of Pearls*.

18. Keen anticipates the modern liberalisation of Sweeney Todd.

19. *The String of Pearls* 29.

20. *The String of Pearls* 8-9.

21. *The String of Pearls* 122-3.

22. *The String of Pearls* 151.

23. Details relate to the Church of St Bartholomew the Great in Smithfield.

24. *The String of Pearls* 274.

25. *The String of Pearls* 276.

26. *The String of Pearls* 96-7.

27. *The String of Pearls* 92-3, 174.

28. In *The String of Pearls* Mrs Lovett is poisoned by Todd (280) so the gruesome murder in my story is invention re-invented.

29. *The String of Pearls* 281.

30. 'Nothing human is alien to me'.

31. In *The String of Pearls* (142) Todd is described as '… some fiend in human shape, who had just completed the destruction of a human soul'.

7 Aaron Kosminski

1. See Philip Sugden, *The Complete History of Jack the Ripper* (1994, revised London: Robinson, 2002) 397-423.

2. Aaron Kosminski's Medical Record. Middlesex County Lunatic Asylum, Colney Hatch Register of Admissions, Males Volume no. 3. Admission no. 11,190. The admitting medical officer's name is given as Dr E Kouchin. In 1894 the real Kosminski was discharged from Colney Hatch and admitted to Leavesden Asylum in Hertfordshire.

3. See Robert House, *Jack the Ripper and the Case for Scotland Yard's Prime Suspect* (NJ: John Wiley and Sons, 2011).

4. 'Facts specified in medical record upon which opinion of insanity is founded' in Kosminski's Medical Record.

5. 'Kosminski, a Polish Jew and resident in Whitechapel. This man became insane owing to many years indulgence in solitary vices'. Report on Jack the Ripper suspects, Melville Mcnaghten, 23 February 1894, MEPO 3/141 f. 180.

6. Arthur G. Morrison, 'Whitechapel', *The Palace Journal* (April 24, 1889) 1022-3.

7. 'Facts specified in medical record upon which opinion of insanity is founded' in Kosminski's Medical Record.

8. 'Leather Apron': the only name linked with the Whitechapel Murders. See 'A noiseless midnight terror', *The Star* (5 September 1888) 3. The apron is the accoutrement of a butcher.

9. From *A Guide to Shechita* (London: Shechita UK, May 2009) 3-5.

10. See *A Guide to Shechita* 6.

11. Deuteronomy 12.21.

12. Transcribed at *Casebook: Jack the Ripper* [Available at https://www.casebook.org/witnesses/frederick-gordon-brown.html] [Accessed 27 September 2018]

13. 'Laws of Slaughtering', from Rabbi Gersion Appel, *The Concise Code of Jewish Law* (New York: Ktav Publishing, 1977) vol. 1. 234-5.

14. *Daily Telegraph* (5 October 1888) 3.

15. Robert House discovered Kosmsinski's birth certificate (11 September 1865) in the Polish State Archives in Poznan. See 'The Kosminski

File', *Casebook: Jack the Ripper* [Available at https://www.casebook.org/dissertations/rip-housekoz.html] [Accessed 27 September 2018]

16. Printed in *Thomson's Weekly News* (1 December 1906). Quoted in Robert House, *Jack the Ripper* 335.

17. See Robert House, *Jack the Ripper* 3-5.

18. Song of Songs, 2.16.

19. *Daily Telegraph* (3 September 1888) 3.

20. See Robert House, *Jack the Ripper* 6-13, and Israel Bartal, *The Jews of Eastern Europe, 1772-1881*, trans. Chaya Naor (University of Pennsylvania Press, 2005).

21. Song of Songs 3.1.

22. Song of Songs 4.9.

23. Song of Songs 4.12.

24. 'Dr. Bond's Post Mortem on Mary Kelly' was lost until returned anonymously to Scotland Yard in 1987. See *Casebook: Jack the Ripper* [Available at https://www.casebook.org/official_documents/pm-kelly.html] [Accessed 28 September 2018]

25. A copy of this famous graffito was appended to the report of Sir Charles Warren, Commissioner of Police of the Metropolis, to the Home Secretary on the Whitechapel Murders. Letter from Charles Warren to Godfrey Lushington, Permanent Under-Secretary of State for the Home Department, 6 November 1888, HO 144/221/A49301C.

26. William Shakespeare, *Macbeth*, 2.3.72-3.

27. *Daily Telegraph* (4 October 1888) 3.

28. A phrase used by Sir Robert Anderson, Assistant Commissioner Metropolitan Police. See Sugden 397-8.

29. Letter from Warren to Lushington, HO 144/221/A49301C.

30. An anachronism. Antonio Moniz pioneered frontal lobotomy in 1935, receiving the Nobel Prize for his work. See his biography at the *Nobel Prize* website [Available at https://www.nobelprize.org/prizes/medicine/1949/moniz/biographical/] [Accessed 28 September 2018]

31. *Reynold's News* (15 September 1946). Quoted at *Casebook: Jack the Ripper* [Available at https://www.casebook.org/police_officials/po-sagar.html] [Accessed 27 September 2018]

32. The 'From Hell' letter was photographed before being lost from the police files. See *Casebook: Jack the Ripper* [Available at https://www.casebook.org/ripper_letters/] [Accessed 27 September 2018]

33. John Milton, *Paradise Lost*, Book 1, ll 64-5.

8 Amelia Dyer

1. Dyer is recorded as singing songs and hymns to herself in prison. See Alison Rattle and Allison Vale, *The Woman who Murdered Babies for Money* (London: Andre Deutsch, 2011) 231. Tom Moore, 'The Last Rose of Summer', published in Thomas Moore, *A Selection of Irish Melodies*, vol. 5 (December 1813). See John Stevenson and Henry Bishop, *Moore's Irish Melodies* (London: Addison, Hollier and Lucas, 1859) 4.

2. Dyer's reply to the Bench when arraigned before magistrates on 4 April 1896. *Weekly Dispatch* (5 April 1896). Quoted Rattle and Vale 189.

3. Oscar Wilde, *The Picture of Dorian Gray*, from *Collected Works*, ed. Vyvyan Holland (London: Collins, 1948, New Edition 1966) 154.

4. Oscar Wilde, *The Importance of Being Ernest*, from *Collected Works* 326.

5. In a letter from Reading Gaol Dyer requested copies of *Barnaby Rudge* and *East Lynne*. See Rattle and Vale 192.

6. See Richard Ellman, *Oscar Wilde* (London: Hamish Hamilton, 1987) 486.

7. Rattle and Vale, 192.

8. Rattle and Vale 192.

9. Oscar Wilde, *De Profundis, Collected Works* 911.

10. Rattle and Vale 54-5.

11. Oscar Wilde and Ada Leverson, *Letters to the Sphinx, with Reminiscences of the Author* (London: Duckworth, 1930) 39-40.

12. Tom Moore, 'The Last Rose of Summer'.

13. H. Montgomery Hyde, *The Trials of Oscar Wilde* (NY: Dover Publications, 1962) 216.

14. A popular Victorian hymn. C.H. Woolson, 'Jesus calls the children dear', in Kelly Dobbs Mickus (ed.) *Hymns for a Pilgrim People* (GIA Publications, 2007) Hymn 166.

15. *The Whole Proceedings of the Queen's Commission of Oyer and Terminer and goal delivery for the City of London, etc., of the Central Criminal Court, held on Monday*

January 7th, 1895, and following days, Eighth Session 1895-1896,725-7. Hereafter cited as *Proceedings of the Central Criminal Court*. See also Rattle and Vale 167-71.

16. Elder Edmund Dumas, 'White', in Benjamin Franklin White and Elisha J. King, *The Sacred Harp* (Philadelphia: S.C. Collins, 1844).

17. Dyer quoted in Rattle and Vale 189.

18. Adapted from Oscar Wilde, 'The Star Child', from *A House of Pomegranates* (1891), *Collected Works* 273.

19. Letters quoted in Rattle and Vale 149-50.

20. *Proceedings of the Central Criminal Court* 729-30.

21. *Proceedings of the Central Criminal Court* 737.

22. *Proceedings of the Central Criminal Court* 740, and Rattle and Vale 238.

23. See Richard Ellman, *Oscar Wilde* (London: Hamish Hamilton, 1987) 485.

24. Ellman 487.

25. Oscar Wilde, 'The Case of Warder Martin: some cruelties of prison life', *Letter to the Daily Chronicle* (28 May 1897), *Collected Works* 958.

26. Wilde, *Collected Works* 959, and Ellman 491.

27. *Proceedings of the Central Criminal Court* 737.

28. *Proceedings of the Central Criminal Court* 740.

29. William Shakespeare, *King Lear*, 5.3.258-9.

30. *Proceedings of the Central Criminal Court* 727-32.

31. Prison Commission File, Record of Execution. Quoted Rattle and Vale 241.

32. Oscar Wilde, *The Soul of Man Under Socialism, Collected Works* 1088.

33. Rattle and Vale 239.

34. Wilde appears to have invented this aphorism extempore in this drama, since I have been unable to trace it.

35. *Proceedings of the Central Criminal Court* 731-2.

36. Matthew 25.35, 40.

37. Matthew 25.41.

38. Oscar Wilde, 'Phrases and Philosophies for the use of the Young' (1994), *Collected Works* 1205.

39. Oscar Wilde, *The Picture of Dorian Gray*, *Collected Works* 45.

40. Oscar Wilde, *The Duchess of Padua* (1883), *Collected Works* 641.

41. William Shakespeare, *Hamlet*, 3.3.38.

42. William Shakespeare, *King Richard II*, 1.1.104-6.

43. Rattle and Vale 241.

9 Heinrich Himmler

1. 'Plenipotentiary'. The title held by the Nazi leader of occupied Denmark.

2. 'Operation Willi'. See Andrew Morton, *The Royals, the Nazis, and the Biggest Cover-Up in History* (London: Michael O'Mara Books, 2015).

3. Oswald Mosely was imprisoned in 1940, and held in Holloway Prison.

4. In fact the Mithraeum was excavated in 1954. See John D. Shepherd, *The Temple of Mithras, London: excavations by W.F. Grimes and A. Williams at the Walbrook* (London: English Heritage, 1998), and W.F. Grimes, *The Excavation of Roman and Medieval London* (London: Routledge and Kegan Paul, 1998), Chapter IV.

5. The Tauroctony discovered at Walbrook can be seen in the Museum of London.

6. See Richard Walter Darre, *Neuadel aus Blut und Boden* (*A New Nobility Based On Blood And Soil*) (München: J.F. Lehmann, 1930).

7. The *Ahnenerbe* ('Ancestral heritage') was a research institute operating within the SS between 1935 and 1945, established by Himmler to propagate theories of Aryan racial supremacy. Hermann Wirth was a Dutch historian and Nazi sympathiser.

8. Himmler quoted in Peter Longerich, *Heinrich Himmler: a Life* (Oxford: Oxford University Press, 2011) 266.

9. Himmler outlined these ideas in his speech (9 June 1942) at the funeral of Reynhard Heydrich, Reich-Protector of Bohemia and Moravia, assassinated by Czech partisans. See also Longerich 271.

10. Himmler quoted Longerich 266.

11. See Montserrat Rico Gongorra, *La Abadia Profanada* (The Desecrated Abbey) (Madrid: Planeta, 2007).

12. The claim was made in Michael Baigent, Richard Leigh and Henry Lincoln, *Holy Blood, Holy Grail* (London: Jonathan Cape, 1982), and subsequently

popularised by Dan Brown in *The Da Vinci Code* (NY: Doubleday, 2003).

13. See Trevor Ravenscroft, *The Spear of Destiny* (London: Neville Spearman, 1972), 329.

14. See Kenneth Hite, *The Nazi Occult* (Oxford: Osprey, 2013) 20.

15. See Eric Kurlander, *Hitler's Monsters: A Supernatural History of the Third Reich* (New Haven: Yale University Press, 2017).

16. Wewelsburg Castel near the city of Paderborn in Westphalia now houses a museum of the SS. See Goodrick-Clarke 177 ff. The *Obergruppenführersaal* and the *Graf* can still be visited.

17. 'Centre of the New World'.

18. A.S. Geden, *Select Passages Illustrating Mithriasm* (London: SPCK, 1925) 51ff.

19. Manfred Claus, *The Roman Cult of Mithras: the God and his Mysteries* (London: Routledge, 2001) 42.

20. A *Tauroctony* (bull-slaying) was always central to the Mithraic mysteries. See David Ulansey, *The Origins of the Mithraic Mysteries: Cosmology and Salvation in the Ancient World* (Oxford: Oxford University Press, 1991) 6.

21. A genuine artefact. See 'Hitler's commemorative timepiece', *Daily Mail* (7 March 2011).

22. The details are taken from the archive film of the funeral, held in the Mosaic Hall of the New Reich Chancellery, Berlin, of Reynhard Heydrich, 9 June 1942. Music from Wagner's *Gotterdamerung* is used as the soundtrack of the film. [Available at https://www.youtube.com/watch?v=V0tXIGerj7I] [Accessed 1 October 2018].

23. Adapted from the eulogy Himmler is seen delivering in the film of Heydrich's funeral. [Available at https://www.youtube.com/watch?v=V0tXIGerj7I] [Accessed 1 October 2018].

24. 'Death's Head', the iconic SS symbol featured on uniform badges and on rings such as those exhibited in the SS Museum at Wewelsburg.

25. Description based on the photograph of Himmler after his suicide by cyanide poisoning, taken by Lance Corporal Guy Adderley of British Intelligence, on 23 May 1945. Previously unseen when sold at auction in March 2011. See *Daily Telegraph* (16 February 2011).

26. From a fragmentary Egyptian papyrus. See William M Brashear, *A Mithraic catechism from Egypt: P. Berol. 21196* (Vienna: Holtzhausens 1992).

27. Marvin Meyer, *The Mithras Liturgy* (London: Scholars Press, 1976).

28. 'Temporary immortality', enlightenment.

29. Photograph of Himmler dead, *Daily Telegraph* (16 February 2011).

30. From the recollections of British Army personnel present at Himmler's death on 23 May 1945. See Paul van Stemman, 'Himmler's Night of Reckoning', *The Independent* (21 May 1995).

10 Tariq Sharmin

1. 'In the name of Allah, Allah is the greatest'.

2. 'O Allah, from You and to You'.

3. 'Forbidden'. 'He has only forbidden to you dead animals, blood, the flesh of swine, and that which has been dedicated to other than Allah'. Quran 16.115.

4. 'O Allah, accept this from me'.

5. The correct method for slaughtering animals by Islamic Law.

6. Quran 5.3.

7. 'Unbelievers'.

8. Quran 5.3.

9. This now notorious anti-semitic mural, 'Freedom for Humanity', painted on a wall in Brick Lane by graffiti artist Kalen Ockerman, was removed by the local council in 2012 following complaints. My description derives from viewing it *in situ* before its removal.

10. The *Takbir* is the Arabic phrase 'Allahu Akhbar', 'God is the greatest'.

11. Islamic times of prayer: Dawn, Noon, Afternoon, Sunset, Nightfall.

12. Quran 2.186.

13. Quran 24.35.

14. The people of Islam.

15. Quran 37.102. 'God willing you will find me obedient'.

11 Postscript: St Bartholomew

1. Bartholomew appears in Matthew, Mark, Luke, and in the Acts of the Apostles.

2. Eusebius, *The Church History*, trans. Paul L. Maier (Grand Rapids: Kregel, 1999, 2007) 166.

3. Alban Butler, *Lives of the Saints, August*, rev. John Cumming (Tunbridge Wells: Burns and Oates, 1998) 232.

4. See for example Jaume Huguet, *The Flaying of St Bartholomew* and two paintings with the same title held in the Wellcome Collection. For Jaume Huguet [Available at https://culturalrites.com/jaume-huguet-1412-1492/]. [Accessed 2 October 2018]. See painting of the Portuguese School, *The Flaying of St Bartholomew* [Available at https://wellcomecollection. org/works/byf5v4f4?query=flaying+of+st+Bartholomew] [Accessed 2 October 2018], and Anonymous, *The Flaying of St Bartholomew* [Available at https://wellcomecollection.org/works/zmxszssf?query=flaying+of+st+ Bartholomew] [Accessed 2 October 2018].

5. Genesis 22.2.

6. Isaiah 53.7.

7. Gregory of Tours, *Glory of the Martyrs*, trans. Raymond van Dam (Liverpool: Liverpool University Press, 1998) 55-6.

8. E A Webb, 'The founder: To 1123', in *The Records of St. Bartholomew's Priory and St. Bartholomew the Great, West Smithfield: Volume 1* (Oxford: Oxford University Press, 1921) 37-55.

9. St Bartholomew appears twice in Michelangelo's *Last Judgement* (1537-41) in the Capella Sistina. The image described appears below and to the right of the figure of Christ in Judgement.

10. Damien Hirst, *St Bartholomew: Exquisite Pain*, permanent exhibition, Church of St Bartholomew the Great, Smithfield. The saint holds a scalpel rather than a skinning knife as in Michelangelo's image.

ABOUT THE AUTHOR

Graham Holderness is the author or editor of some 60 books, with overall sales of tens of thousands. His work can be divided into three strands: (1) literary criticism, theory and scholarship, especially in Shakespeare studies; (2) the pioneering of an innovative new method of 'creative criticism'; and (3) creative writing in fiction, poetry and drama. His poetry collection *Craeft* received a Poetry Book Society award in 2002. His play *Wholly Writ* was performed at Shakespeare's Globe, and by Royal Shakespeare company actors in Stratford-upon-Avon. He has published two novels: *The Prince of Denmark* (2001) and *Black and Deep Desires: William Shakespeare Vampire Hunter* (2015). His publishers have included Penguin, Cambridge University Press, Bloomsbury, Palgrave Macmillan, Routledge, Manchester University Press, and Lion Books.

EER will also publish his other new study, *Samurai Shakespeare*, in Spring 2020, and new editions of two of his works: *Textual Shakespeare* and *The Prince of Denmark*.

Lightning Source UK Ltd.
Milton Keynes UK
UKHW040608241119
354120UK00003B/19/P